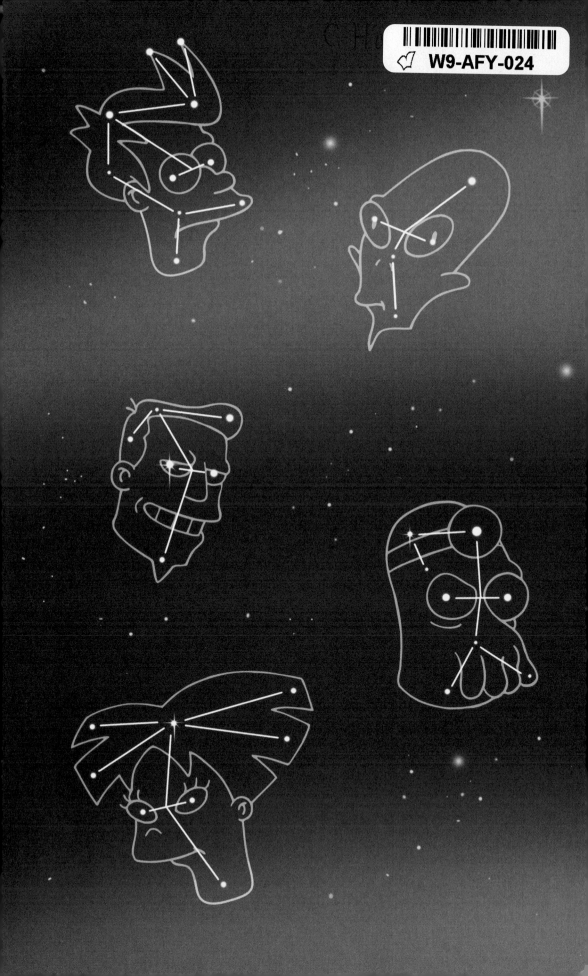

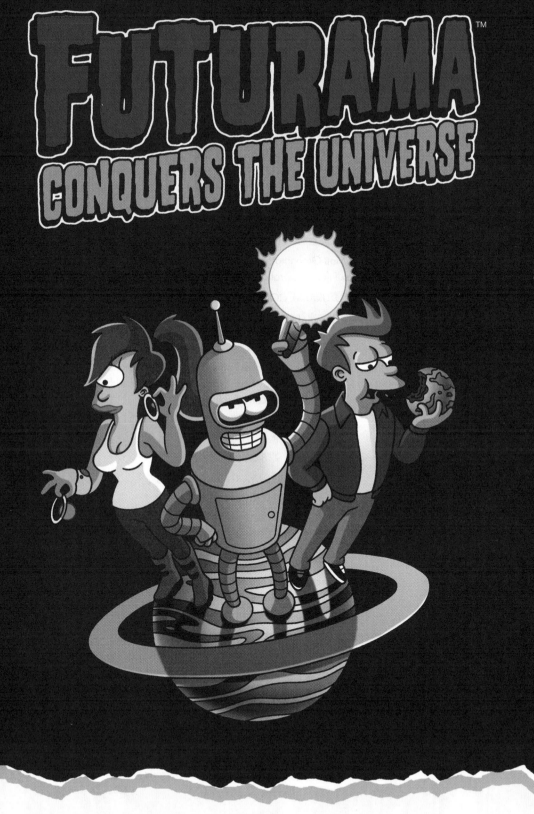

# FUTURAMA™
## CONQUERS THE UNIVERSE

**HARPER**

NEW YORK • LONDON • TORONTO • SYDNEY

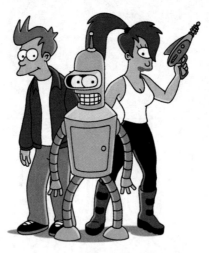

FUTURAMA CONQUERS THE UNIVERSE

 For information address
HarperCollins Publishers,
10 East 53rd Street, New York, NY 10022.

FIRST EDITION

ISBN: 978-0-06-143069-5

07 08 09 10 11 QWM 10 9 8 7 6 5 4 3 2 1

Publisher: Matt Groening
Creative Director: Bill Morrison
Managing Editor: Terry Delegeane
Director of Operations: Robert Zaugh
Art Director: Nathan Kane
Art Director Special Projects: Serban Cristescu
Production Manager: Christopher Ungar
Legal Guardian: Susan A. Grode

Trade Paperback Concepts and Design: Serban Cristescu

Trade Paperback Cover Art: Serban Cristescu, Chia-Hsien Jason Ho, Bill Morrison, Mike Rote

HarperCollins Editors: Hope Innelli, Jeremy Cesarec

Contributing Artists:

Karen Bates, Serban Cristescu, John Delaney, Chia-Hsien Jason Ho, Nathan Kane, Mike Kazaleh, Tom King, James Lloyd, Joey Mason, Bill Morrison, Phyllis Novin, Andrew Pepoy, Mike Rote, Steve Steere Jr., Chris Ungar

Contributing Writers:
Ian Boothby, Eric Rogers, Patric M. Verrone

PRINTED IN CANADA

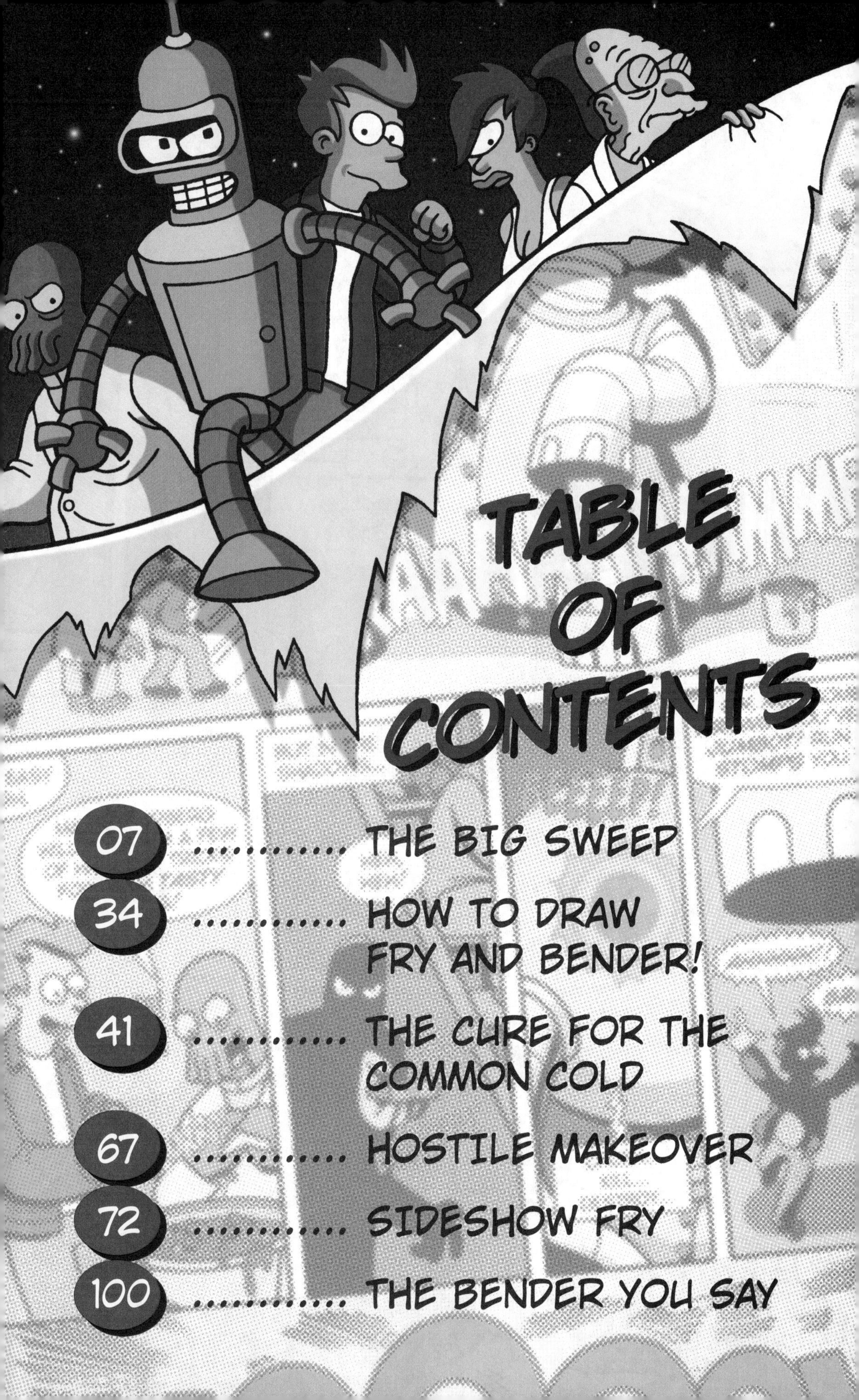

# TABLE OF CONTENTS

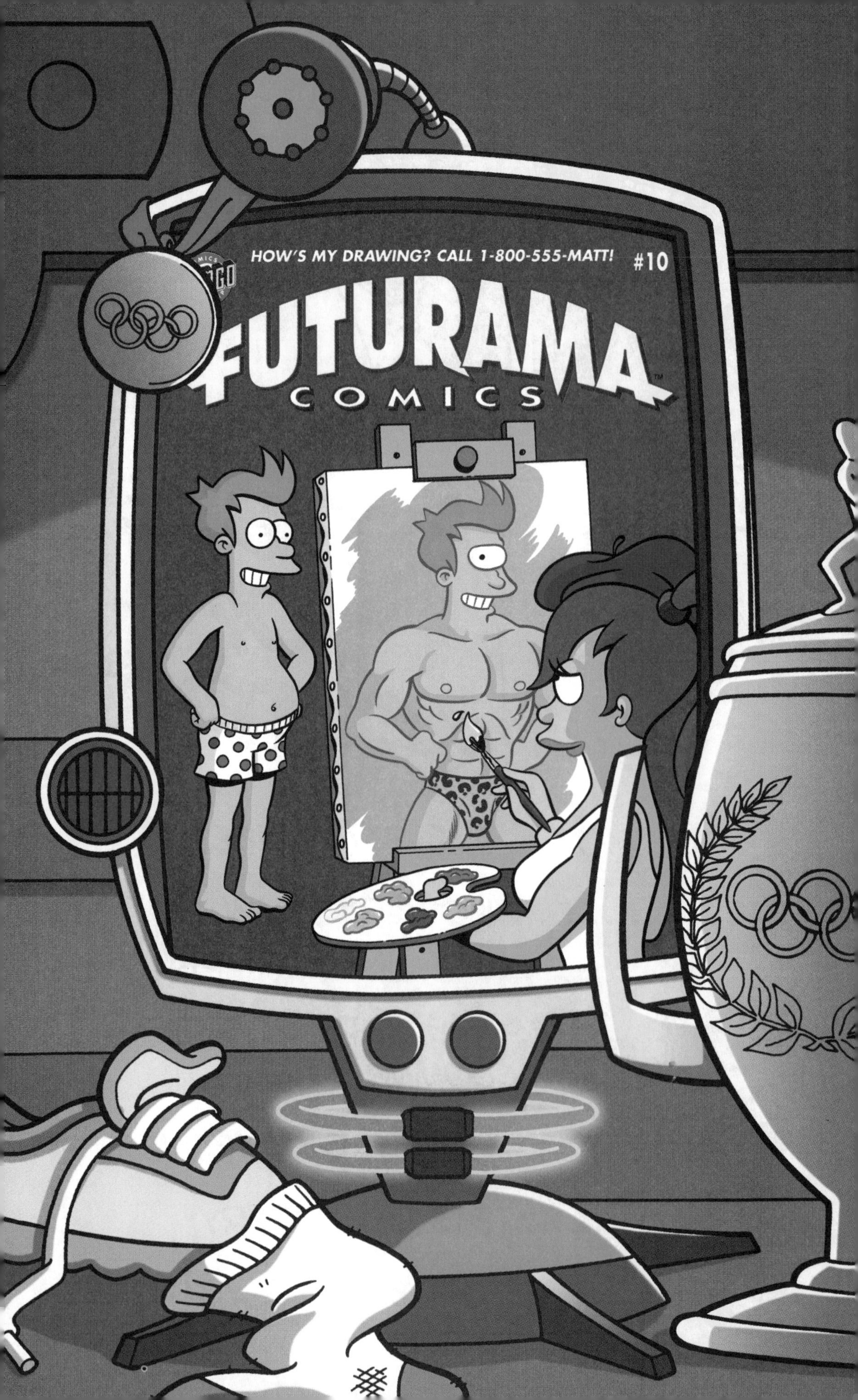
HOW'S MY DRAWING? CALL 1-800-555-MATT!
#10
FUTURAMA
COMICS

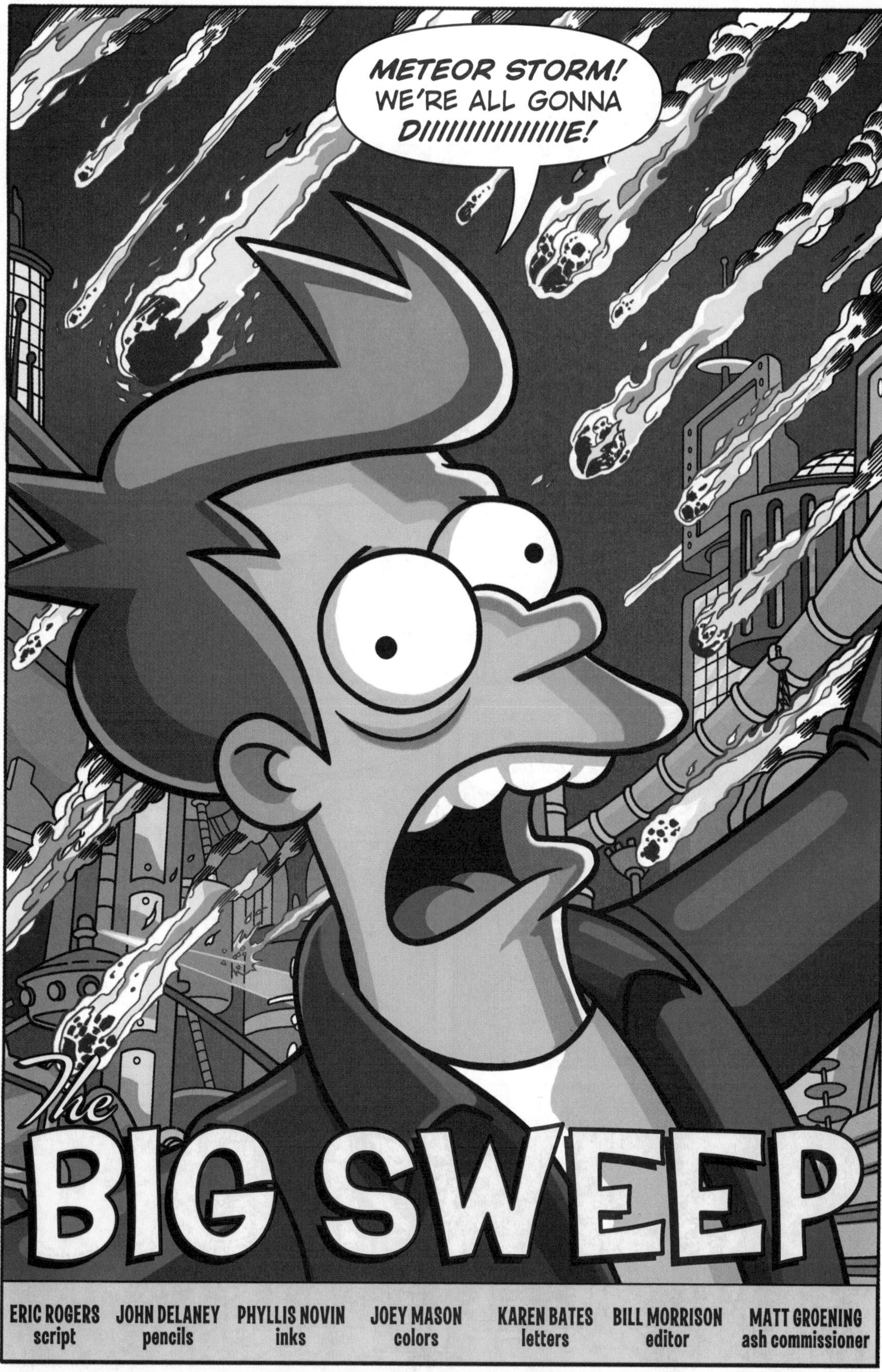
METEOR STORM! WE'RE ALL GONNA DIIIIIIIIIIIIIIIIIIE!
The
BIG SWEEP

ERIC ROGERS script | JOHN DELANEY pencils | PHYLLIS NOVIN inks | JOEY MASON colors | KAREN BATES letters | BILL MORRISON editor | MATT GROENING ash commissioner

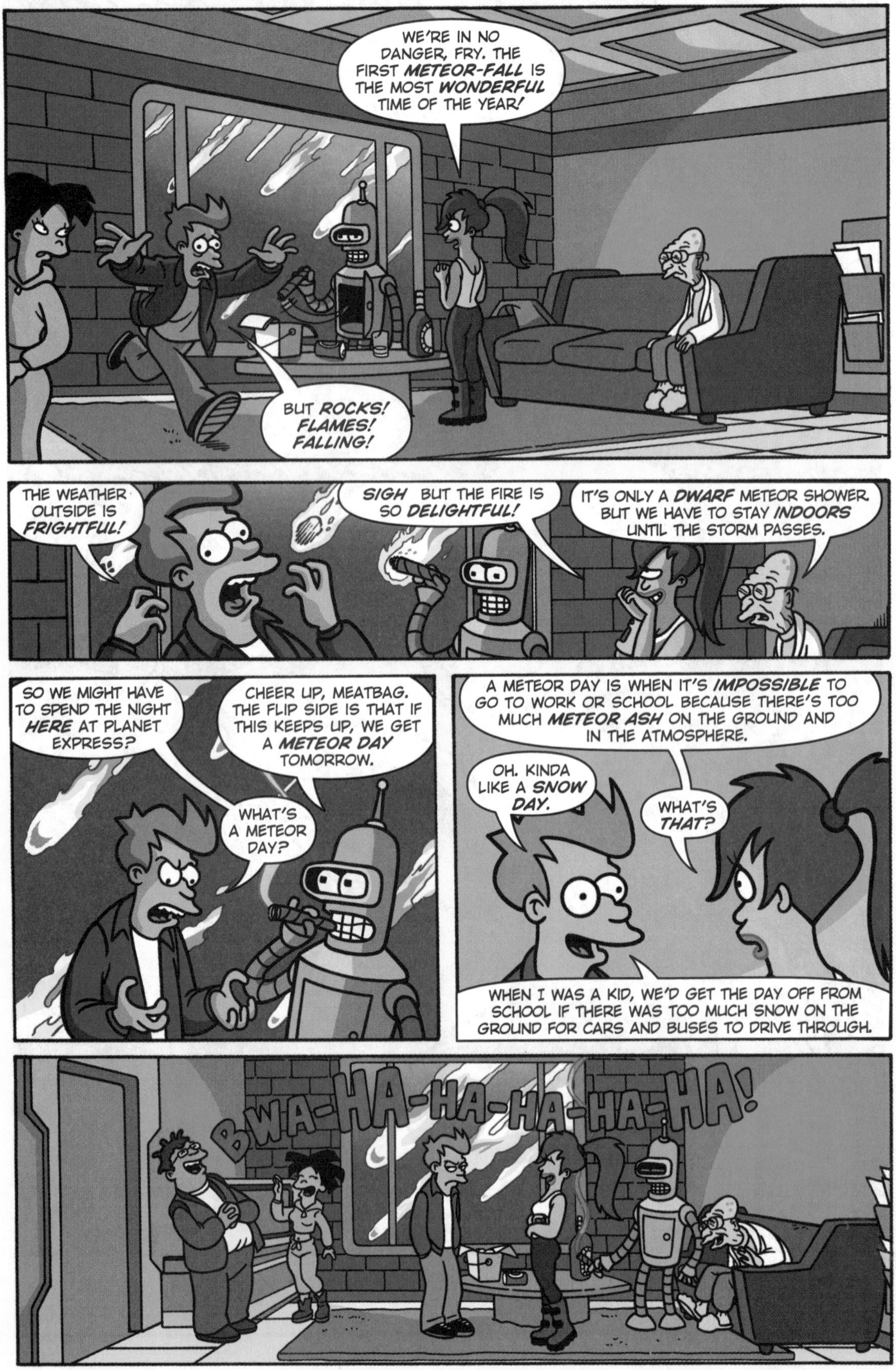
WE'RE IN NO DANGER, FRY. THE FIRST METEOR-FALL IS THE MOST WONDERFUL TIME OF THE YEAR!
BUT ROCKS! FLAMES! FALLING!
THE WEATHER OUTSIDE IS FRIGHTFUL!
SIGH BUT THE FIRE IS SO DELIGHTFUL!
IT'S ONLY A DWARF METEOR SHOWER. BUT WE HAVE TO STAY INDOORS UNTIL THE STORM PASSES.
SO WE MIGHT HAVE TO SPEND THE NIGHT HERE AT PLANET EXPRESS?
CHEER UP, MEATBAG. THE FLIP SIDE IS THAT IF THIS KEEPS UP, WE GET A METEOR DAY TOMORROW.
WHAT'S A METEOR DAY?
A METEOR DAY IS WHEN IT'S IMPOSSIBLE TO GO TO WORK OR SCHOOL BECAUSE THERE'S TOO MUCH METEOR ASH ON THE GROUND AND IN THE ATMOSPHERE.
OH. KINDA LIKE A SNOW DAY.
WHAT'S THAT?
WHEN I WAS A KID, WE'D GET THE DAY OFF FROM SCHOOL IF THERE WAS TOO MUCH SNOW ON THE GROUND FOR CARS AND BUSES TO DRIVE THROUGH.
BWA-HA-HA-HA-HA-HA!

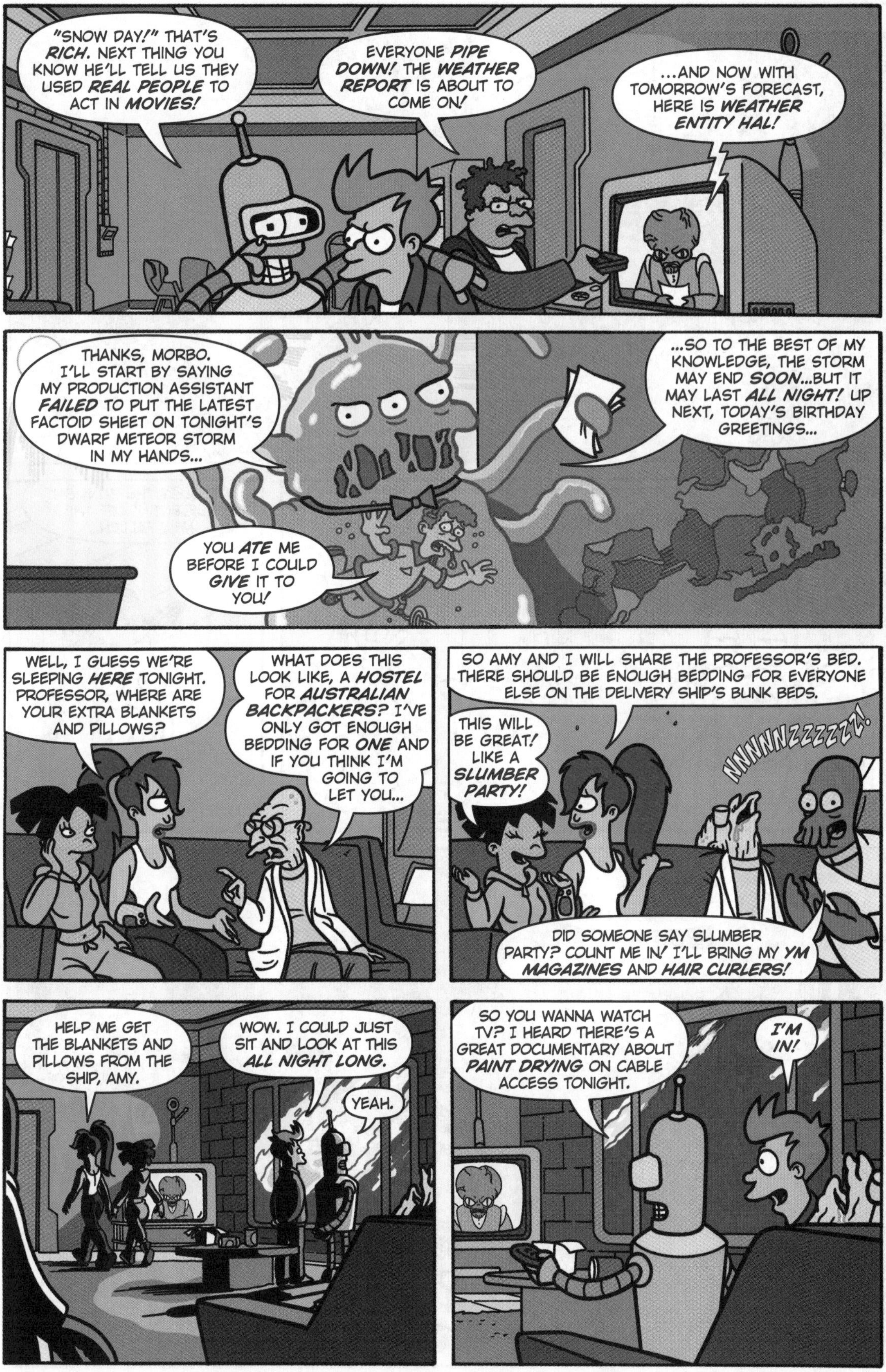
"SNOW DAY!" THAT'S RICH. NEXT THING YOU KNOW HE'LL TELL US THEY USED REAL PEOPLE TO ACT IN MOVIES!
EVERYONE PIPE DOWN! THE WEATHER REPORT IS ABOUT TO COME ON!
...AND NOW WITH TOMORROW'S FORECAST, HERE IS WEATHER ENTITY HAL!
THANKS, MORBO. I'LL START BY SAYING MY PRODUCTION ASSISTANT FAILED TO PUT THE LATEST FACTOID SHEET ON TONIGHT'S DWARF METEOR STORM IN MY HANDS...
YOU ATE ME BEFORE I COULD GIVE IT TO YOU!
...SO TO THE BEST OF MY KNOWLEDGE, THE STORM MAY END SOON...BUT IT MAY LAST ALL NIGHT! UP NEXT, TODAY'S BIRTHDAY GREETINGS...
WELL, I GUESS WE'RE SLEEPING HERE TONIGHT. PROFESSOR, WHERE ARE YOUR EXTRA BLANKETS AND PILLOWS?
WHAT DOES THIS LOOK LIKE, A HOSTEL FOR AUSTRALIAN BACKPACKERS? I'VE ONLY GOT ENOUGH BEDDING FOR ONE AND IF YOU THINK I'M GOING TO LET YOU...
SO AMY AND I WILL SHARE THE PROFESSOR'S BED. THERE SHOULD BE ENOUGH BEDDING FOR EVERYONE ELSE ON THE DELIVERY SHIP'S BUNK BEDS.
THIS WILL BE GREAT! LIKE A SLUMBER PARTY!
NNNNNZZZZZZ!
DID SOMEONE SAY SLUMBER PARTY? COUNT ME IN! I'LL BRING MY YM MAGAZINES AND HAIR CURLERS!
HELP ME GET THE BLANKETS AND PILLOWS FROM THE SHIP, AMY.
WOW. I COULD JUST SIT AND LOOK AT THIS ALL NIGHT LONG.
YEAH.
SO YOU WANNA WATCH TV? I HEARD THERE'S A GREAT DOCUMENTARY ABOUT PAINT DRYING ON CABLE ACCESS TONIGHT.
I'M IN!

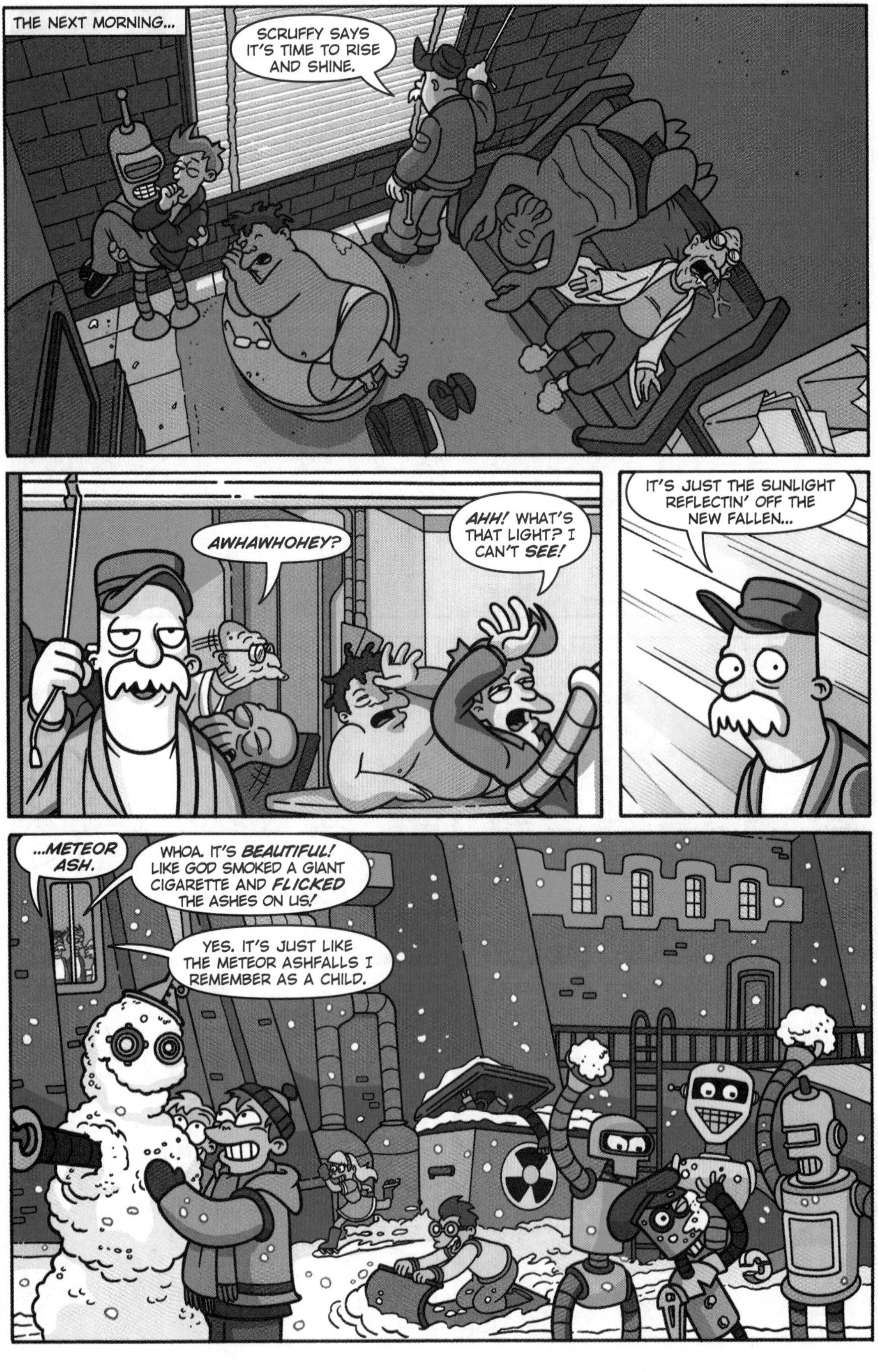
THE NEXT MORNING...
SCRUFFY SAYS IT'S TIME TO RISE AND SHINE.
AWHAWHOHEY?
AHH! WHAT'S THAT LIGHT? I CAN'T SEE!
IT'S JUST THE SUNLIGHT REFLECTIN' OFF THE NEW FALLEN...
...METEOR ASH.
WHOA. IT'S BEAUTIFUL! LIKE GOD SMOKED A GIANT CIGARETTE AND FLICKED THE ASHES ON US!
YES. IT'S JUST LIKE THE METEOR ASHFALLS I REMEMBER AS A CHILD.

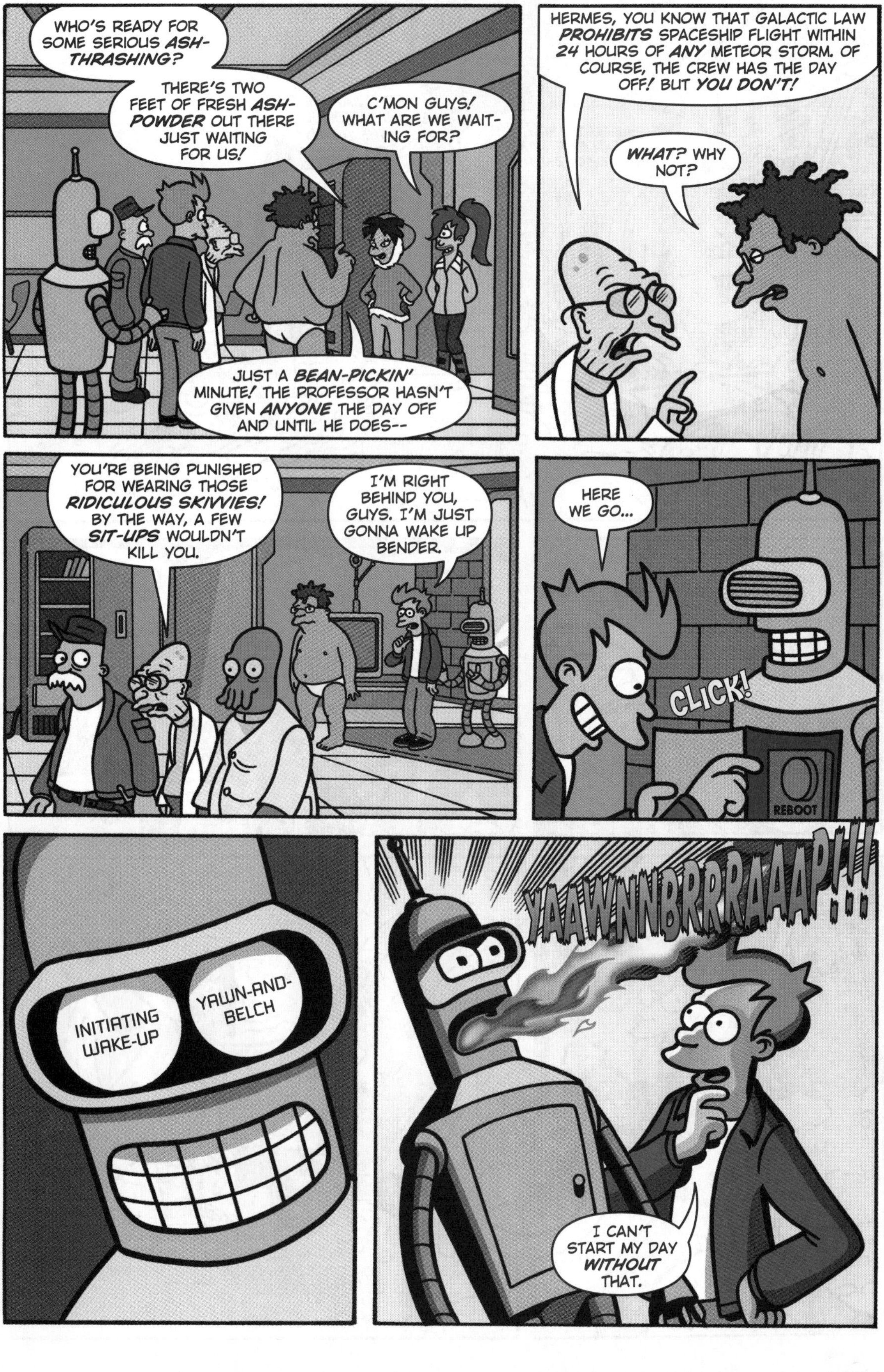
WHO'S READY FOR SOME SERIOUS ASH-THRASHING?
THERE'S TWO FEET OF FRESH ASH-POWDER OUT THERE JUST WAITING FOR US!
C'MON GUYS! WHAT ARE WE WAIT-ING FOR?
JUST A BEAN-PICKIN' MINUTE! THE PROFESSOR HASN'T GIVEN ANYONE THE DAY OFF AND UNTIL HE DOES--
HERMES, YOU KNOW THAT GALACTIC LAW PROHIBITS SPACESHIP FLIGHT WITHIN 24 HOURS OF ANY METEOR STORM. OF COURSE, THE CREW HAS THE DAY OFF! BUT YOU DON'T!
WHAT? WHY NOT?
YOU'RE BEING PUNISHED FOR WEARING THOSE RIDICULOUS SKIVVIES! BY THE WAY, A FEW SIT-UPS WOULDN'T KILL YOU.
I'M RIGHT BEHIND YOU, GUYS. I'M JUST GONNA WAKE UP BENDER.
HERE WE GO...
CLICK!
REBOOT
INITIATING WAKE-UP
YAWN-AND-BELCH
YAAWNNBRRRAAAP!!!
I CAN'T START MY DAY WITHOUT THAT.

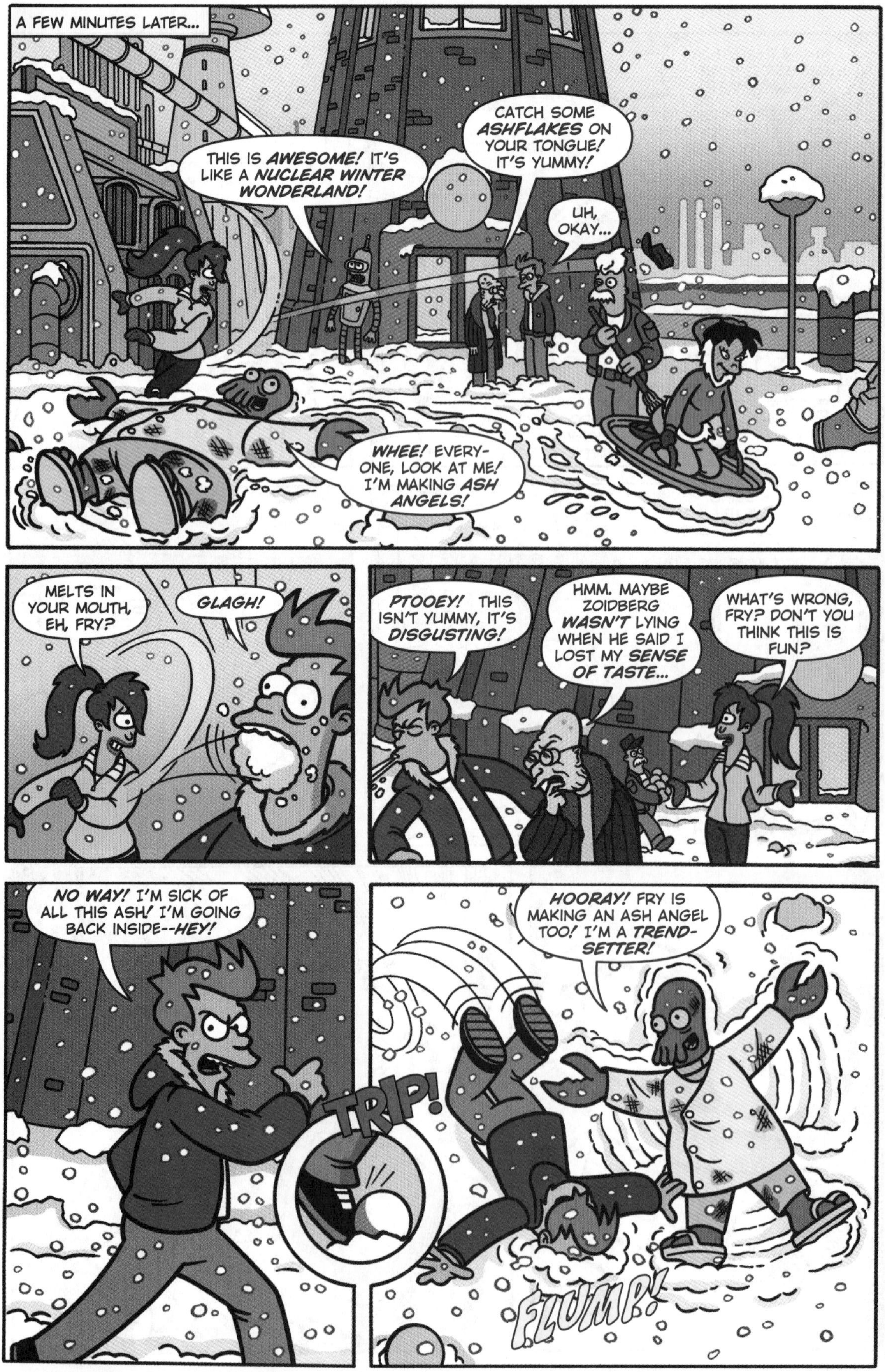
A FEW MINUTES LATER...
THIS IS AWESOME! IT'S LIKE A NUCLEAR WINTER WONDERLAND!
CATCH SOME ASHFLAKES ON YOUR TONGUE! IT'S YUMMY!
UH, OKAY...
WHEE! EVERY-ONE, LOOK AT ME! I'M MAKING ASH ANGELS!
MELTS IN YOUR MOUTH, EH, FRY?
GLAGH!
PTOOEY! THIS ISN'T YUMMY, IT'S DISGUSTING!
HMM. MAYBE ZOIDBERG WASN'T LYING WHEN HE SAID I LOST MY SENSE OF TASTE...
WHAT'S WRONG, FRY? DON'T YOU THINK THIS IS FUN?
NO WAY! I'M SICK OF ALL THIS ASH! I'M GOING BACK INSIDE--HEY!
TRIP!
HOORAY! FRY IS MAKING AN ASH ANGEL TOO! I'M A TREND-SETTER!
FLUMP!

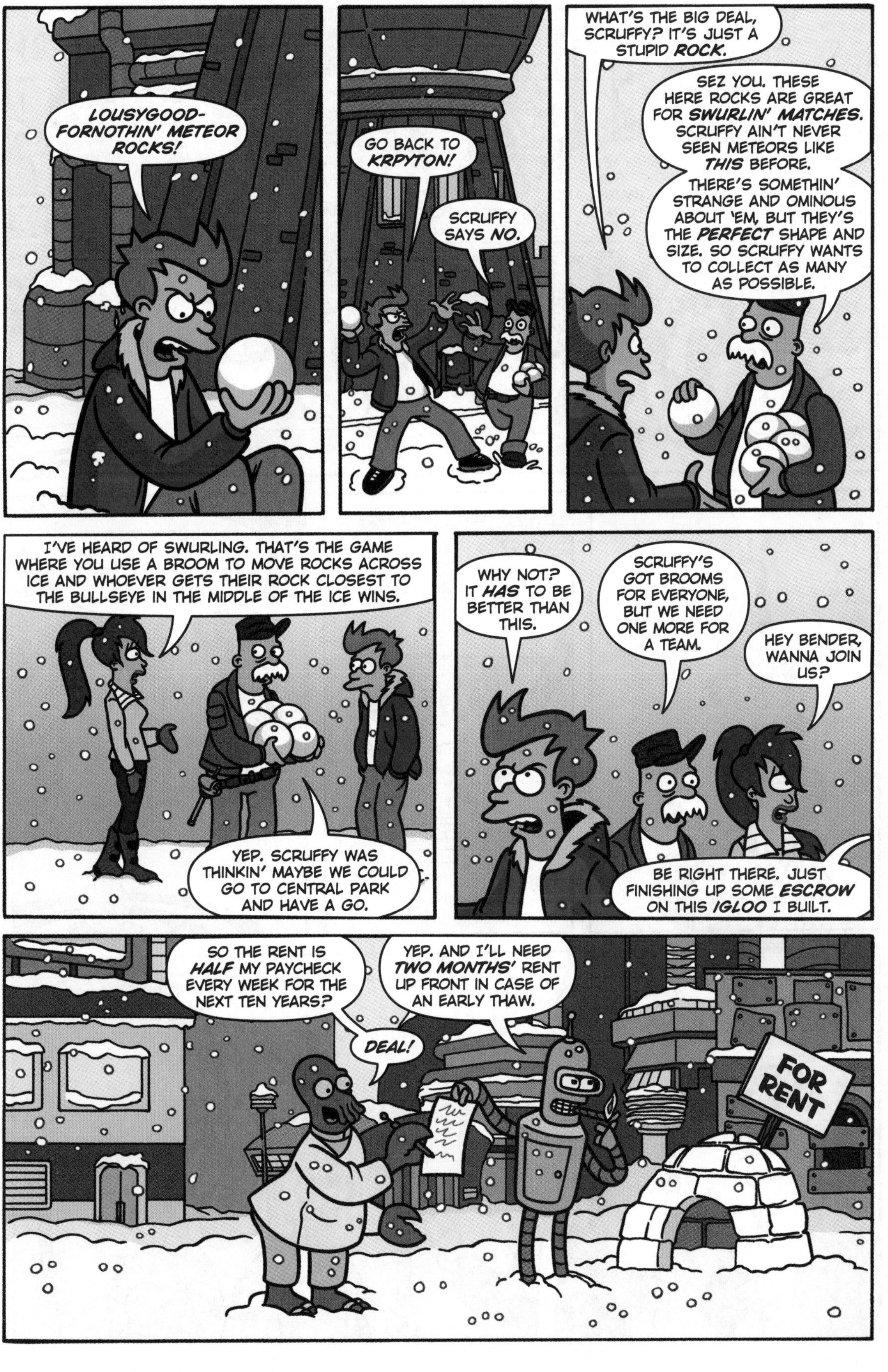

LOUSYGOOD-FORNOTHIN' METEOR ROCKS!
GO BACK TO KRPYTON!
SCRUFFY SAYS NO.
WHAT'S THE BIG DEAL, SCRUFFY? IT'S JUST A STUPID ROCK.
SEZ YOU. THESE HERE ROCKS ARE GREAT FOR SWURLIN' MATCHES. SCRUFFY AIN'T NEVER SEEN METEORS LIKE THIS BEFORE.
THERE'S SOMETHIN' STRANGE AND OMINOUS ABOUT 'EM, BUT THEY'S THE PERFECT SHAPE AND SIZE. SO SCRUFFY WANTS TO COLLECT AS MANY AS POSSIBLE.
I'VE HEARD OF SWURLING. THAT'S THE GAME WHERE YOU USE A BROOM TO MOVE ROCKS ACROSS ICE AND WHOEVER GETS THEIR ROCK CLOSEST TO THE BULLSEYE IN THE MIDDLE OF THE ICE WINS.
YEP. SCRUFFY WAS THINKIN' MAYBE WE COULD GO TO CENTRAL PARK AND HAVE A GO.
WHY NOT? IT HAS TO BE BETTER THAN THIS.
SCRUFFY'S GOT BROOMS FOR EVERYONE, BUT WE NEED ONE MORE FOR A TEAM.
HEY BENDER, WANNA JOIN US?
BE RIGHT THERE. JUST FINISHING UP SOME ESCROW ON THIS IGLOO I BUILT.
SO THE RENT IS HALF MY PAYCHECK EVERY WEEK FOR THE NEXT TEN YEARS?
DEAL!
YEP. AND I'LL NEED TWO MONTHS' RENT UP FRONT IN CASE OF AN EARLY THAW.
FOR RENT

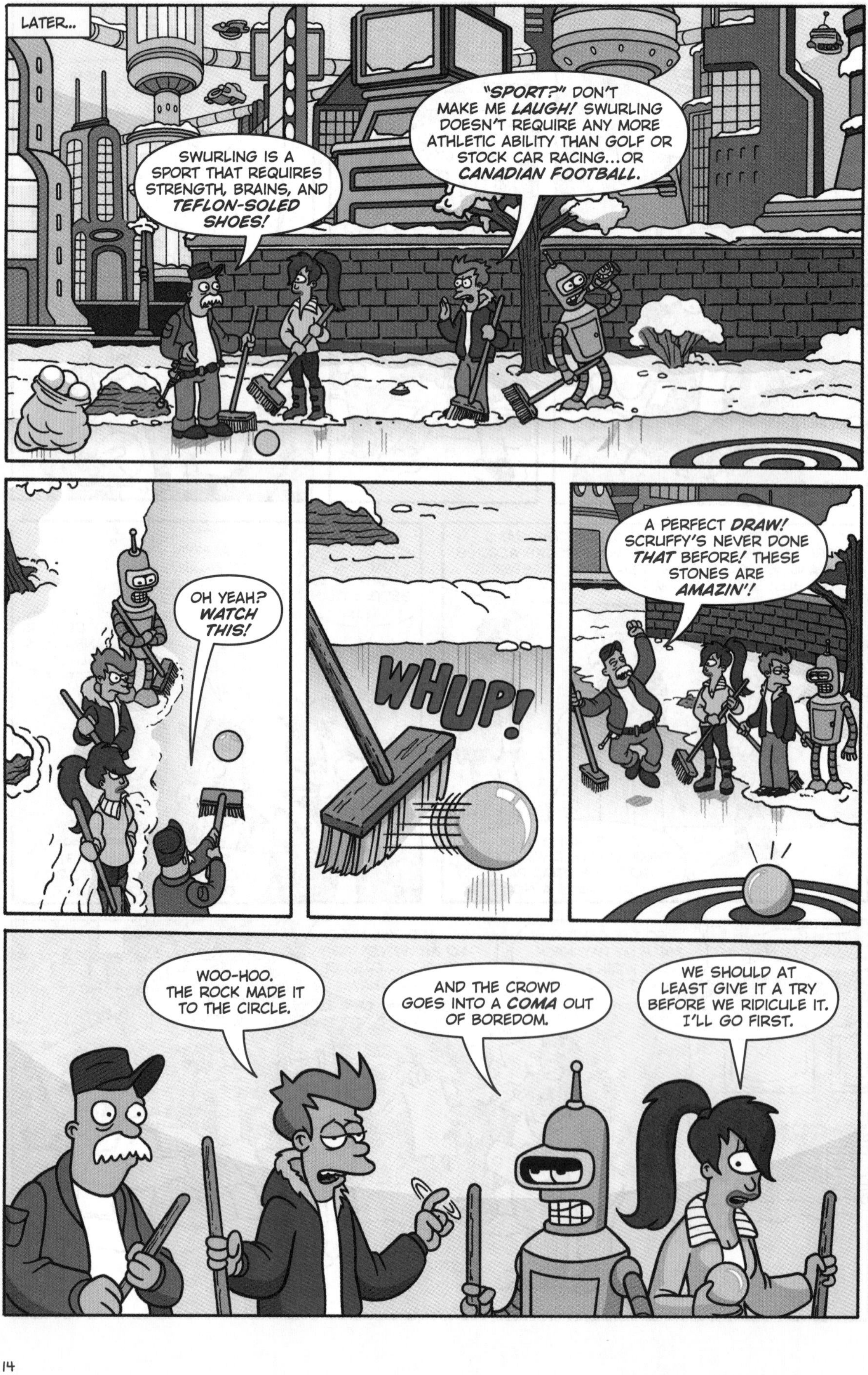
LATER...
SWURLING IS A SPORT THAT REQUIRES STRENGTH, BRAINS, AND TEFLON-SOLED SHOES!
"SPORT?" DON'T MAKE ME LAUGH! SWURLING DOESN'T REQUIRE ANY MORE ATHLETIC ABILITY THAN GOLF OR STOCK CAR RACING...OR CANADIAN FOOTBALL.
OH YEAH? WATCH THIS!
WHUP!
A PERFECT DRAW! SCRUFFY'S NEVER DONE THAT BEFORE! THESE STONES ARE AMAZIN'!
WOO-HOO. THE ROCK MADE IT TO THE CIRCLE.
AND THE CROWD GOES INTO A COMA OUT OF BOREDOM.
WE SHOULD AT LEAST GIVE IT A TRY BEFORE WE RIDICULE IT. I'LL GO FIRST.

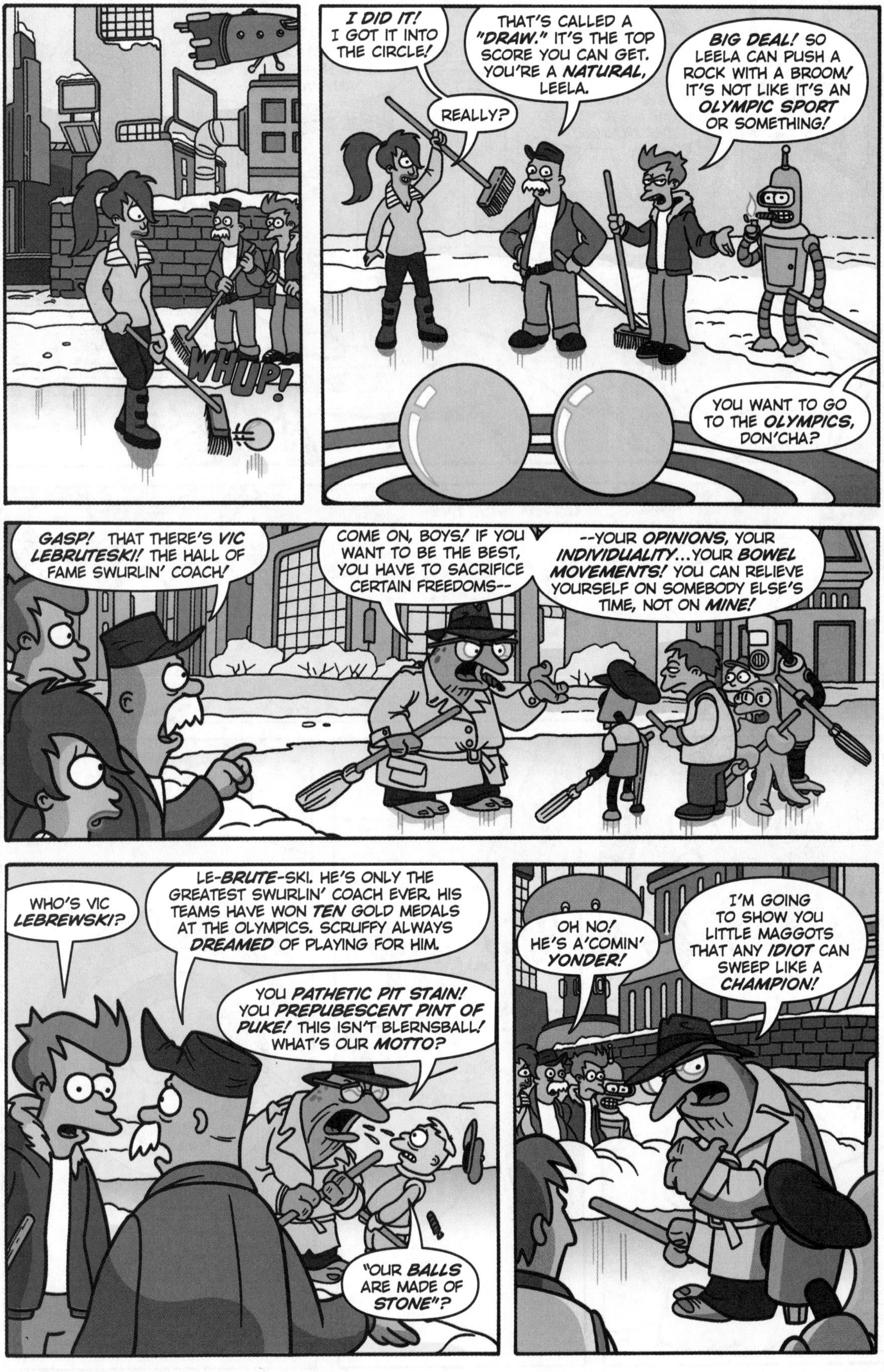
WHUP!
I DID IT! I GOT IT INTO THE CIRCLE!
THAT'S CALLED A "DRAW." IT'S THE TOP SCORE YOU CAN GET. YOU'RE A NATURAL, LEELA.
REALLY?
BIG DEAL! SO LEELA CAN PUSH A ROCK WITH A BROOM! IT'S NOT LIKE IT'S AN OLYMPIC SPORT OR SOMETHING!
YOU WANT TO GO TO THE OLYMPICS, DON'CHA?
GASP! THAT THERE'S VIC LEBRUTESKI! THE HALL OF FAME SWURLIN' COACH!
COME ON, BOYS! IF YOU WANT TO BE THE BEST, YOU HAVE TO SACRIFICE CERTAIN FREEDOMS--
--YOUR OPINIONS, YOUR INDIVIDUALITY...YOUR BOWEL MOVEMENTS! YOU CAN RELIEVE YOURSELF ON SOMEBODY ELSE'S TIME, NOT ON MINE!
WHO'S VIC LEBREWSKI?
LE-BRUTE-SKI. HE'S ONLY THE GREATEST SWURLIN' COACH EVER. HIS TEAMS HAVE WON TEN GOLD MEDALS AT THE OLYMPICS. SCRUFFY ALWAYS DREAMED OF PLAYING FOR HIM.
YOU PATHETIC PIT STAIN! YOU PREPUBESCENT PINT OF PUKE! THIS ISN'T BLERNSBALL! WHAT'S OUR MOTTO?
"OUR BALLS ARE MADE OF STONE"?
OH NO! HE'S A'COMIN' YONDER!
I'M GOING TO SHOW YOU LITTLE MAGGOTS THAT ANY IDIOT CAN SWEEP LIKE A CHAMPION!

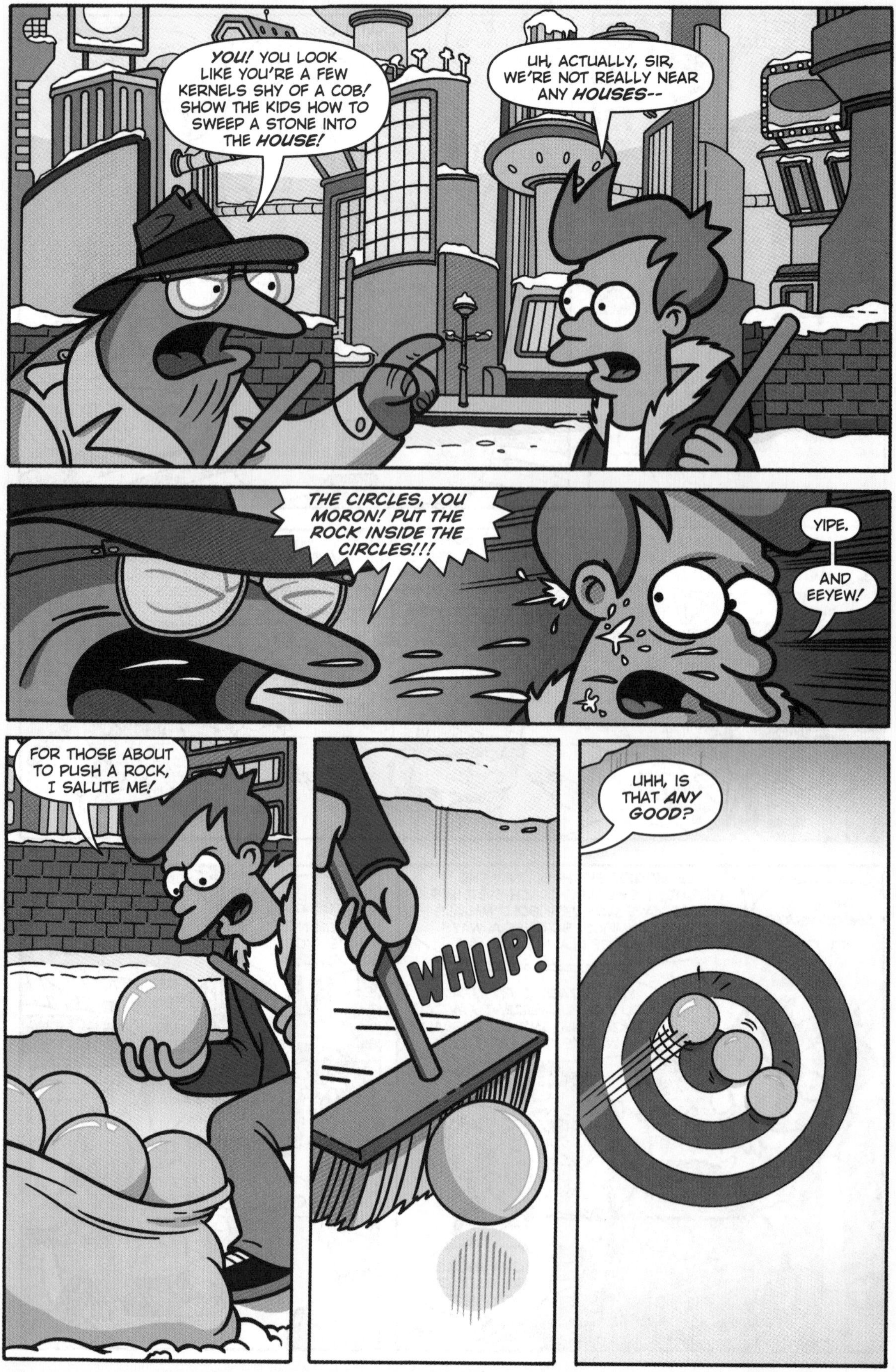
YOU! YOU LOOK LIKE YOU'RE A FEW KERNELS SHY OF A COB! SHOW THE KIDS HOW TO SWEEP A STONE INTO THE HOUSE!
UH, ACTUALLY, SIR, WE'RE NOT REALLY NEAR ANY HOUSES--
THE CIRCLES, YOU MORON! PUT THE ROCK INSIDE THE CIRCLES!!!
YIPE.
AND EEYEW!
FOR THOSE ABOUT TO PUSH A ROCK, I SALUTE ME!
WHUP!
UHH, IS THAT ANY GOOD?

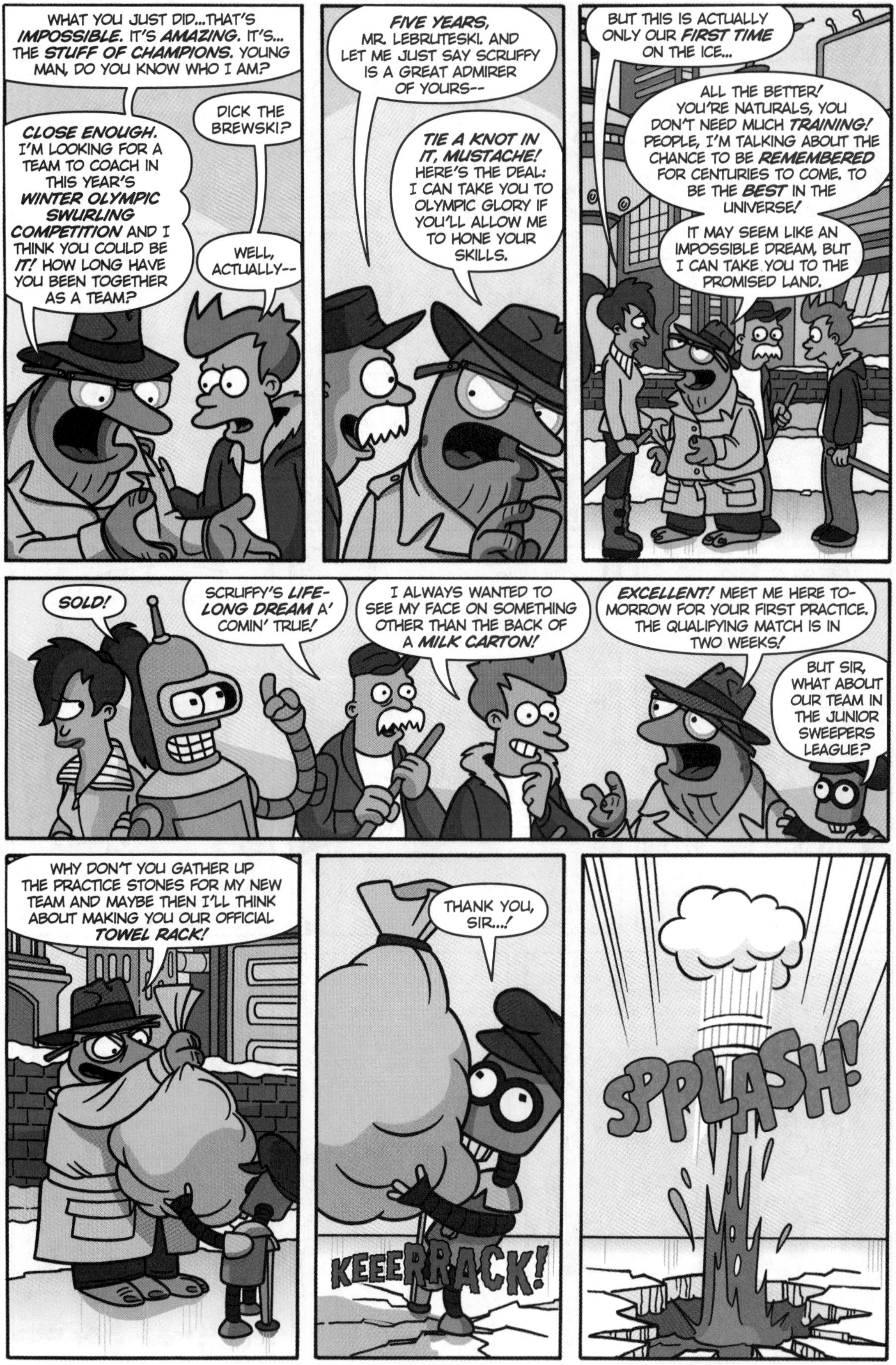
WHAT YOU JUST DID...THAT'S IMPOSSIBLE. IT'S AMAZING. IT'S... THE STUFF OF CHAMPIONS. YOUNG MAN, DO YOU KNOW WHO I AM?
DICK THE BREWSKI?
CLOSE ENOUGH. I'M LOOKING FOR A TEAM TO COACH IN THIS YEAR'S WINTER OLYMPIC SWURLING COMPETITION AND I THINK YOU COULD BE IT! HOW LONG HAVE YOU BEEN TOGETHER AS A TEAM?
WELL, ACTUALLY--
FIVE YEARS, MR. LEBRUTESKI. AND LET ME JUST SAY SCRUFFY IS A GREAT ADMIRER OF YOURS--
TIE A KNOT IN IT, MUSTACHE! HERE'S THE DEAL: I CAN TAKE YOU TO OLYMPIC GLORY IF YOU'LL ALLOW ME TO HONE YOUR SKILLS.
BUT THIS IS ACTUALLY ONLY OUR FIRST TIME ON THE ICE...
ALL THE BETTER! YOU'RE NATURALS, YOU DON'T NEED MUCH TRAINING! PEOPLE, I'M TALKING ABOUT THE CHANCE TO BE REMEMBERED FOR CENTURIES TO COME. TO BE THE BEST IN THE UNIVERSE!
IT MAY SEEM LIKE AN IMPOSSIBLE DREAM, BUT I CAN TAKE YOU TO THE PROMISED LAND.
SOLD!
SCRUFFY'S LIFE-LONG DREAM A' COMIN' TRUE!
I ALWAYS WANTED TO SEE MY FACE ON SOMETHING OTHER THAN THE BACK OF A MILK CARTON!
EXCELLENT! MEET ME HERE TO-MORROW FOR YOUR FIRST PRACTICE. THE QUALIFYING MATCH IS IN TWO WEEKS!
BUT SIR, WHAT ABOUT OUR TEAM IN THE JUNIOR SWEEPERS LEAGUE?
WHY DON'T YOU GATHER UP THE PRACTICE STONES FOR MY NEW TEAM AND MAYBE THEN I'LL THINK ABOUT MAKING YOU OUR OFFICIAL TOWEL RACK!
THANK YOU, SIR...!
KEEERRACK!
SPPLASH!

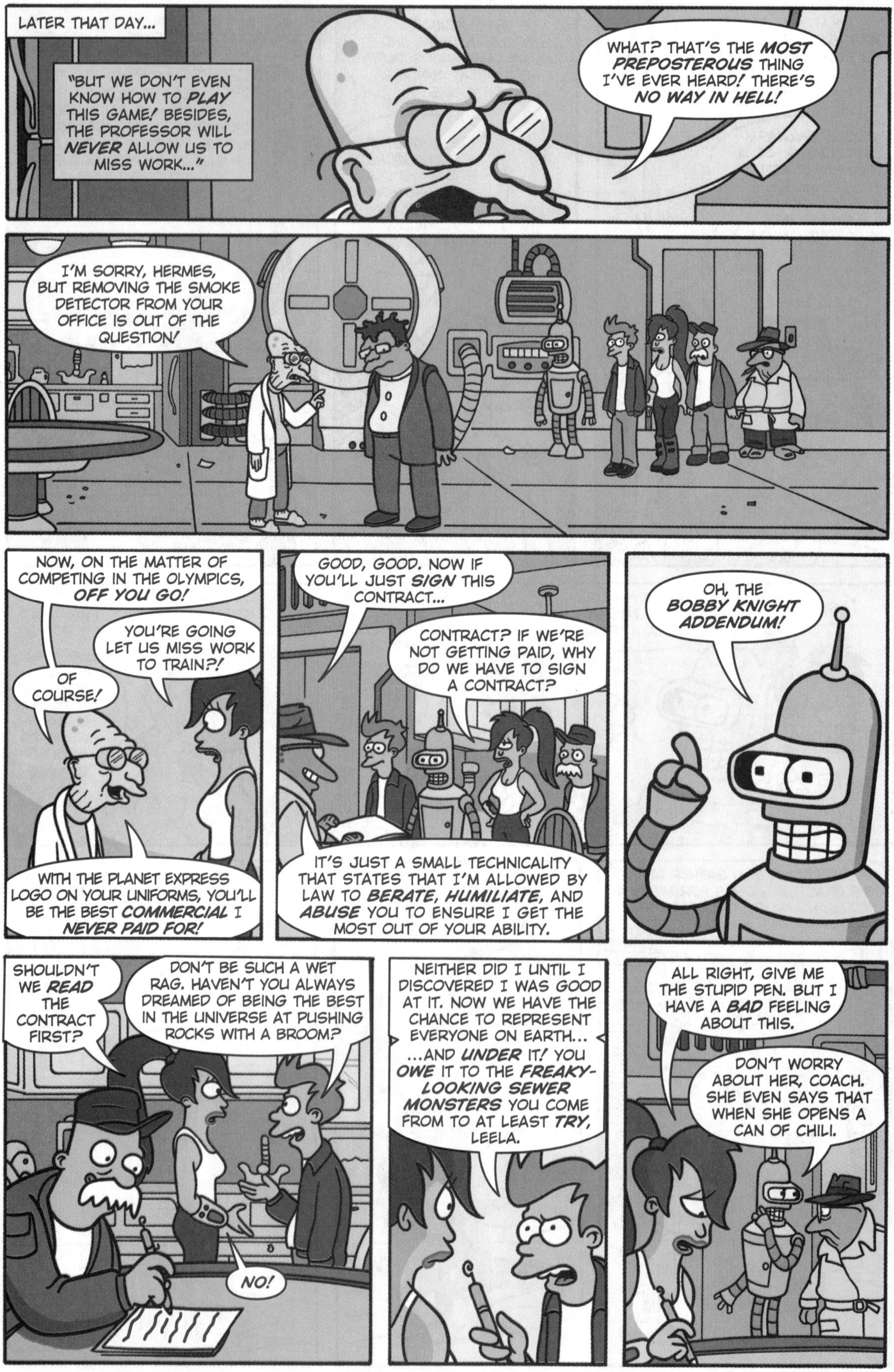

LATER THAT DAY...
"BUT WE DON'T EVEN KNOW HOW TO PLAY THIS GAME! BESIDES, THE PROFESSOR WILL NEVER ALLOW US TO MISS WORK..."
WHAT? THAT'S THE MOST PREPOSTEROUS THING I'VE EVER HEARD! THERE'S NO WAY IN HELL!
I'M SORRY, HERMES, BUT REMOVING THE SMOKE DETECTOR FROM YOUR OFFICE IS OUT OF THE QUESTION!
NOW, ON THE MATTER OF COMPETING IN THE OLYMPICS, OFF YOU GO!
YOU'RE GOING LET US MISS WORK TO TRAIN?!
OF COURSE!
WITH THE PLANET EXPRESS LOGO ON YOUR UNIFORMS, YOU'LL BE THE BEST COMMERCIAL I NEVER PAID FOR!
GOOD, GOOD. NOW IF YOU'LL JUST SIGN THIS CONTRACT...
CONTRACT? IF WE'RE NOT GETTING PAID, WHY DO WE HAVE TO SIGN A CONTRACT?
IT'S JUST A SMALL TECHNICALITY THAT STATES THAT I'M ALLOWED BY LAW TO BERATE, HUMILIATE, AND ABUSE YOU TO ENSURE I GET THE MOST OUT OF YOUR ABILITY.
OH, THE BOBBY KNIGHT ADDENDUM!
SHOULDN'T WE READ THE CONTRACT FIRST?
DON'T BE SUCH A WET RAG. HAVEN'T YOU ALWAYS DREAMED OF BEING THE BEST IN THE UNIVERSE AT PUSHING ROCKS WITH A BROOM?
NO!
NEITHER DID I UNTIL I DISCOVERED I WAS GOOD AT IT. NOW WE HAVE THE CHANCE TO REPRESENT EVERYONE ON EARTH...
...AND UNDER IT! YOU OWE IT TO THE FREAKY-LOOKING SEWER MONSTERS YOU COME FROM TO AT LEAST TRY, LEELA.
ALL RIGHT, GIVE ME THE STUPID PEN. BUT I HAVE A BAD FEELING ABOUT THIS.
DON'T WORRY ABOUT HER, COACH. SHE EVEN SAYS THAT WHEN SHE OPENS A CAN OF CHILI.

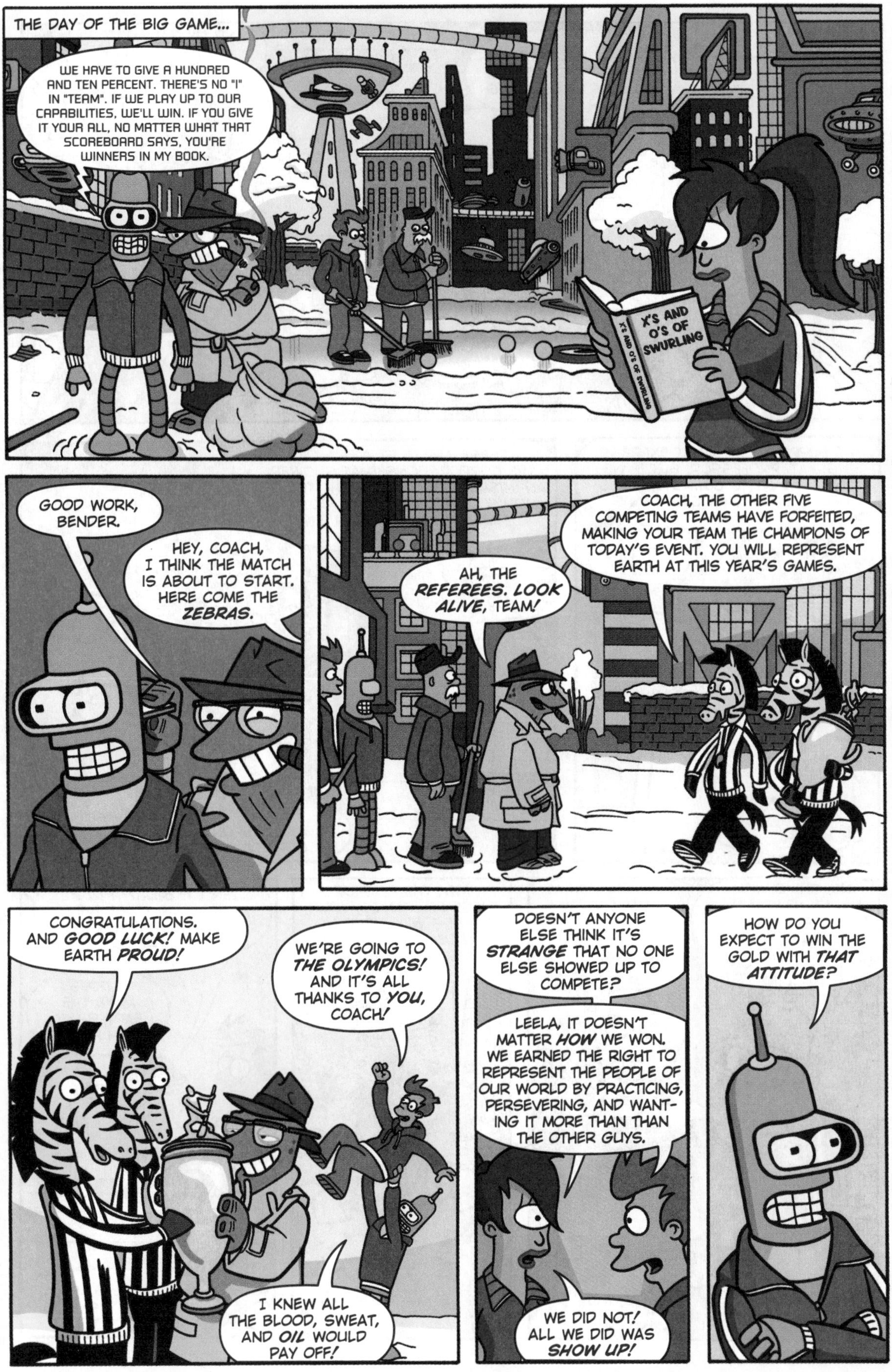
THE DAY OF THE BIG GAME...
WE HAVE TO GIVE A HUNDRED AND TEN PERCENT. THERE'S NO "I" IN "TEAM". IF WE PLAY UP TO OUR CAPABILITIES, WE'LL WIN. IF YOU GIVE IT YOUR ALL, NO MATTER WHAT THAT SCOREBOARD SAYS, YOU'RE WINNERS IN MY BOOK.
X'S AND O'S OF SWURLING
GOOD WORK, BENDER.
HEY, COACH, I THINK THE MATCH IS ABOUT TO START. HERE COME THE ZEBRAS.
AH, THE REFEREES. LOOK ALIVE, TEAM!
COACH, THE OTHER FIVE COMPETING TEAMS HAVE FORFEITED, MAKING YOUR TEAM THE CHAMPIONS OF TODAY'S EVENT. YOU WILL REPRESENT EARTH AT THIS YEAR'S GAMES.
CONGRATULATIONS. AND GOOD LUCK! MAKE EARTH PROUD!
WE'RE GOING TO THE OLYMPICS! AND IT'S ALL THANKS TO YOU, COACH!
I KNEW ALL THE BLOOD, SWEAT, AND OIL WOULD PAY OFF!
DOESN'T ANYONE ELSE THINK IT'S STRANGE THAT NO ONE ELSE SHOWED UP TO COMPETE?
LEELA, IT DOESN'T MATTER HOW WE WON. WE EARNED THE RIGHT TO REPRESENT THE PEOPLE OF OUR WORLD BY PRACTICING, PERSEVERING, AND WANTING IT MORE THAN THAN THE OTHER GUYS.
WE DID NOT! ALL WE DID WAS SHOW UP!
HOW DO YOU EXPECT TO WIN THE GOLD WITH THAT ATTITUDE?

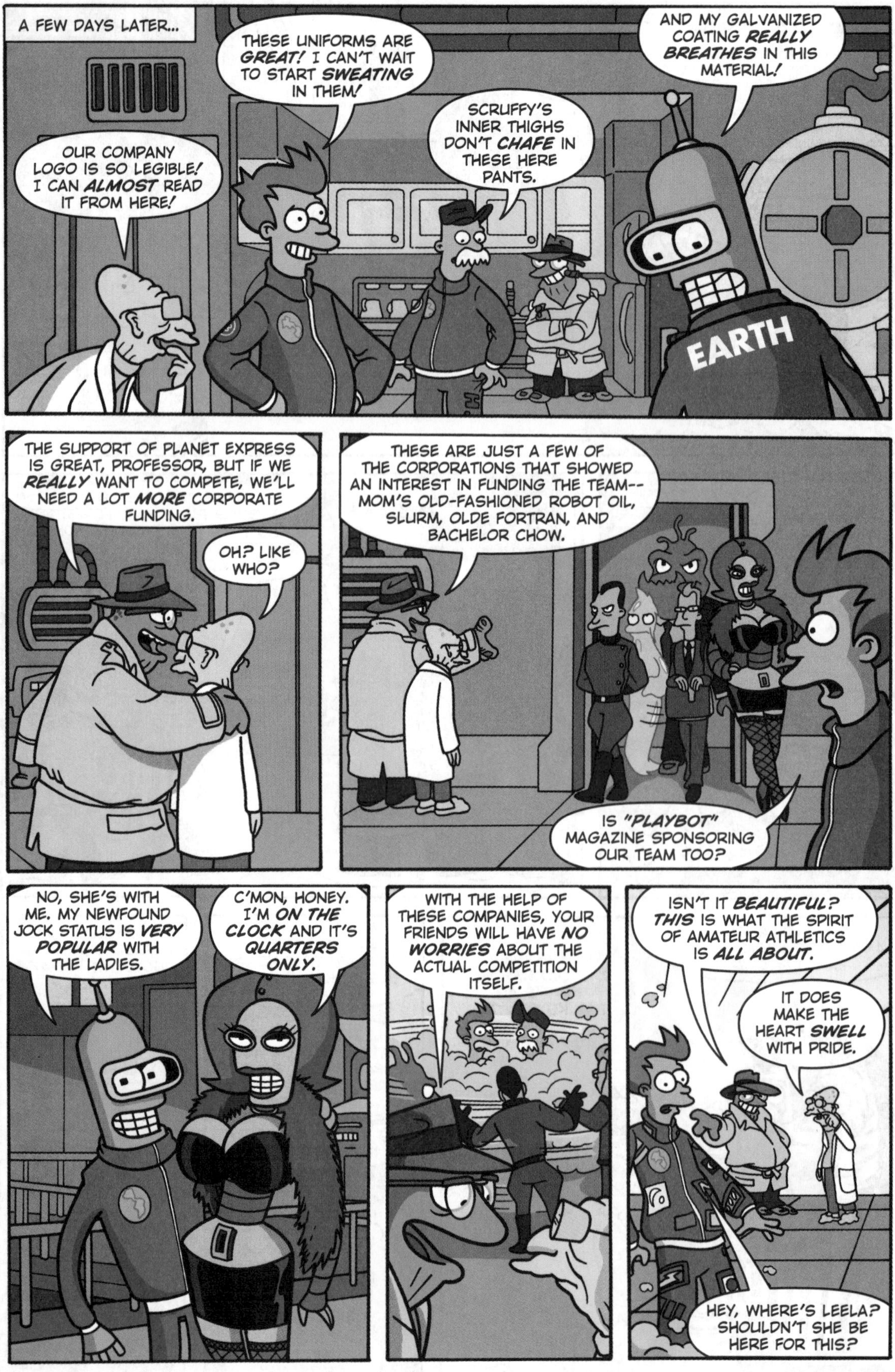
A FEW DAYS LATER...
THESE UNIFORMS ARE GREAT! I CAN'T WAIT TO START SWEATING IN THEM!
OUR COMPANY LOGO IS SO LEGIBLE! I CAN ALMOST READ IT FROM HERE!
SCRUFFY'S INNER THIGHS DON'T CHAFE IN THESE HERE PANTS.
AND MY GALVANIZED COATING REALLY BREATHES IN THIS MATERIAL!
EARTH
THE SUPPORT OF PLANET EXPRESS IS GREAT, PROFESSOR, BUT IF WE REALLY WANT TO COMPETE, WE'LL NEED A LOT MORE CORPORATE FUNDING.
OH? LIKE WHO?
THESE ARE JUST A FEW OF THE CORPORATIONS THAT SHOWED AN INTEREST IN FUNDING THE TEAM-- MOM'S OLD-FASHIONED ROBOT OIL, SLURM, OLDE FORTRAN, AND BACHELOR CHOW.
IS "PLAYBOT" MAGAZINE SPONSORING OUR TEAM TOO?
NO, SHE'S WITH ME. MY NEWFOUND JOCK STATUS IS VERY POPULAR WITH THE LADIES.
C'MON, HONEY. I'M ON THE CLOCK AND IT'S QUARTERS ONLY.
WITH THE HELP OF THESE COMPANIES, YOUR FRIENDS WILL HAVE NO WORRIES ABOUT THE ACTUAL COMPETITION ITSELF.
ISN'T IT BEAUTIFUL? THIS IS WHAT THE SPIRIT OF AMATEUR ATHLETICS IS ALL ABOUT.
IT DOES MAKE THE HEART SWELL WITH PRIDE.
HEY, WHERE'S LEELA? SHOULDN'T SHE BE HERE FOR THIS?

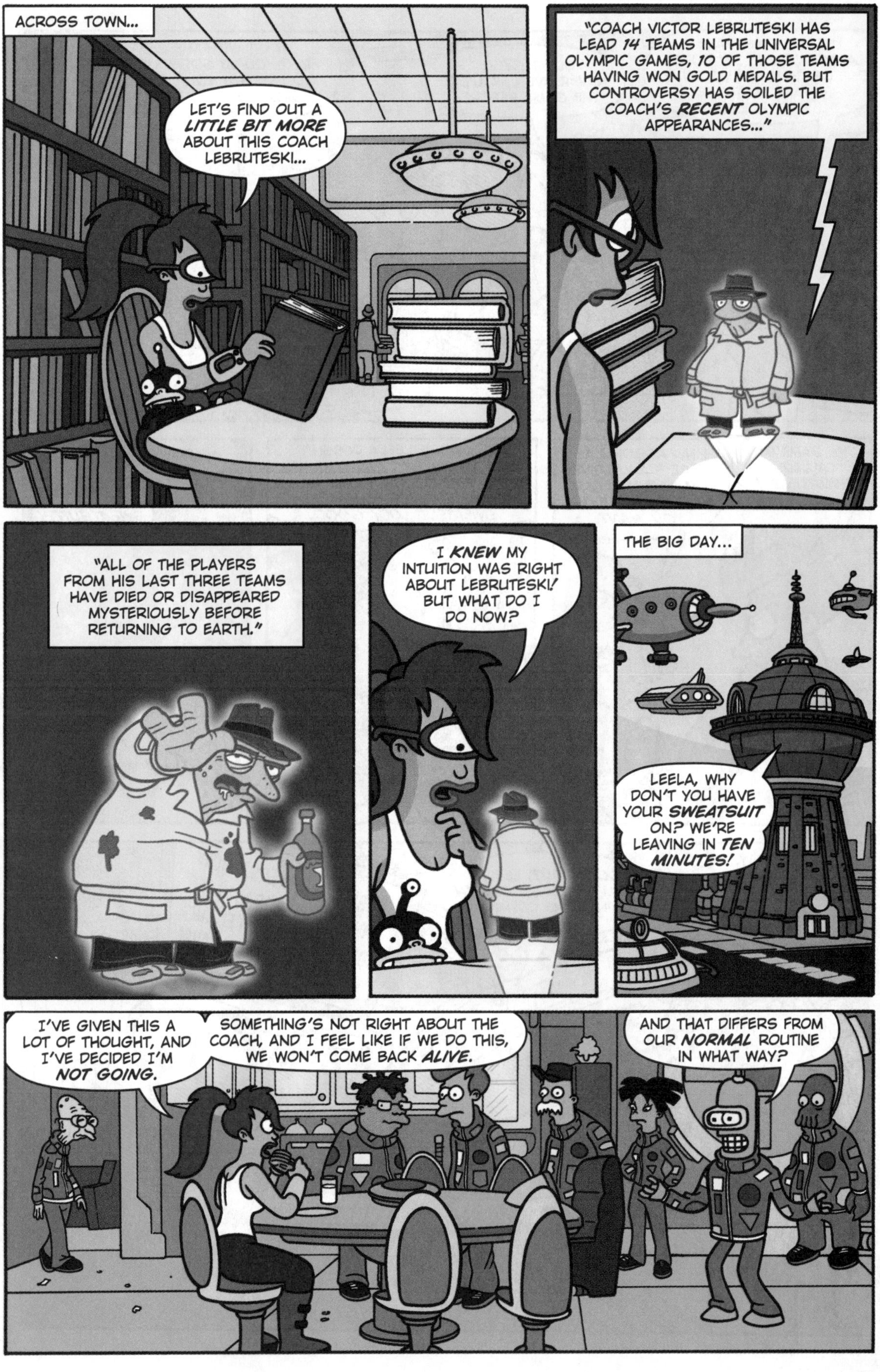
ACROSS TOWN...
LET'S FIND OUT A LITTLE BIT MORE ABOUT THIS COACH LEBRUTESKI...
"COACH VICTOR LEBRUTESKI HAS LEAD 14 TEAMS IN THE UNIVERSAL OLYMPIC GAMES, 10 OF THOSE TEAMS HAVING WON GOLD MEDALS. BUT CONTROVERSY HAS SOILED THE COACH'S RECENT OLYMPIC APPEARANCES..."
"ALL OF THE PLAYERS FROM HIS LAST THREE TEAMS HAVE DIED OR DISAPPEARED MYSTERIOUSLY BEFORE RETURNING TO EARTH."
I KNEW MY INTUITION WAS RIGHT ABOUT LEBRUTESKI! BUT WHAT DO I DO NOW?
THE BIG DAY...
LEELA, WHY DON'T YOU HAVE YOUR SWEATSUIT ON? WE'RE LEAVING IN TEN MINUTES!
I'VE GIVEN THIS A LOT OF THOUGHT, AND I'VE DECIDED I'M NOT GOING.
SOMETHING'S NOT RIGHT ABOUT THE COACH, AND I FEEL LIKE IF WE DO THIS, WE WON'T COME BACK ALIVE.
AND THAT DIFFERS FROM OUR NORMAL ROUTINE IN WHAT WAY?

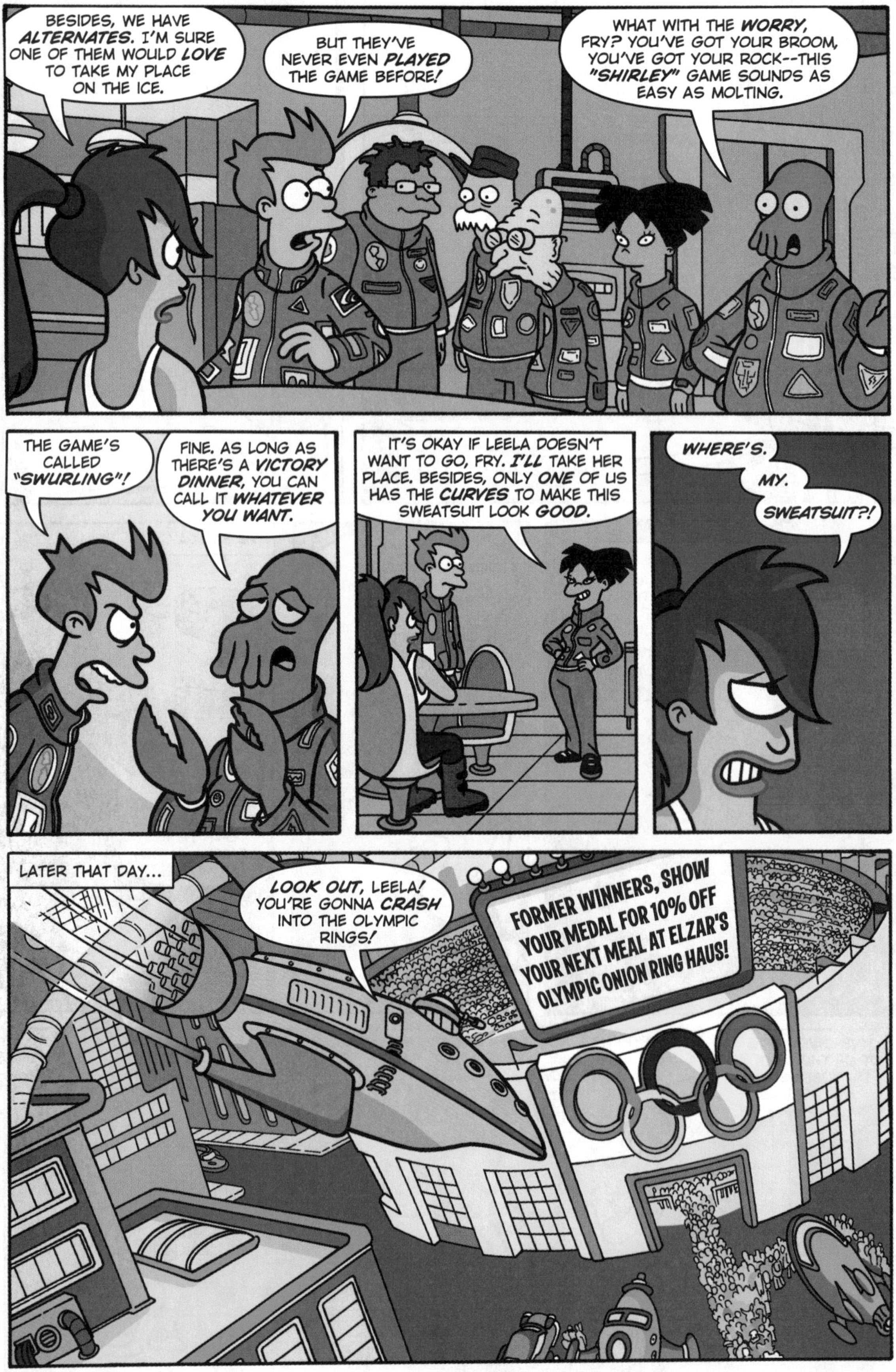
BESIDES, WE HAVE ALTERNATES. I'M SURE ONE OF THEM WOULD LOVE TO TAKE MY PLACE ON THE ICE.
BUT THEY'VE NEVER EVEN PLAYED THE GAME BEFORE!
WHAT WITH THE WORRY, FRY? YOU'VE GOT YOUR BROOM, YOU'VE GOT YOUR ROCK--THIS "SHIRLEY" GAME SOUNDS AS EASY AS MOLTING.
THE GAME'S CALLED "SWURLING"!
FINE. AS LONG AS THERE'S A VICTORY DINNER, YOU CAN CALL IT WHATEVER YOU WANT.
IT'S OKAY IF LEELA DOESN'T WANT TO GO, FRY. I'LL TAKE HER PLACE. BESIDES, ONLY ONE OF US HAS THE CURVES TO MAKE THIS SWEATSUIT LOOK GOOD.
WHERE'S.
MY.
SWEATSUIT?!
LATER THAT DAY...
LOOK OUT, LEELA! YOU'RE GONNA CRASH INTO THE OLYMPIC RINGS!
FORMER WINNERS, SHOW YOUR MEDAL FOR 10% OFF YOUR NEXT MEAL AT ELZAR'S OLYMPIC ONION RING HAUS!

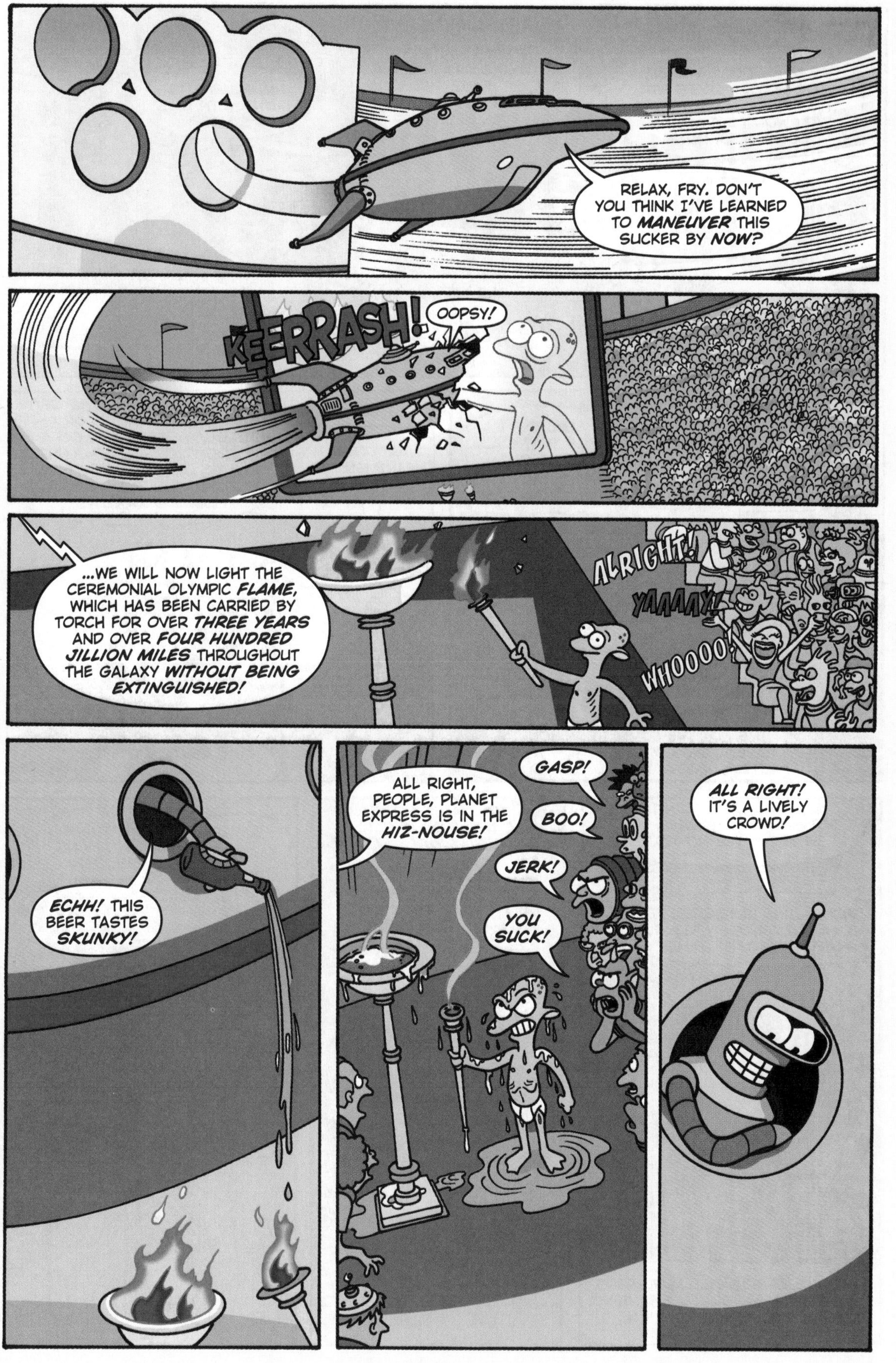
RELAX, FRY. DON'T YOU THINK I'VE LEARNED TO MANEUVER THIS SUCKER BY NOW?
KEERRASH!
OOPSY!
...WE WILL NOW LIGHT THE CEREMONIAL OLYMPIC FLAME, WHICH HAS BEEN CARRIED BY TORCH FOR OVER THREE YEARS AND OVER FOUR HUNDRED JILLION MILES THROUGHOUT THE GALAXY WITHOUT BEING EXTINGUISHED!
ALRIGHT!
YAAAAY!
WHOOOO!
ECHH! THIS BEER TASTES SKUNKY!
ALL RIGHT, PEOPLE, PLANET EXPRESS IS IN THE HIZ-NOUSE!
GASP!
BOO!
JERK!
YOU SUCK!
ALL RIGHT! IT'S A LIVELY CROWD!

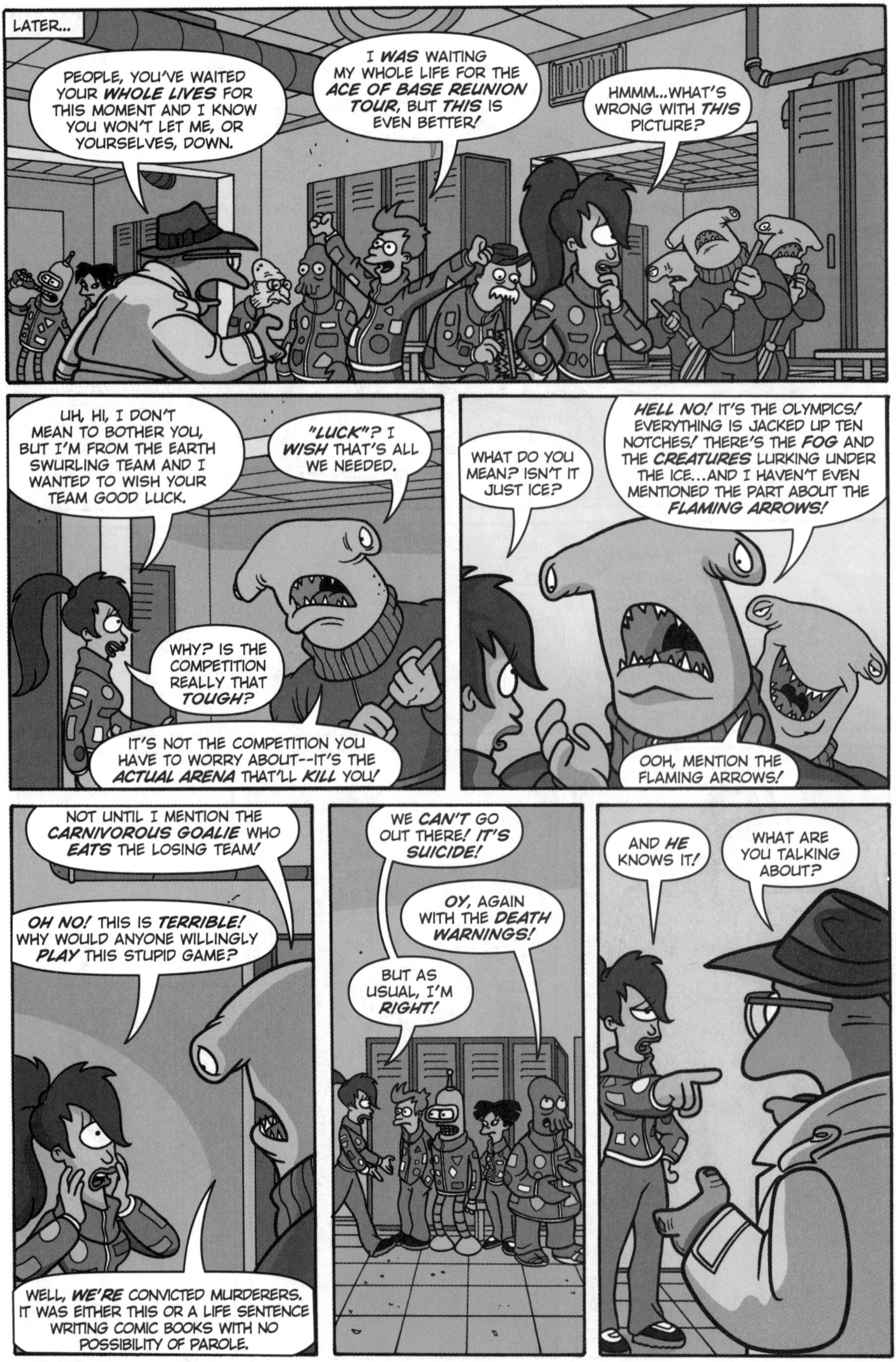
LATER...
PEOPLE, YOU'VE WAITED YOUR WHOLE LIVES FOR THIS MOMENT AND I KNOW YOU WON'T LET ME, OR YOURSELVES, DOWN.
I WAS WAITING MY WHOLE LIFE FOR THE ACE OF BASE REUNION TOUR, BUT THIS IS EVEN BETTER!
HMMM...WHAT'S WRONG WITH THIS PICTURE?
UH, HI, I DON'T MEAN TO BOTHER YOU, BUT I'M FROM THE EARTH SWURLING TEAM AND I WANTED TO WISH YOUR TEAM GOOD LUCK.
"LUCK"? I WISH THAT'S ALL WE NEEDED.
WHY? IS THE COMPETITION REALLY THAT TOUGH?
IT'S NOT THE COMPETITION YOU HAVE TO WORRY ABOUT--IT'S THE ACTUAL ARENA THAT'LL KILL YOU!
WHAT DO YOU MEAN? ISN'T IT JUST ICE?
HELL NO! IT'S THE OLYMPICS! EVERYTHING IS JACKED UP TEN NOTCHES! THERE'S THE FOG AND THE CREATURES LURKING UNDER THE ICE...AND I HAVEN'T EVEN MENTIONED THE PART ABOUT THE FLAMING ARROWS!
OOH, MENTION THE FLAMING ARROWS!
NOT UNTIL I MENTION THE CARNIVOROUS GOALIE WHO EATS THE LOSING TEAM!
OH NO! THIS IS TERRIBLE! WHY WOULD ANYONE WILLINGLY PLAY THIS STUPID GAME?
WELL, WE'RE CONVICTED MURDERERS. IT WAS EITHER THIS OR A LIFE SENTENCE WRITING COMIC BOOKS WITH NO POSSIBILITY OF PAROLE.
WE CAN'T GO OUT THERE! IT'S SUICIDE!
OY, AGAIN WITH THE DEATH WARNINGS!
BUT AS USUAL, I'M RIGHT!
AND HE KNOWS IT!
WHAT ARE YOU TALKING ABOUT?

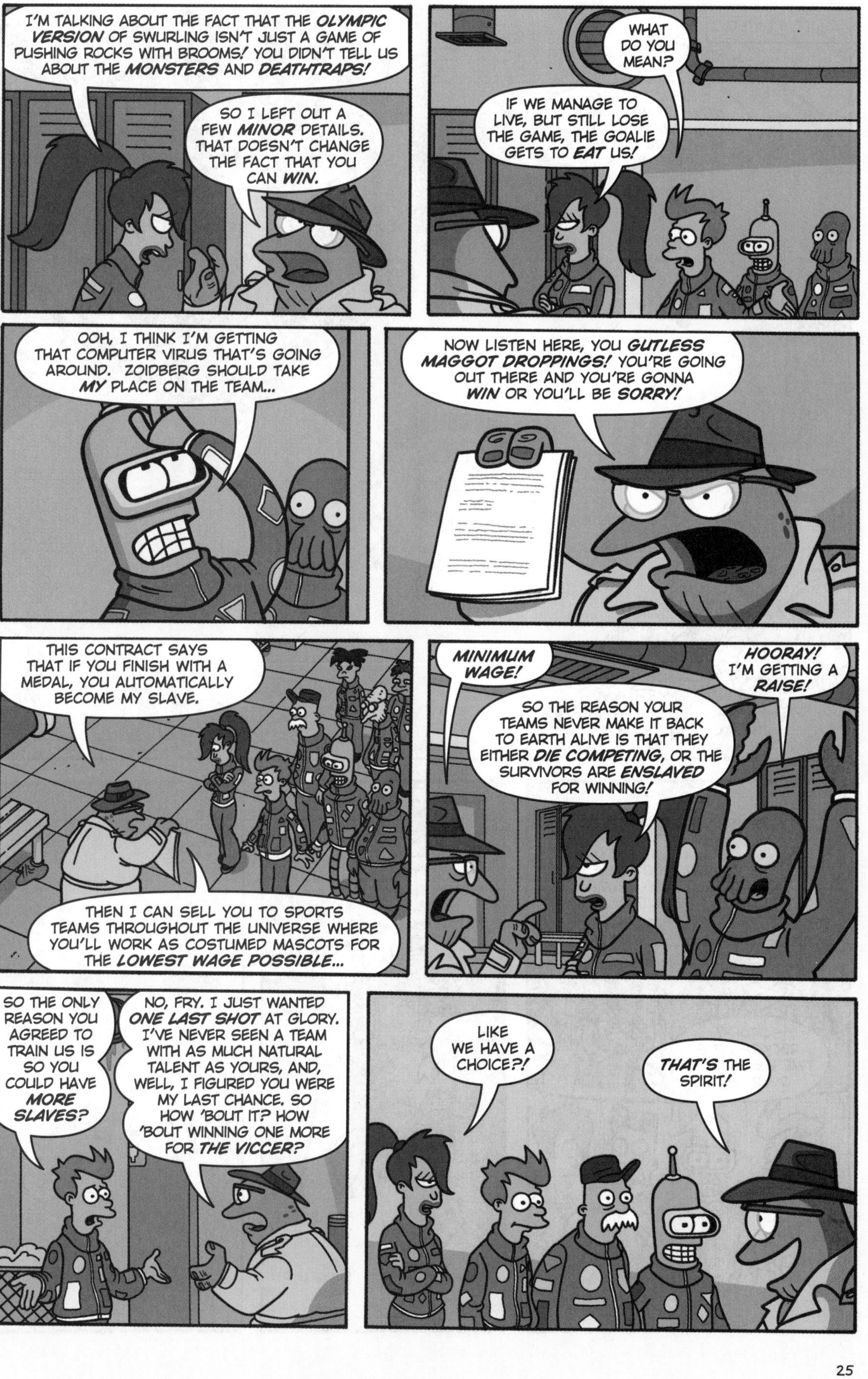
I'M TALKING ABOUT THE FACT THAT THE OLYMPIC VERSION OF SWURLING ISN'T JUST A GAME OF PUSHING ROCKS WITH BROOMS! YOU DIDN'T TELL US ABOUT THE MONSTERS AND DEATHTRAPS!
SO I LEFT OUT A FEW MINOR DETAILS. THAT DOESN'T CHANGE THE FACT THAT YOU CAN WIN.
WHAT DO YOU MEAN?
IF WE MANAGE TO LIVE, BUT STILL LOSE THE GAME, THE GOALIE GETS TO EAT US!
OOH, I THINK I'M GETTING THAT COMPUTER VIRUS THAT'S GOING AROUND. ZOIDBERG SHOULD TAKE MY PLACE ON THE TEAM...
NOW LISTEN HERE, YOU GUTLESS MAGGOT DROPPINGS! YOU'RE GOING OUT THERE AND YOU'RE GONNA WIN OR YOU'LL BE SORRY!
THIS CONTRACT SAYS THAT IF YOU FINISH WITH A MEDAL, YOU AUTOMATICALLY BECOME MY SLAVE.
THEN I CAN SELL YOU TO SPORTS TEAMS THROUGHOUT THE UNIVERSE WHERE YOU'LL WORK AS COSTUMED MASCOTS FOR THE LOWEST WAGE POSSIBLE...
MINIMUM WAGE!
HOORAY! I'M GETTING A RAISE!
SO THE REASON YOUR TEAMS NEVER MAKE IT BACK TO EARTH ALIVE IS THAT THEY EITHER DIE COMPETING, OR THE SURVIVORS ARE ENSLAVED FOR WINNING!
SO THE ONLY REASON YOU AGREED TO TRAIN US IS SO YOU COULD HAVE MORE SLAVES?
NO, FRY. I JUST WANTED ONE LAST SHOT AT GLORY. I'VE NEVER SEEN A TEAM WITH AS MUCH NATURAL TALENT AS YOURS, AND, WELL, I FIGURED YOU WERE MY LAST CHANCE. SO HOW 'BOUT IT? HOW 'BOUT WINNING ONE MORE FOR THE VICCER?
LIKE WE HAVE A CHOICE?!
THAT'S THE SPIRIT!

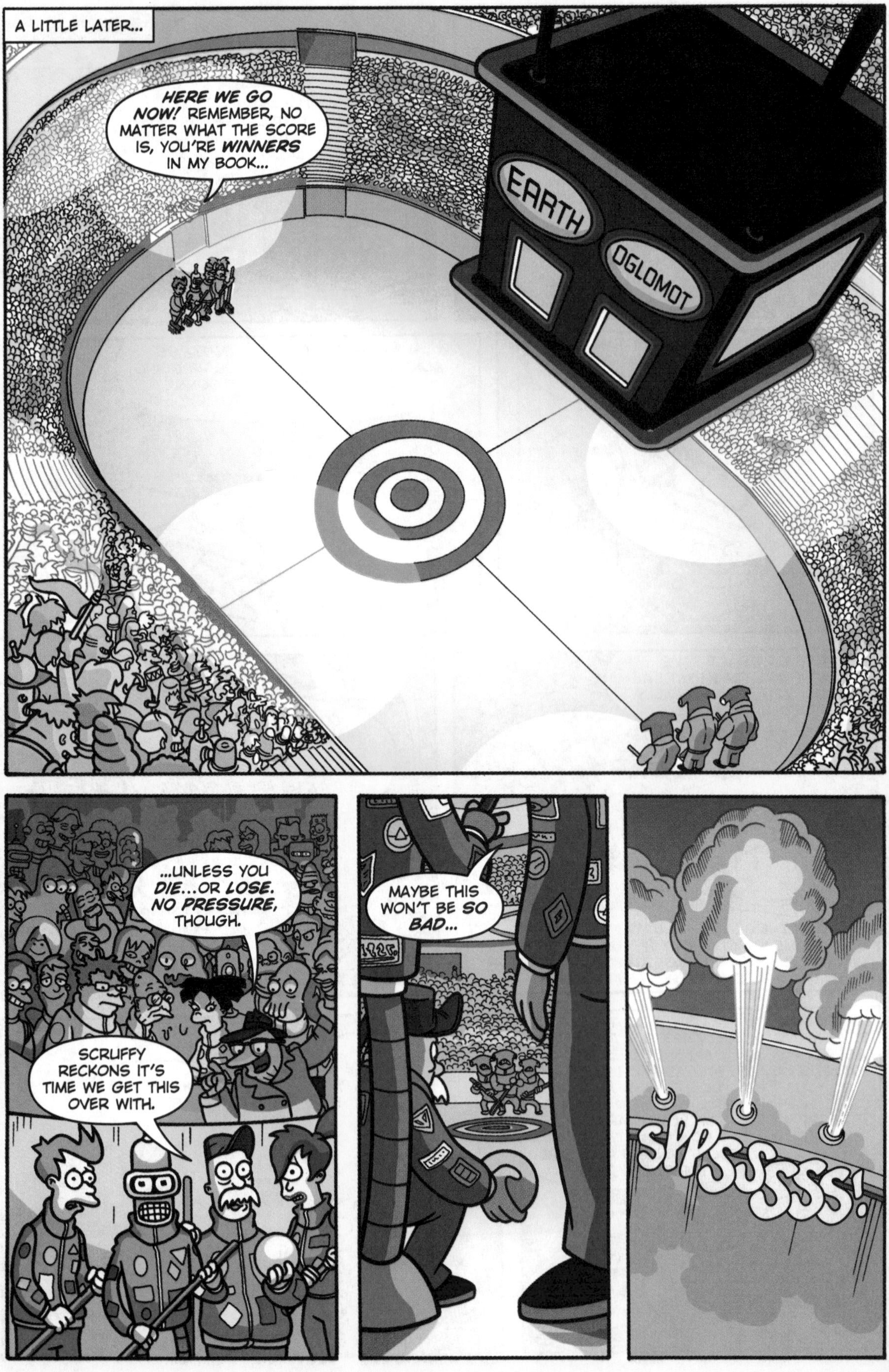
A LITTLE LATER...
HERE WE GO NOW! REMEMBER, NO MATTER WHAT THE SCORE IS, YOU'RE WINNERS IN MY BOOK...
EARTH
OGLOMOT
...UNLESS YOU DIE...OR LOSE. NO PRESSURE, THOUGH.
SCRUFFY RECKONS IT'S TIME WE GET THIS OVER WITH.
MAYBE THIS WON'T BE SO BAD...
SPPSSSSSS!

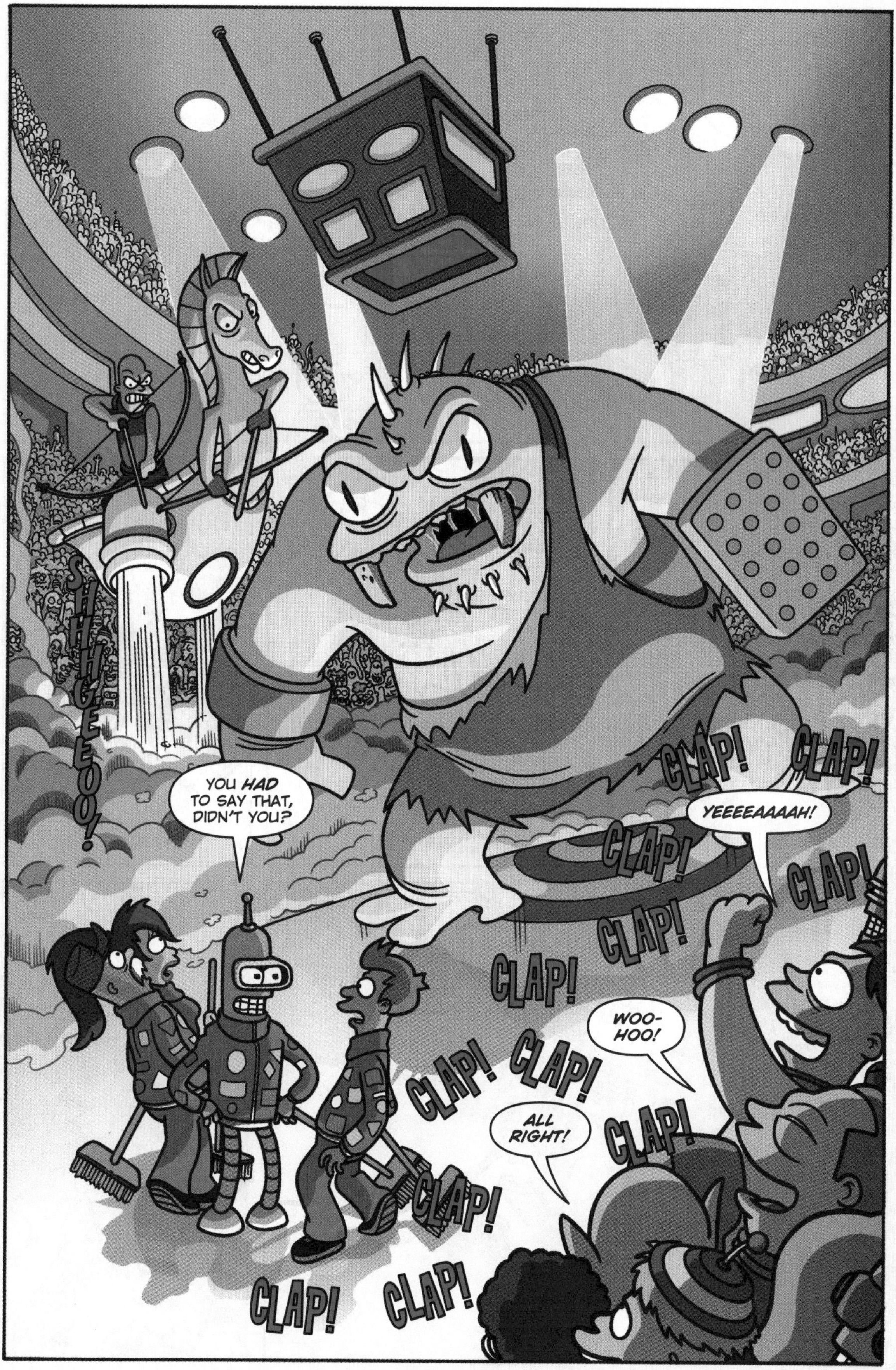
SHHGEEOOO!
YOU HAD TO SAY THAT, DIDN'T YOU?
CLAP! CLAP!
YEEEEAAAAH!
CLAP!
CLAP!
CLAP!
CLAP!
WOO-HOO!
CLAP! CLAP!
ALL RIGHT!
CLAP!
CLAP!
CLAP! CLAP!

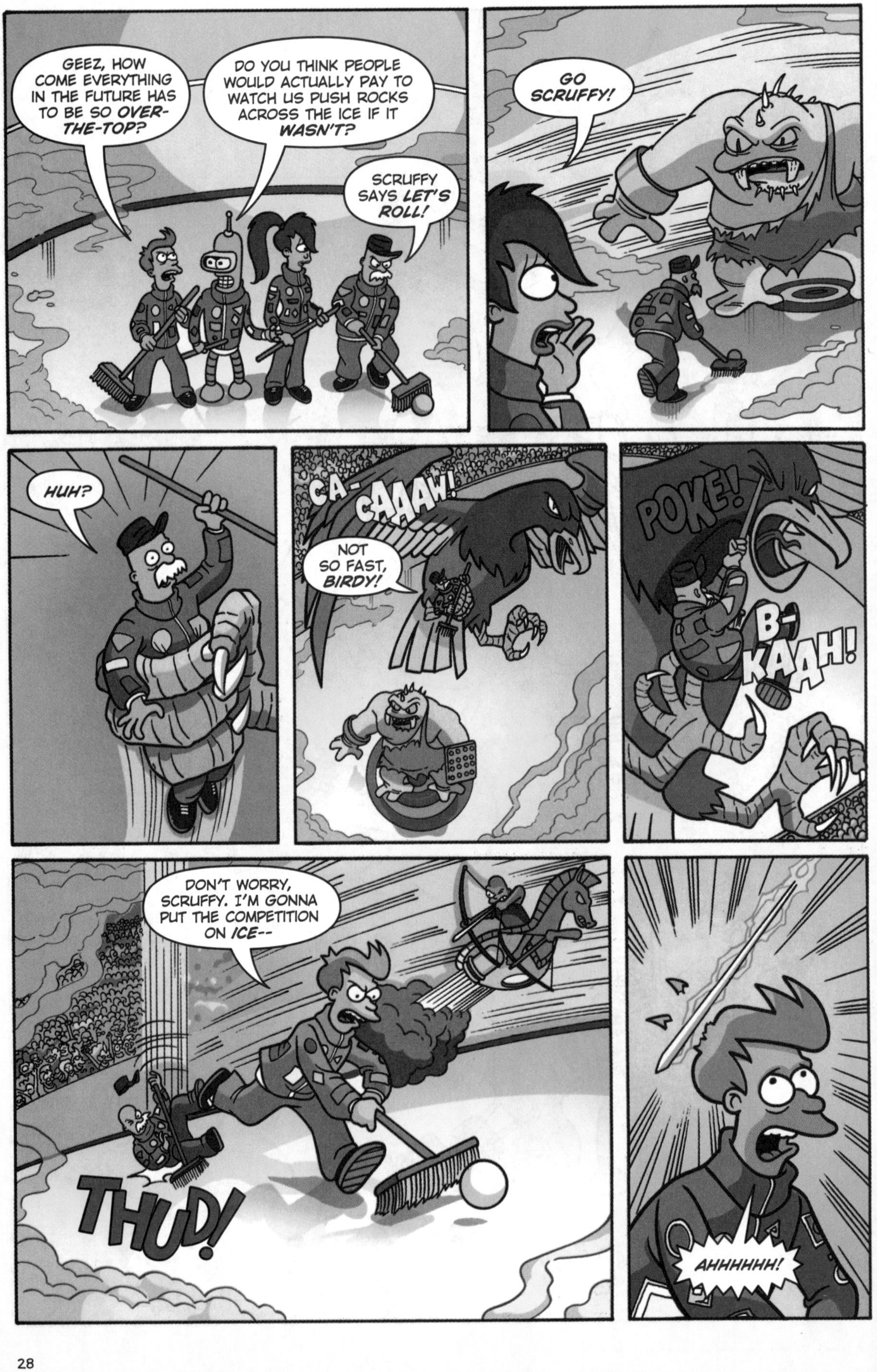
GEEZ, HOW COME EVERYTHING IN THE FUTURE HAS TO BE SO OVER-THE-TOP?
DO YOU THINK PEOPLE WOULD ACTUALLY PAY TO WATCH US PUSH ROCKS ACROSS THE ICE IF IT WASN'T?
SCRUFFY SAYS LET'S ROLL!
GO SCRUFFY!
HUH?
CA-CAAAW!
NOT SO FAST, BIRDY!
POKE!
B-KAAH!
DON'T WORRY, SCRUFFY. I'M GONNA PUT THE COMPETITION ON ICE--
THUD!
AHHHHHH!

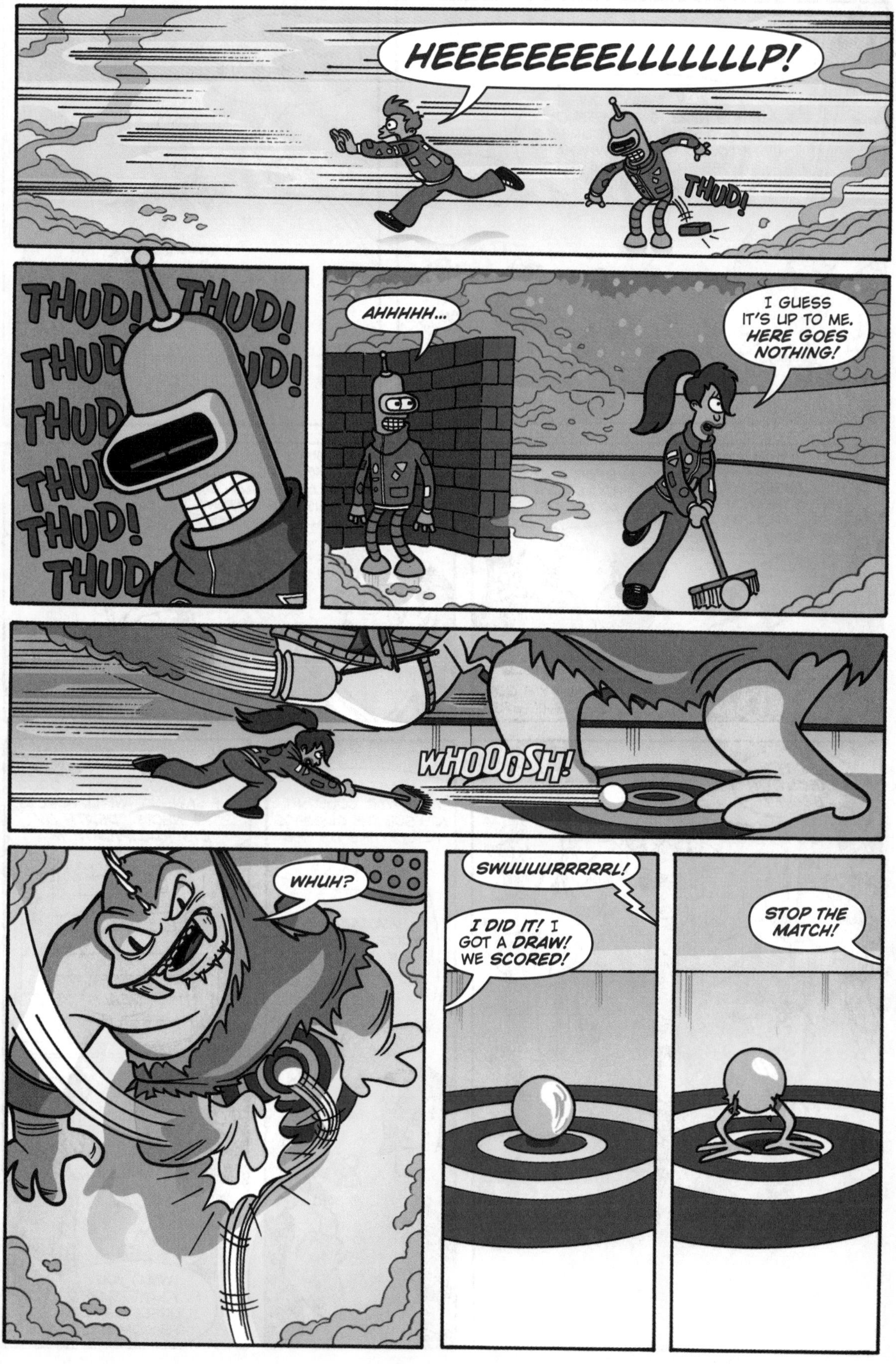
HEEEEEEEELLLLLLLP!
THUD!
THUD! THUD!
THUD! THUD!
THUD
THUD
THUD!
THUD
AHHHHH...
I GUESS IT'S UP TO ME. HERE GOES NOTHING!
WHOOOSH!
WHUH?
SWUUUURRRRRL!
I DID IT! I GOT A DRAW! WE SCORED!
STOP THE MATCH!

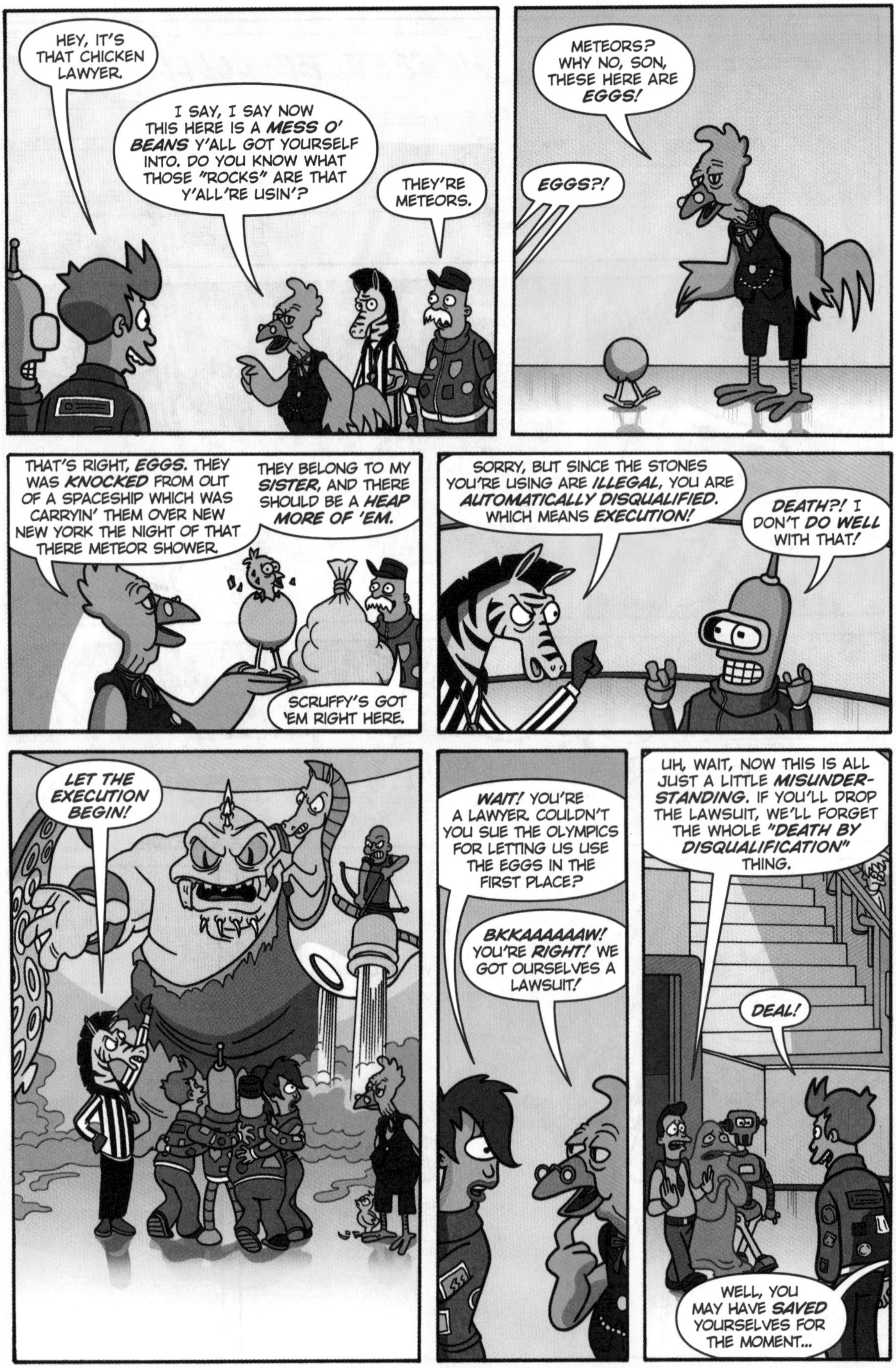
HEY, IT'S THAT CHICKEN LAWYER.
I SAY, I SAY NOW THIS HERE IS A MESS O' BEANS Y'ALL GOT YOURSELF INTO. DO YOU KNOW WHAT THOSE "ROCKS" ARE THAT Y'ALL'RE USIN'?
THEY'RE METEORS.
METEORS? WHY NO, SON, THESE HERE ARE EGGS!
EGGS?!
THAT'S RIGHT, EGGS. THEY WAS KNOCKED FROM OUT OF A SPACESHIP WHICH WAS CARRYIN' THEM OVER NEW NEW YORK THE NIGHT OF THAT THERE METEOR SHOWER.
THEY BELONG TO MY SISTER, AND THERE SHOULD BE A HEAP MORE OF 'EM.
SCRUFFY'S GOT 'EM RIGHT HERE.
SORRY, BUT SINCE THE STONES YOU'RE USING ARE ILLEGAL, YOU ARE AUTOMATICALLY DISQUALIFIED. WHICH MEANS EXECUTION!
DEATH?! I DON'T DO WELL WITH THAT!
LET THE EXECUTION BEGIN!
WAIT! YOU'RE A LAWYER. COULDN'T YOU SUE THE OLYMPICS FOR LETTING US USE THE EGGS IN THE FIRST PLACE?
BKKAAAAAAW! YOU'RE RIGHT! WE GOT OURSELVES A LAWSUIT!
UH, WAIT, NOW THIS IS ALL JUST A LITTLE MISUNDERSTANDING. IF YOU'LL DROP THE LAWSUIT, WE'LL FORGET THE WHOLE "DEATH BY DISQUALIFICATION" THING.
DEAL!
WELL, YOU MAY HAVE SAVED YOURSELVES FOR THE MOMENT...

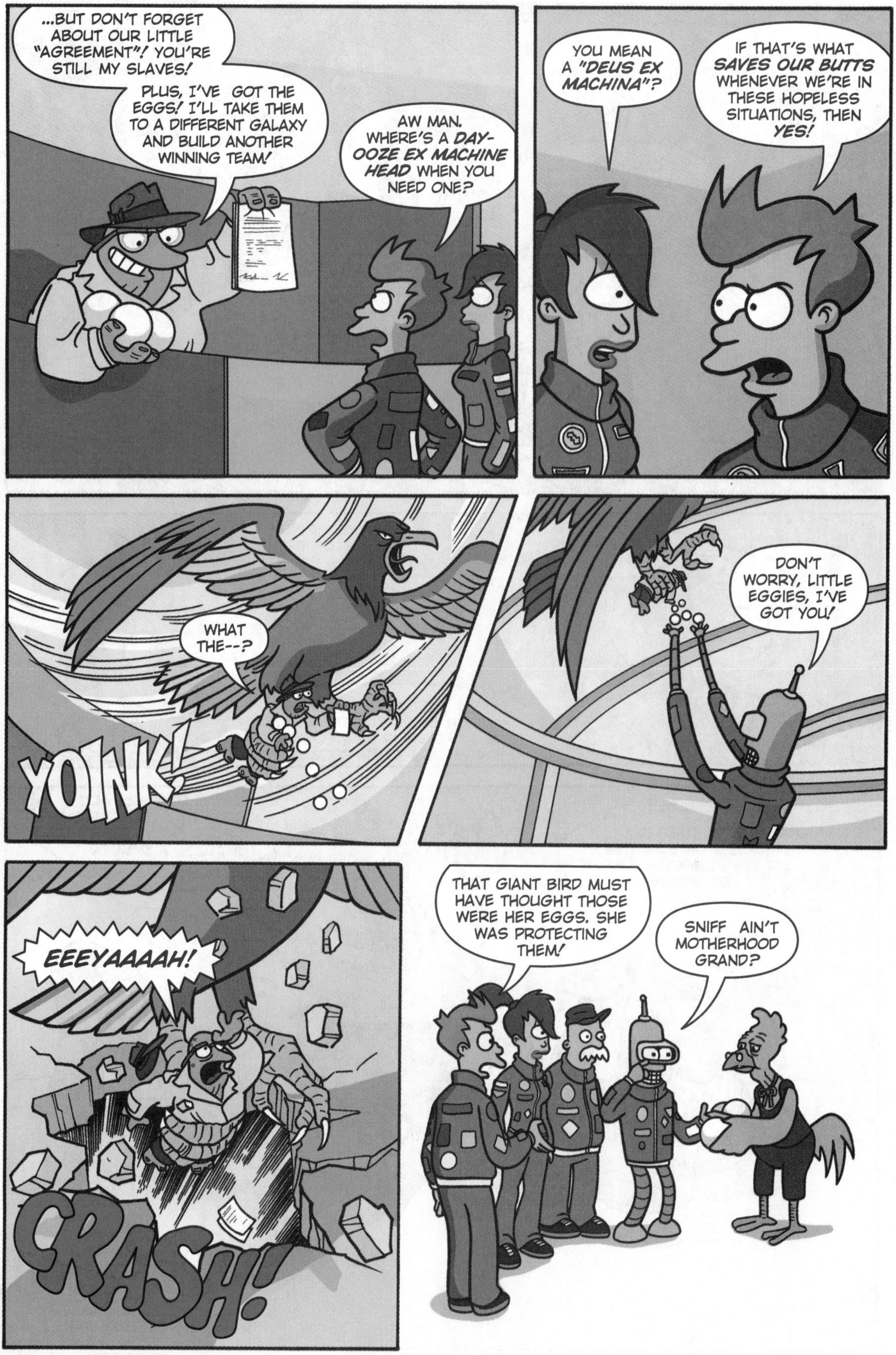
...BUT DON'T FORGET ABOUT OUR LITTLE "AGREEMENT"! YOU'RE STILL MY SLAVES!
PLUS, I'VE GOT THE EGGS! I'LL TAKE THEM TO A DIFFERENT GALAXY AND BUILD ANOTHER WINNING TEAM!
AW MAN. WHERE'S A DAY-OOZE EX MACHINE HEAD WHEN YOU NEED ONE?
YOU MEAN A "DEUS EX MACHINA"?
IF THAT'S WHAT SAVES OUR BUTTS WHENEVER WE'RE IN THESE HOPELESS SITUATIONS, THEN YES!
WHAT THE--?
YOINK!
DON'T WORRY, LITTLE EGGIES, I'VE GOT YOU!
EEEYAAAAH!
CRASH!
THAT GIANT BIRD MUST HAVE THOUGHT THOSE WERE HER EGGS. SHE WAS PROTECTING THEM!
SNIFF AIN'T MOTHERHOOD GRAND?

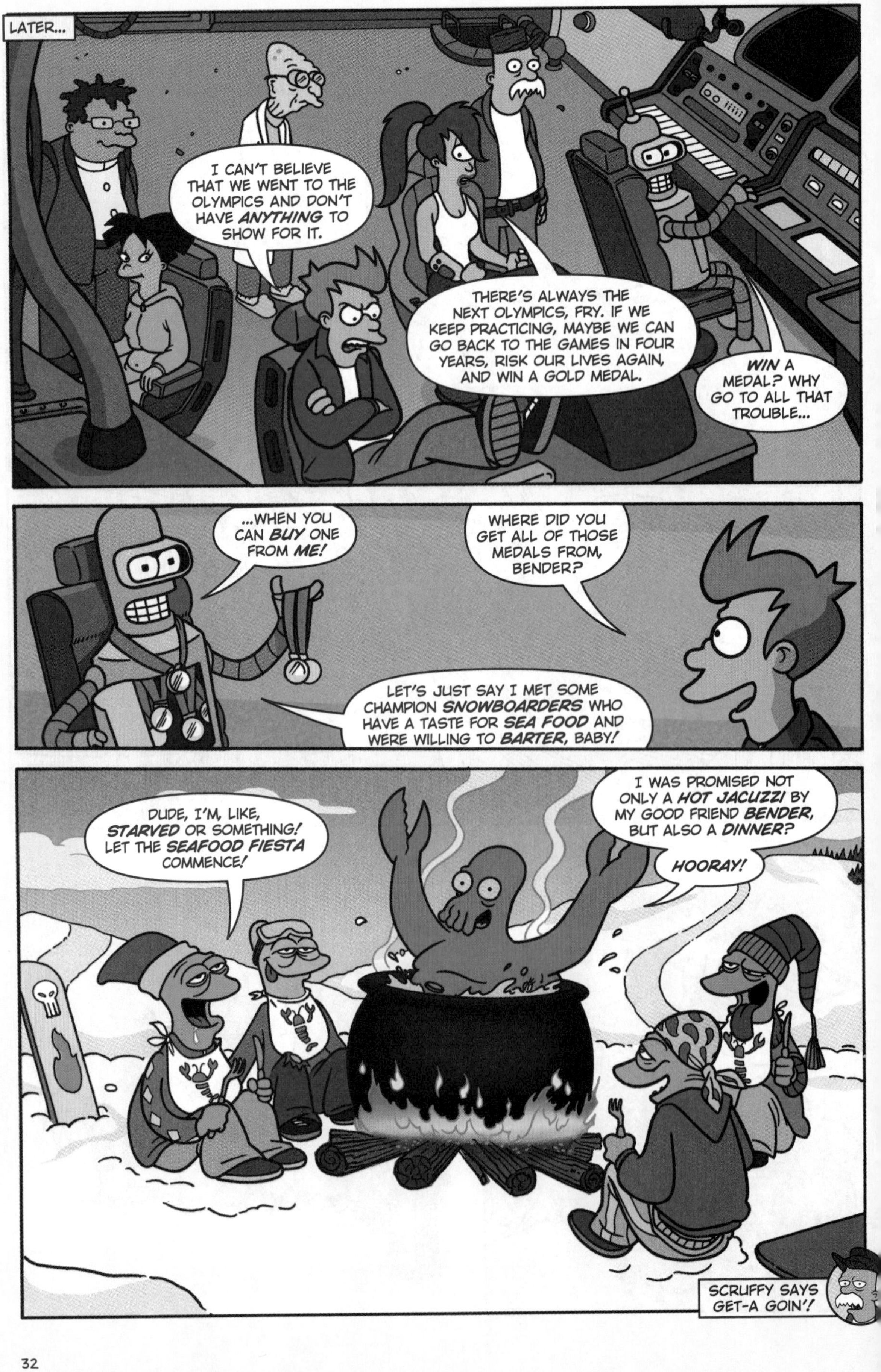
LATER...
I CAN'T BELIEVE THAT WE WENT TO THE OLYMPICS AND DON'T HAVE *ANYTHING* TO SHOW FOR IT.
THERE'S ALWAYS THE NEXT OLYMPICS, FRY. IF WE KEEP PRACTICING, MAYBE WE CAN GO BACK TO THE GAMES IN FOUR YEARS, RISK OUR LIVES AGAIN, AND WIN A GOLD MEDAL.
*WIN* A MEDAL? WHY GO TO ALL THAT TROUBLE...
...WHEN YOU CAN *BUY* ONE FROM *ME!*
WHERE DID YOU GET ALL OF THOSE MEDALS FROM, BENDER?
LET'S JUST SAY I MET SOME CHAMPION *SNOWBOARDERS* WHO HAVE A TASTE FOR *SEA FOOD* AND WERE WILLING TO *BARTER*, BABY!
DUDE, I'M, LIKE, *STARVED* OR SOMETHING! LET THE *SEAFOOD FIESTA* COMMENCE!
I WAS PROMISED NOT ONLY A *HOT JACUZZI* BY MY GOOD FRIEND *BENDER*, BUT ALSO A *DINNER?*
*HOORAY!*
SCRUFFY SAYS GET-A GOIN'!

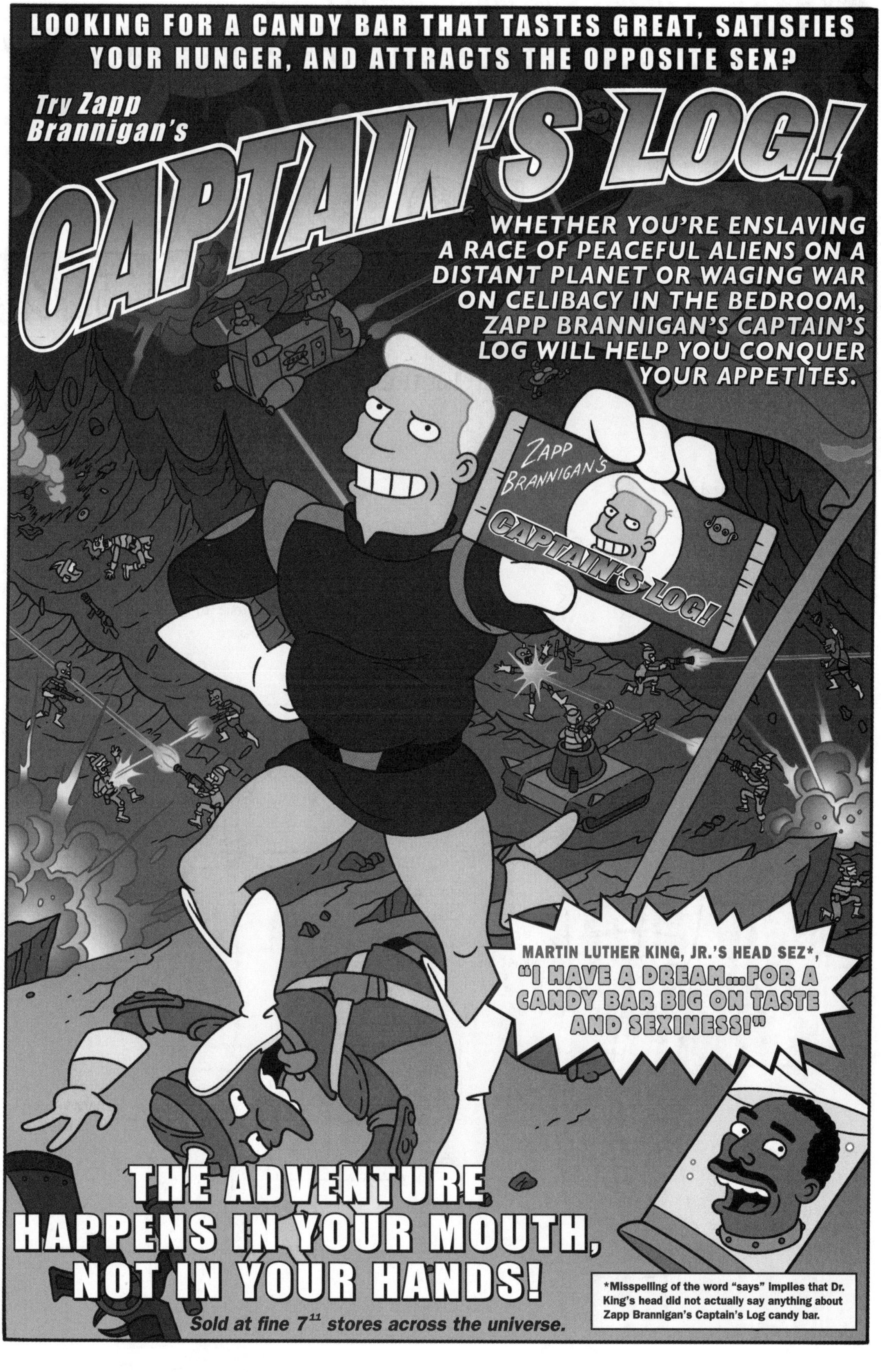
LOOKING FOR A CANDY BAR THAT TASTES GREAT, SATISFIES YOUR HUNGER, AND ATTRACTS THE OPPOSITE SEX?
Try Zapp Brannigan's
CAPTAIN'S LOG!
WHETHER YOU'RE ENSLAVING A RACE OF PEACEFUL ALIENS ON A DISTANT PLANET OR WAGING WAR ON CELIBACY IN THE BEDROOM, ZAPP BRANNIGAN'S CAPTAIN'S LOG WILL HELP YOU CONQUER YOUR APPETITES.
ZAPP BRANNIGAN'S CAPTAIN'S LOG!
MARTIN LUTHER KING, JR.'S HEAD SEZ*, "I HAVE A DREAM...FOR A CANDY BAR BIG ON TASTE AND SEXINESS!"
THE ADVENTURE HAPPENS IN YOUR MOUTH, NOT IN YOUR HANDS!
Sold at fine 7-11 stores across the universe.
*Misspelling of the word "says" implies that Dr. King's head did not actually say anything about Zapp Brannigan's Captain's Log candy bar.

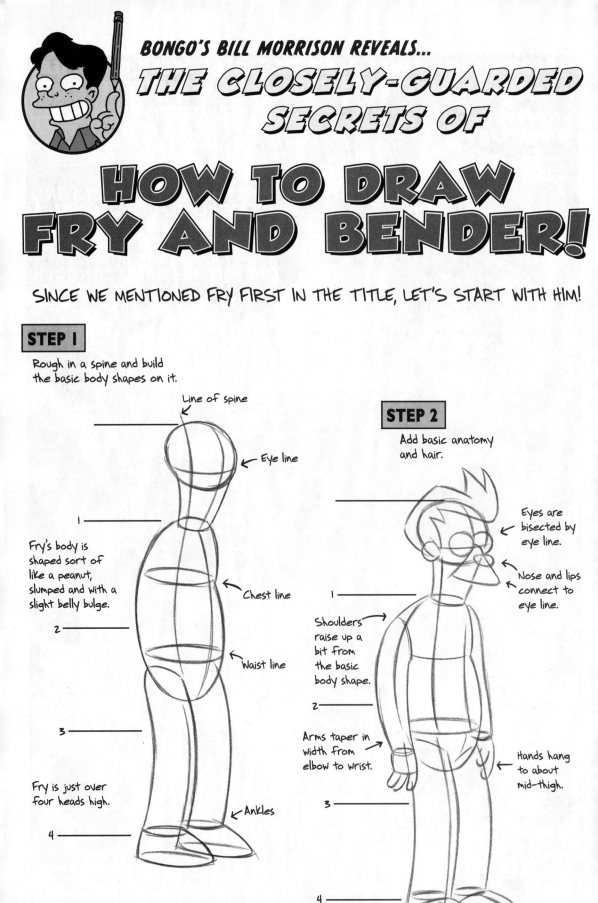

BONGO'S BILL MORRISON REVEALS...

# THE CLOSELY-GUARDED SECRETS OF

# HOW TO DRAW FRY AND BENDER!

SINCE WE MENTIONED FRY FIRST IN THE TITLE, LET'S START WITH HIM!

## STEP 1

Rough in a spine and build the basic body shapes on it.

Line of spine

Eye line

1 ———

Fry's body is shaped sort of like a peanut, slumped and with a slight belly bulge.

2 ———

Chest line

Waist line

3 ———

Fry is just over four heads high.

4 ———

Ankles

## STEP 2

Add basic anatomy and hair.

Eyes are bisected by eye line.

Nose and lips connect to eye line.

1 ———

Shoulders raise up a bit from the basic body shape.

2 ———

Arms taper in width from elbow to wrist.

Hands hang to about mid-thigh.

3 ———

4 ———

Shoes have thick soles. →

34

## STEP 3

Add clothing and details.

1

2

Jacket has a → thickness to it.

3

4

Two lines indicate ← the shoelaces.

## STEP 4

Clean up your lines and add color.

# NOW LET'S TAKE A CLOSER LOOK AT FRY'S HEAD!

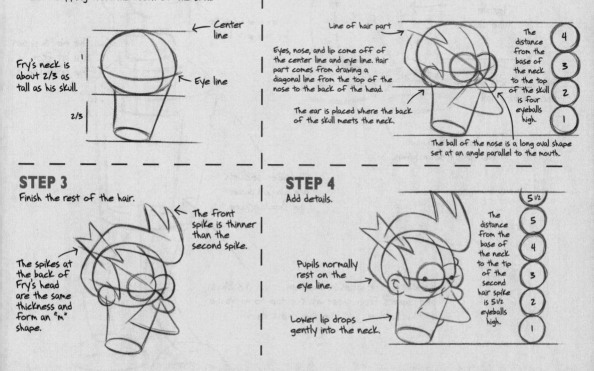

## STEP 1

Start with an oval for the skull. Then draw the neck dropping from the front of the skull.

← Center line

Fry's neck is about 2/3 as tall as his skull.

← Eye line

## STEP 2

Add facial features and hair.

Line of hair part →

Eyes, nose, and lip come off of the center line and eye line. Hair part comes from drawing a diagonal line from the top of the nose to the back of the head.

The ear is placed where the back of the skull meets the neck.

The distance from the base of the neck to the top of the skull is four eyeballs high.

4
3
2
1

The ball of the nose is a long oval shape set at an angle parallel to the mouth.

## STEP 3

Finish the rest of the hair.

← The front spike is thinner than the second spike.

The spikes at the back of Fry's head are the same thickness and form an "m" shape.

## STEP 4

Add details.

Pupils normally rest on the eye line. →

Lower lip drops → gently into the neck.

The distance from the base of the neck to the tip of the second hair spike is 5½ eyeballs high.

5½
5
4
3
2
1

# GOT IT? OKAY, NOW LET'S DRAW BENDER!

**STEP 1** Draw the basic body shapes.

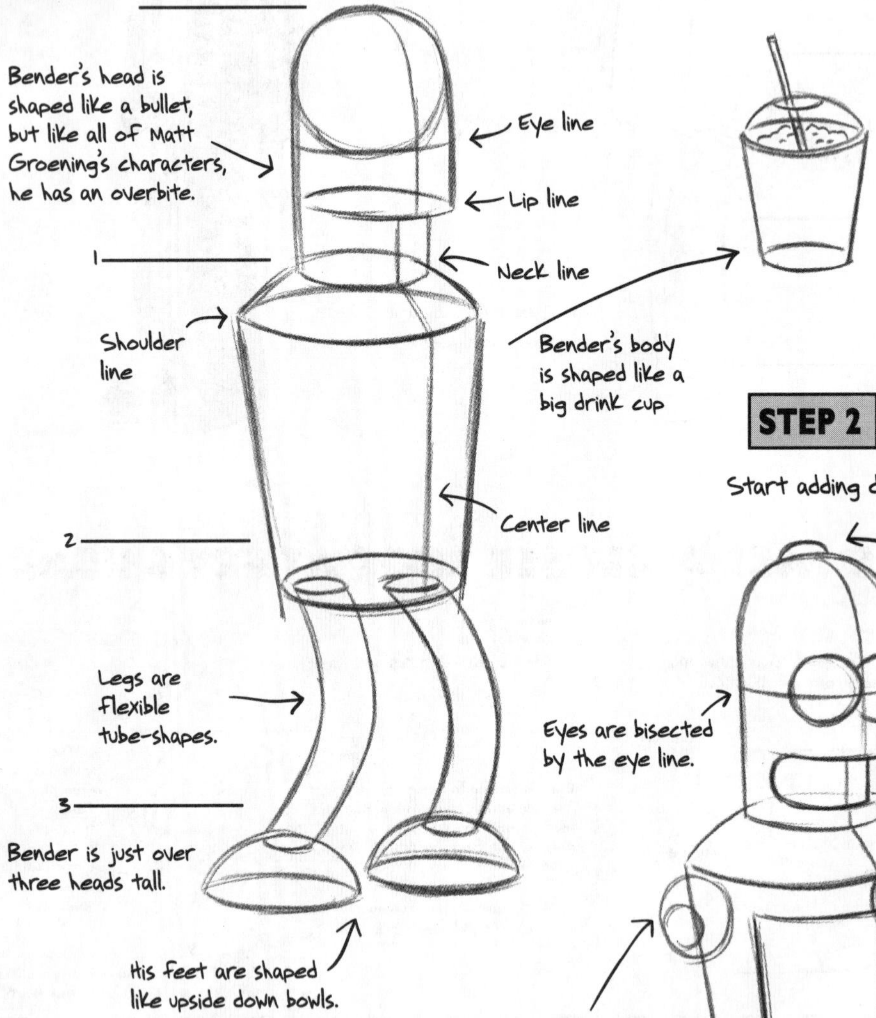

Bender's head is shaped like a bullet, but like all of Matt Groening's characters, he has an overbite.
Eye line
Lip line
1
Neck line
Shoulder line
Bender's body is shaped like a big drink cup
Center line
2
Legs are flexible tube-shapes.
3
Bender is just over three heads tall.
His feet are shaped like upside down bowls.


**STEP 2**

Start adding details.

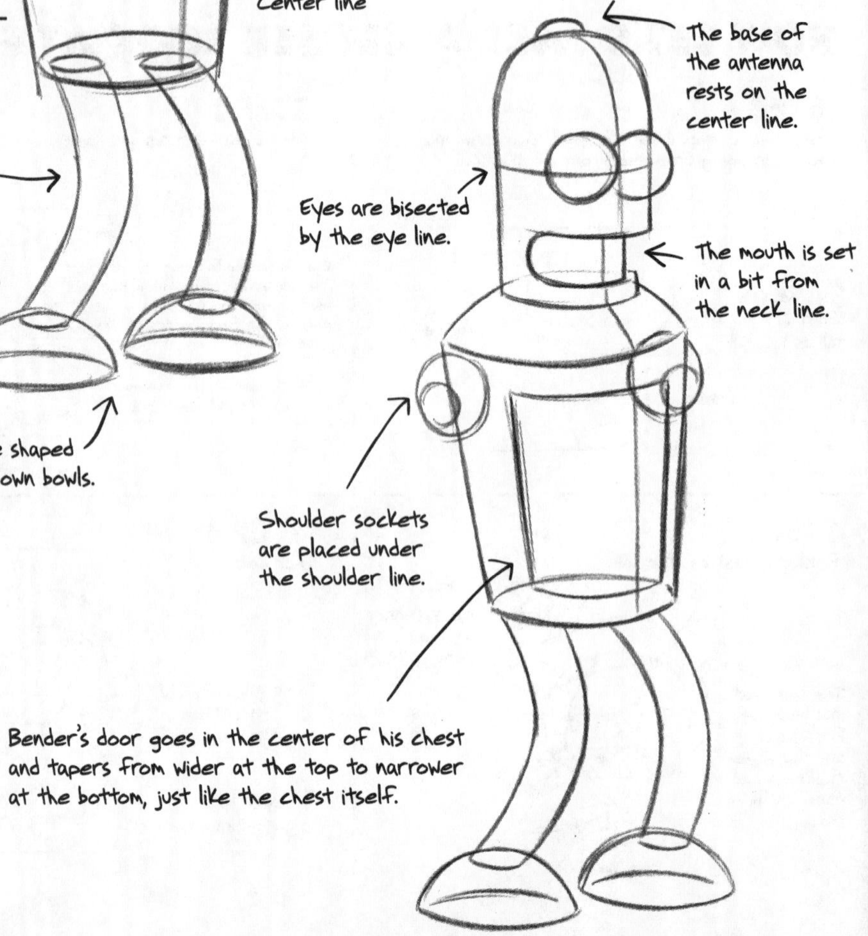

The base of the antenna rests on the center line.
Eyes are bisected by the eye line.
The mouth is set in a bit from the neck line.
Shoulder sockets are placed under the shoulder line.
Bender's door goes in the center of his chest and tapers from wider at the top to narrower at the bottom, just like the chest itself.

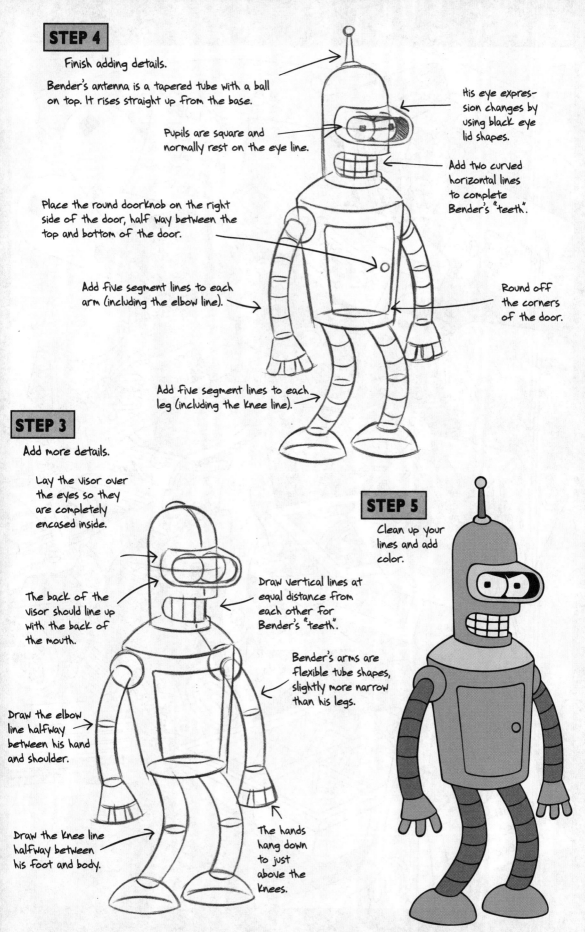

## STEP 4

Finish adding details.

Bender's antenna is a tapered tube with a ball on top. It rises straight up from the base.

Pupils are square and normally rest on the eye line.

Place the round doorknob on the right side of the door, half way between the top and bottom of the door.

Add five segment lines to each arm (including the elbow line).

Add five segment lines to each leg (including the knee line).

His eye expression changes by using black eye lid shapes.

Add two curved horizontal lines to complete Bender's "teeth".

Round off the corners of the door.

## STEP 3

Add more details.

Lay the visor over the eyes so they are completely encased inside.

The back of the visor should line up with the back of the mouth.

Draw the elbow line halfway between his hand and shoulder.

Draw the knee line halfway between his foot and body.

Draw vertical lines at equal distance from each other for Bender's "teeth".

Bender's arms are flexible tube shapes, slightly more narrow than his legs.

The hands hang down to just above the knees.

## STEP 5

Clean up your lines and add color.

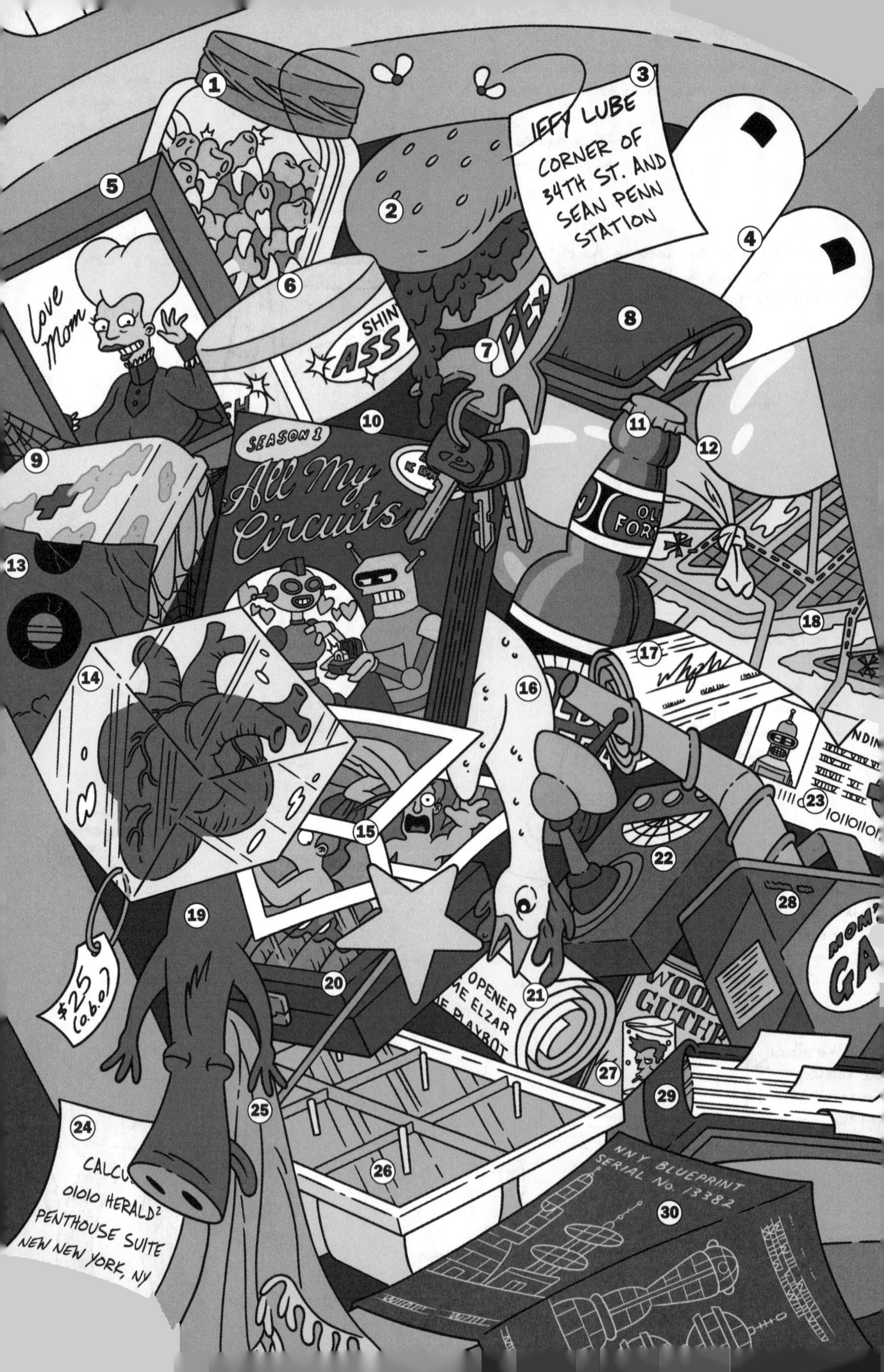

JEFY LUBE
CORNER OF 34TH ST. AND SEAN PENN STATION
Love Mom
SEASON 1
All My Circuits
ASS
$25 (o.b.o.)
OPENER
ELZAR
PLAYBOT
CALCU
01010 HERALD²
PENTHOUSE SUITE
NEW NEW YORK, NY
NNY BLUEPRINT
SERIAL No. 13382

# Let's see... WHAT'S IN BENDER'S CHEST!

1. Collection of Gold Teeth from Grave-Robbed Corpses
2. Hermes' Manwich
3. Calculon's Favorite Oil Change Shop
4. Extra Pair of Eyes
5. Photo of MOM
6. Shiny Metal Brand® Ass Polish
7. Duplicate Set of Keys to Planet Express Ship
8. Fry's Wallet
9. First Aid Kit (never been used)
10. "All My Circuits: Season One" DVD set
11. Beer
12. Water Balloons Filled with Slurm™
13. Little Black Disk (with phone numbers of loose fembots)
14. Some Guy's Heart
15. Compromising Photos of Fry
16. Rubber Chicken
17. Restraining Order to Stay Away from Calculon
18. Calculon's Path from Home to Work
19. Forgotten Spice Weasel (dead)
20. Cigar Humidor
21. X-mas List for Robot Santa
22. Gay-dar Satellite Controls
23. Bending License
24. Calculon's Address
25. "Gender Bender" Tu-tu and Wand
26. Booze-cicles
27. Professor's Folk Music CD (Woody Guthrie's Head Live at Headstock)
28. Gasoline Can
29. Elzar's Personal Cookbook
30. Blueprint Diagram of Bank of New New York

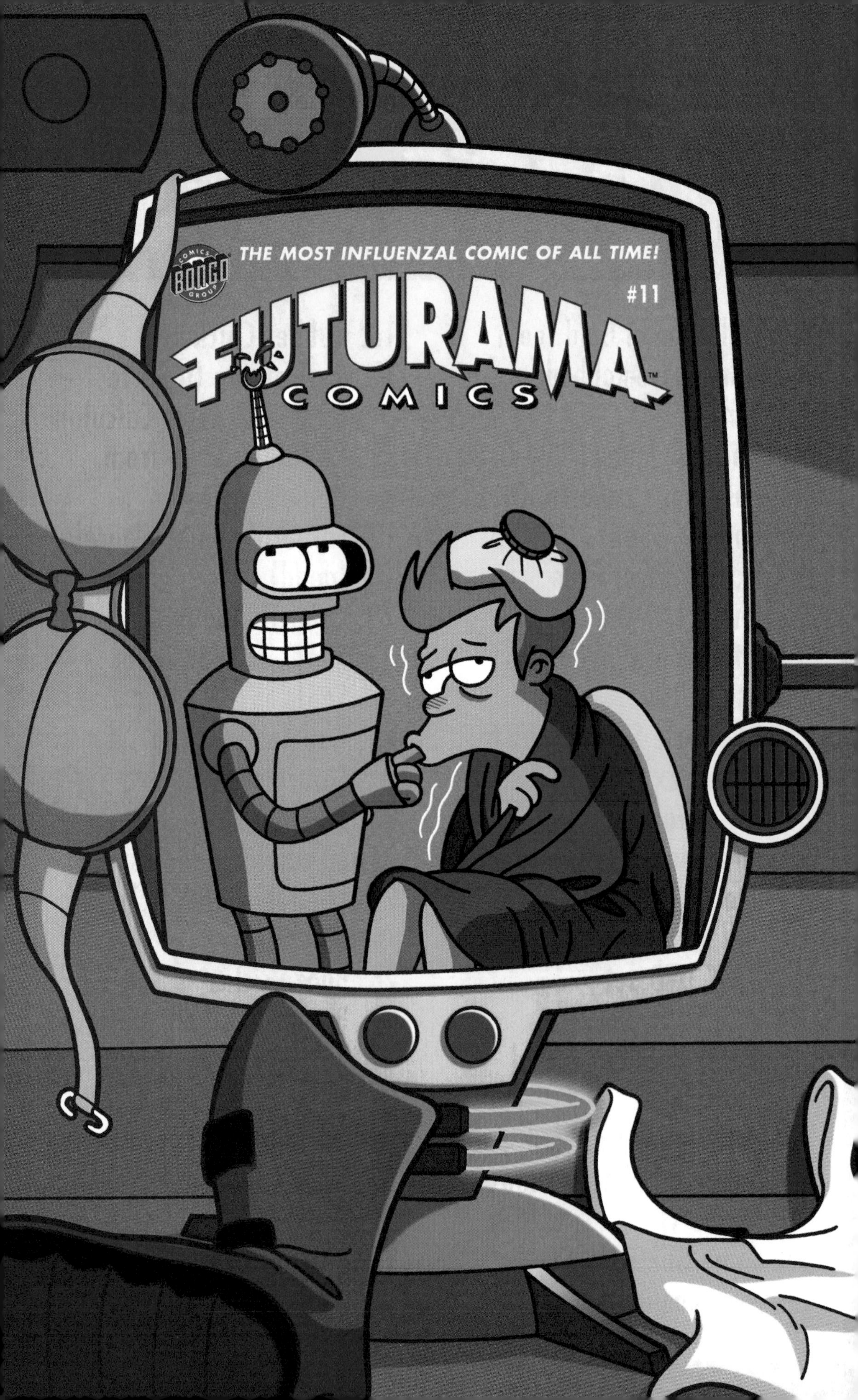
BONGO COMICS GROUP
THE MOST INFLUENZAL COMIC OF ALL TIME!
#11
FUTURAMA COMICS™

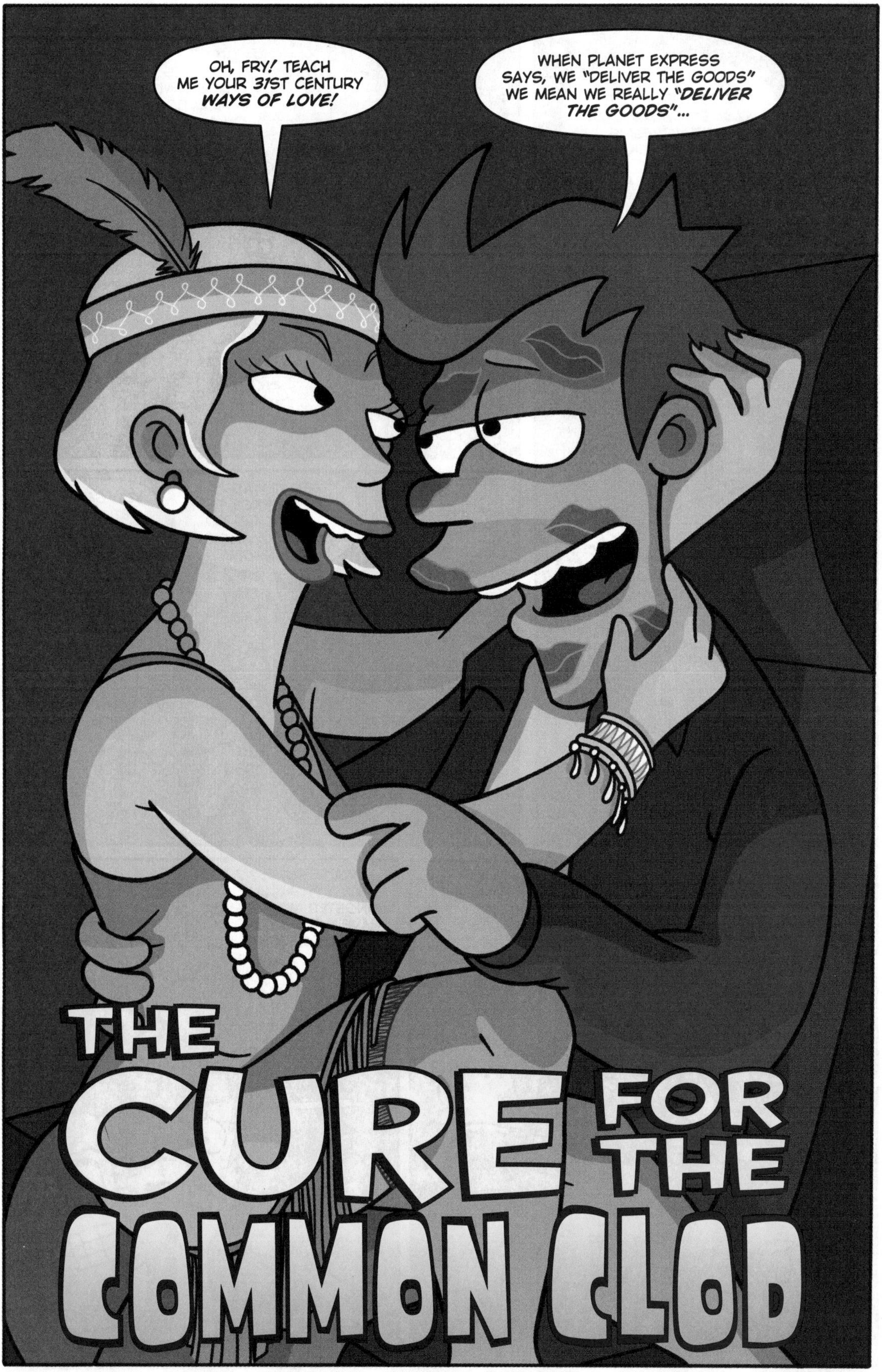
OH, FRY! TEACH ME YOUR 31ST CENTURY WAYS OF LOVE!
WHEN PLANET EXPRESS SAYS, WE "DELIVER THE GOODS" WE MEAN WE REALLY "DELIVER THE GOODS"...
THE CURE FOR THE COMMON CLOD

**PATRIC M. VERRONE** SCRIPT · **TOM KING** PENCILS · **PHYLLIS NOVIN** INKS · **JOEY MASON** COLORS · **KAREN BATES** LETTERS · **BILL MORRISON** EDITOR · **MATT GROENING** DR. FEEL GOOD

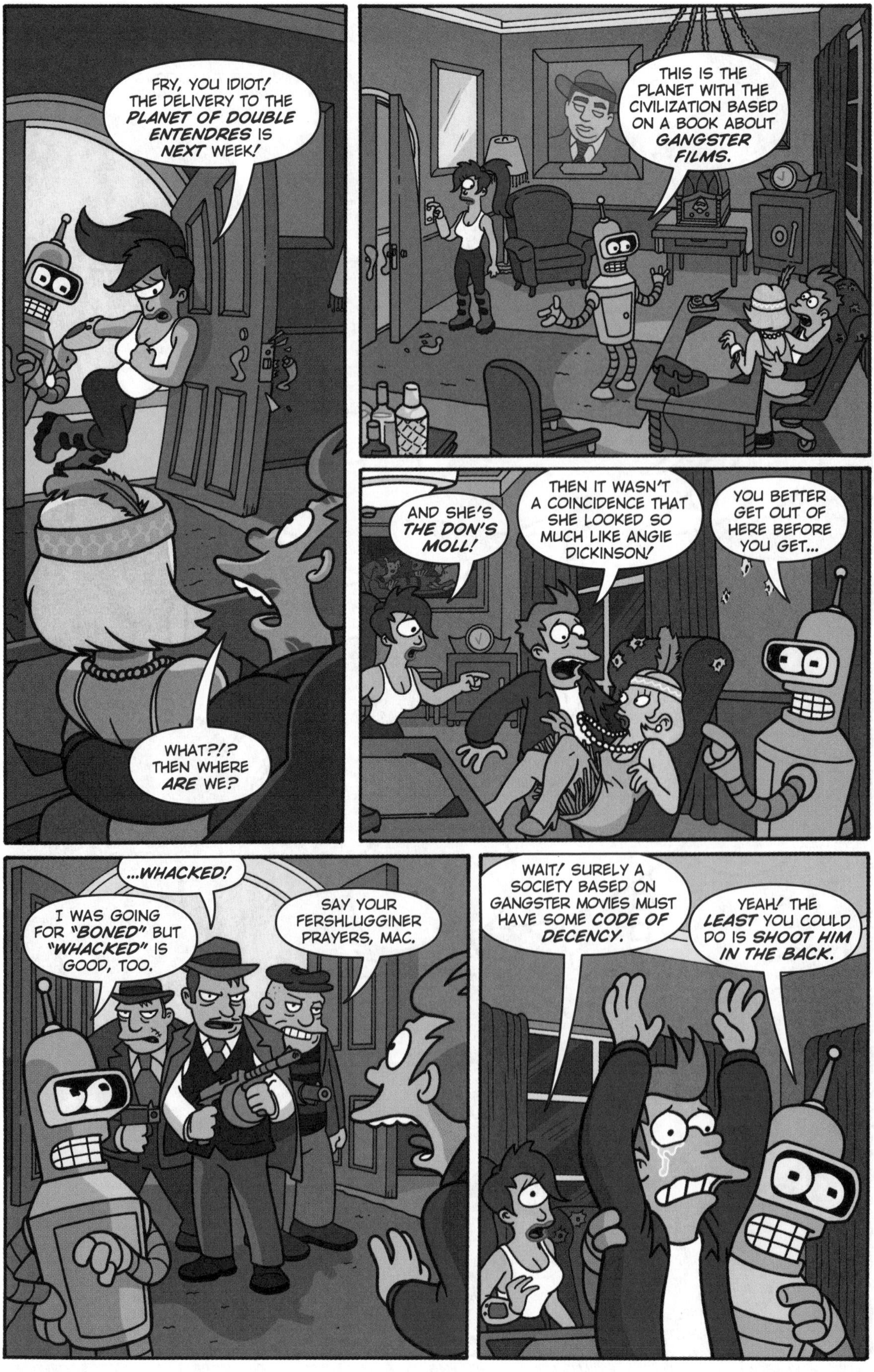
FRY, YOU IDIOT! THE DELIVERY TO THE PLANET OF DOUBLE ENTENDRES IS NEXT WEEK!
WHAT?!? THEN WHERE ARE WE?
THIS IS THE PLANET WITH THE CIVILIZATION BASED ON A BOOK ABOUT GANGSTER FILMS.
AND SHE'S THE DON'S MOLL!
THEN IT WASN'T A COINCIDENCE THAT SHE LOOKED SO MUCH LIKE ANGIE DICKINSON!
YOU BETTER GET OUT OF HERE BEFORE YOU GET...
...WHACKED!
I WAS GOING FOR "BONED" BUT "WHACKED" IS GOOD, TOO.
SAY YOUR FERSHLUGGINER PRAYERS, MAC.
WAIT! SURELY A SOCIETY BASED ON GANGSTER MOVIES MUST HAVE SOME CODE OF DECENCY.
YEAH! THE LEAST YOU COULD DO IS SHOOT HIM IN THE BACK.

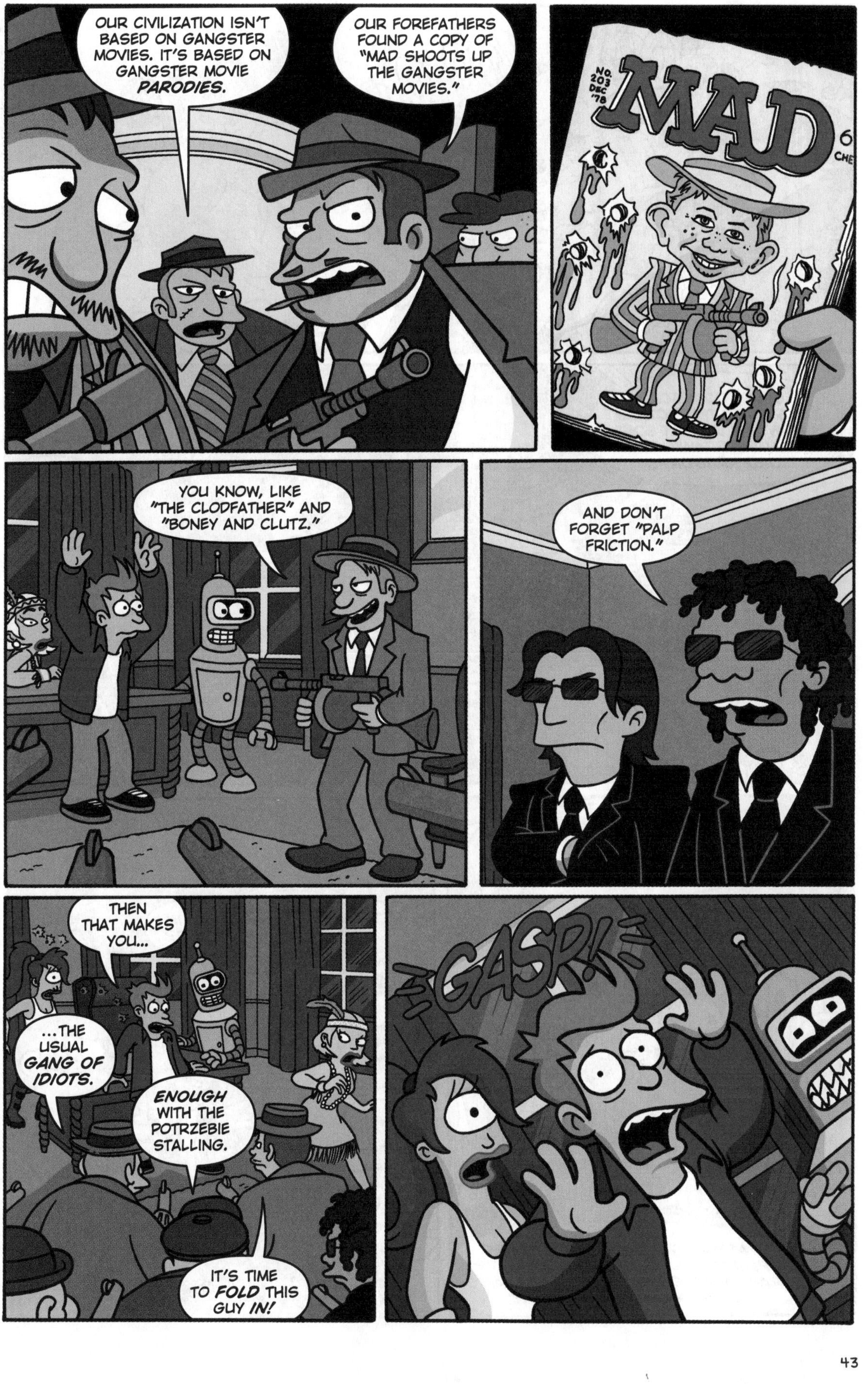

OUR CIVILIZATION ISN'T BASED ON GANGSTER MOVIES. IT'S BASED ON GANGSTER MOVIE *PARODIES*.
OUR FOREFATHERS FOUND A COPY OF "MAD SHOOTS UP THE GANGSTER MOVIES."
NO. 203 DEC '78
MAD
YOU KNOW, LIKE "THE CLODFATHER" AND "BONEY AND CLUTZ."
AND DON'T FORGET "PALP FRICTION."
THEN THAT MAKES YOU...
...THE USUAL *GANG OF IDIOTS*.
*ENOUGH* WITH THE POTRZEBIE STALLING.
IT'S TIME TO *FOLD* THIS GUY *IN!*
GASP!

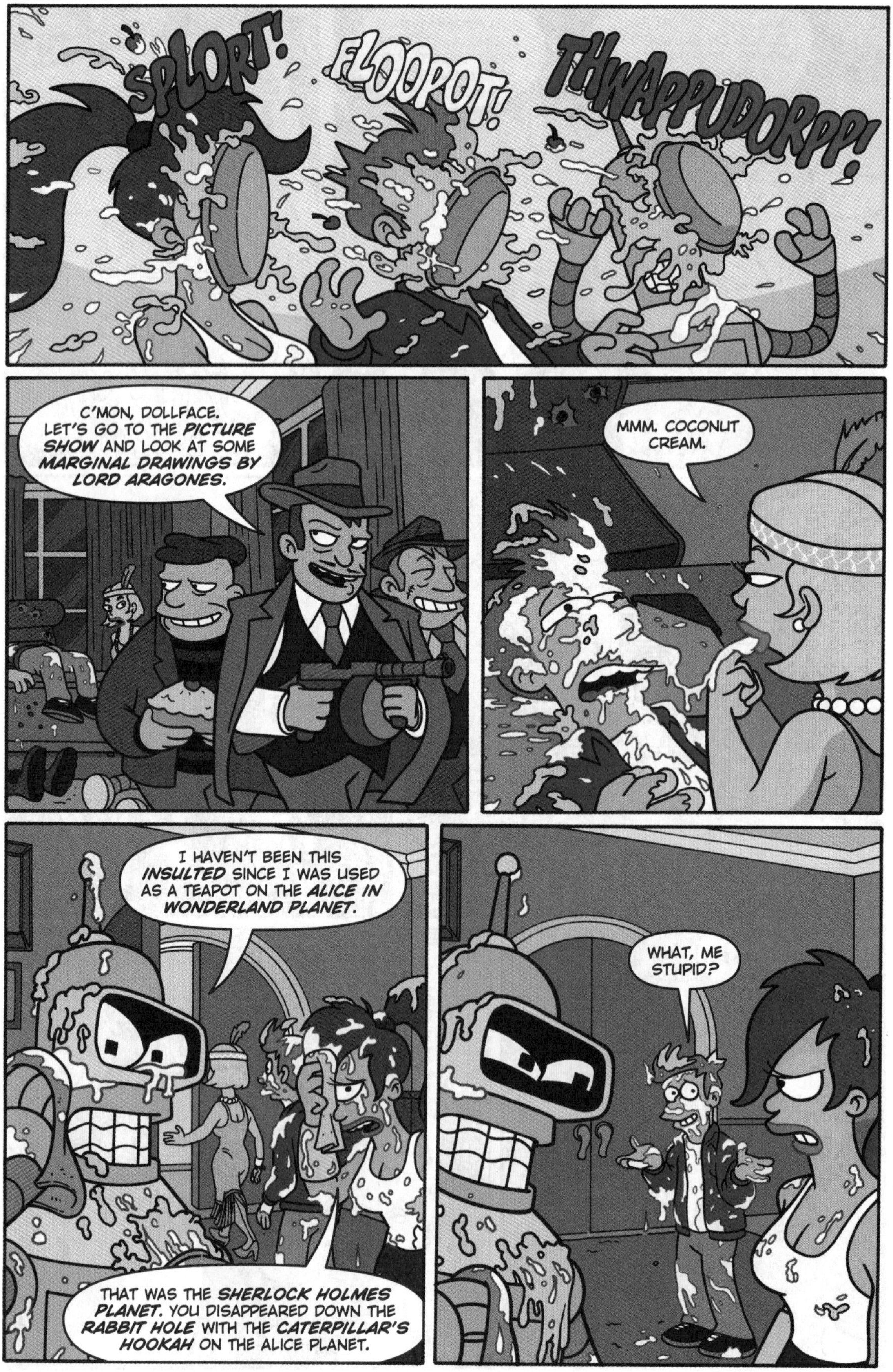
SPLORT!
FLOOPOT!
THWAPPUDORPP!
C'MON, DOLLFACE. LET'S GO TO THE PICTURE SHOW AND LOOK AT SOME MARGINAL DRAWINGS BY LORD ARAGONES.
MMM. COCONUT CREAM.
I HAVEN'T BEEN THIS INSULTED SINCE I WAS USED AS A TEAPOT ON THE ALICE IN WONDERLAND PLANET.
THAT WAS THE SHERLOCK HOLMES PLANET. YOU DISAPPEARED DOWN THE RABBIT HOLE WITH THE CATERPILLAR'S HOOKAH ON THE ALICE PLANET.
WHAT, ME STUPID?

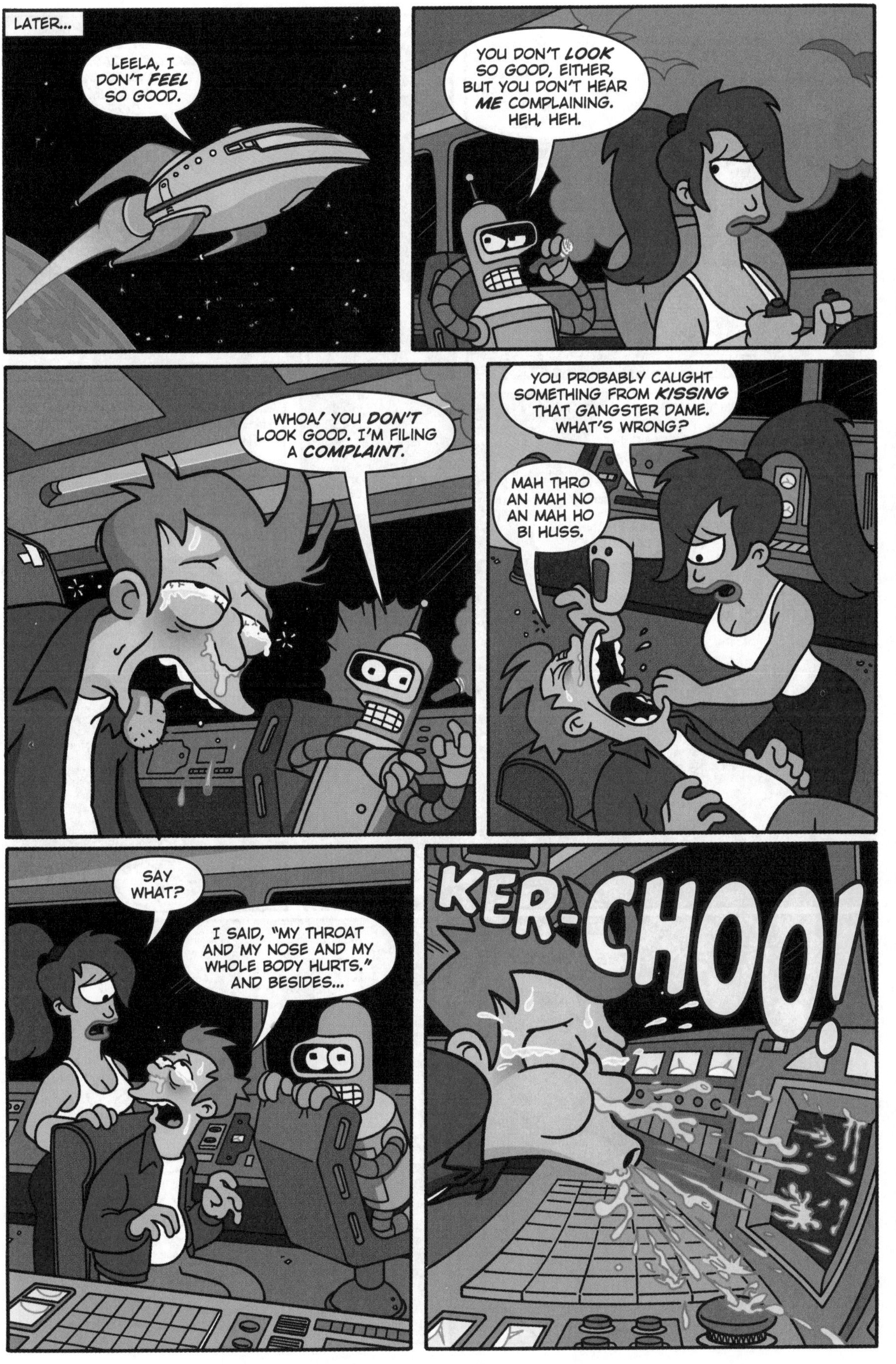
LATER...
LEELA, I DON'T FEEL SO GOOD.
YOU DON'T LOOK SO GOOD, EITHER, BUT YOU DON'T HEAR ME COMPLAINING. HEH, HEH.
WHOA! YOU DON'T LOOK GOOD. I'M FILING A COMPLAINT.
YOU PROBABLY CAUGHT SOMETHING FROM KISSING THAT GANGSTER DAME. WHAT'S WRONG?
MAH THRO AN MAH NO AN MAH HO BI HUSS.
SAY WHAT?
I SAID, "MY THROAT AND MY NOSE AND MY WHOLE BODY HURTS." AND BESIDES...
KER-CHOO!

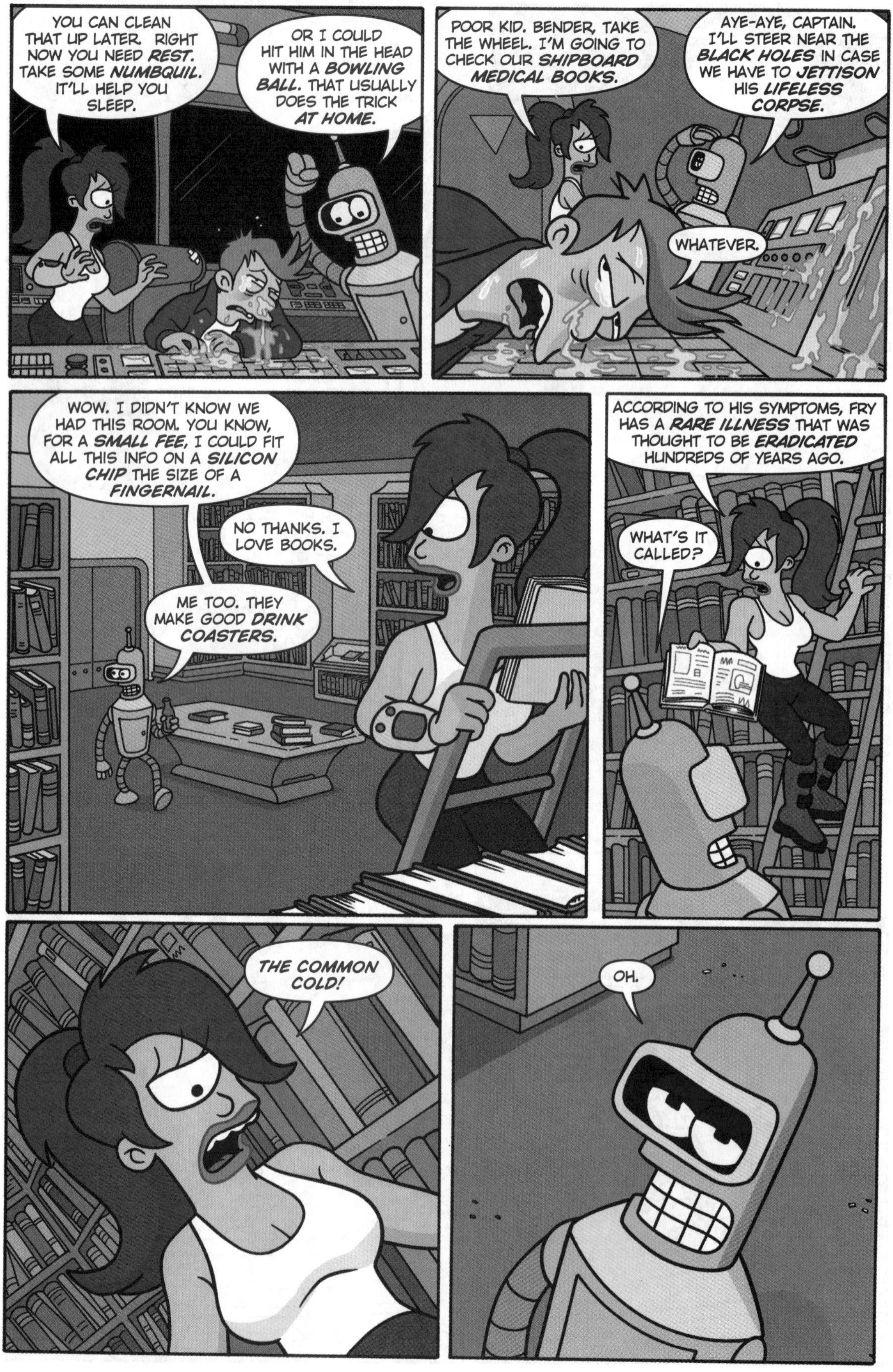

YOU CAN CLEAN THAT UP LATER. RIGHT NOW YOU NEED REST. TAKE SOME NUMBQUIL. IT'LL HELP YOU SLEEP.
OR I COULD HIT HIM IN THE HEAD WITH A BOWLING BALL. THAT USUALLY DOES THE TRICK AT HOME.
POOR KID. BENDER, TAKE THE WHEEL. I'M GOING TO CHECK OUR SHIPBOARD MEDICAL BOOKS.
AYE-AYE, CAPTAIN. I'LL STEER NEAR THE BLACK HOLES IN CASE WE HAVE TO JETTISON HIS LIFELESS CORPSE.
WHATEVER.
WOW. I DIDN'T KNOW WE HAD THIS ROOM. YOU KNOW, FOR A SMALL FEE, I COULD FIT ALL THIS INFO ON A SILICON CHIP THE SIZE OF A FINGERNAIL.
NO THANKS. I LOVE BOOKS.
ME TOO. THEY MAKE GOOD DRINK COASTERS.
ACCORDING TO HIS SYMPTOMS, FRY HAS A RARE ILLNESS THAT WAS THOUGHT TO BE ERADICATED HUNDREDS OF YEARS AGO.
WHAT'S IT CALLED?
THE COMMON COLD!
OH.

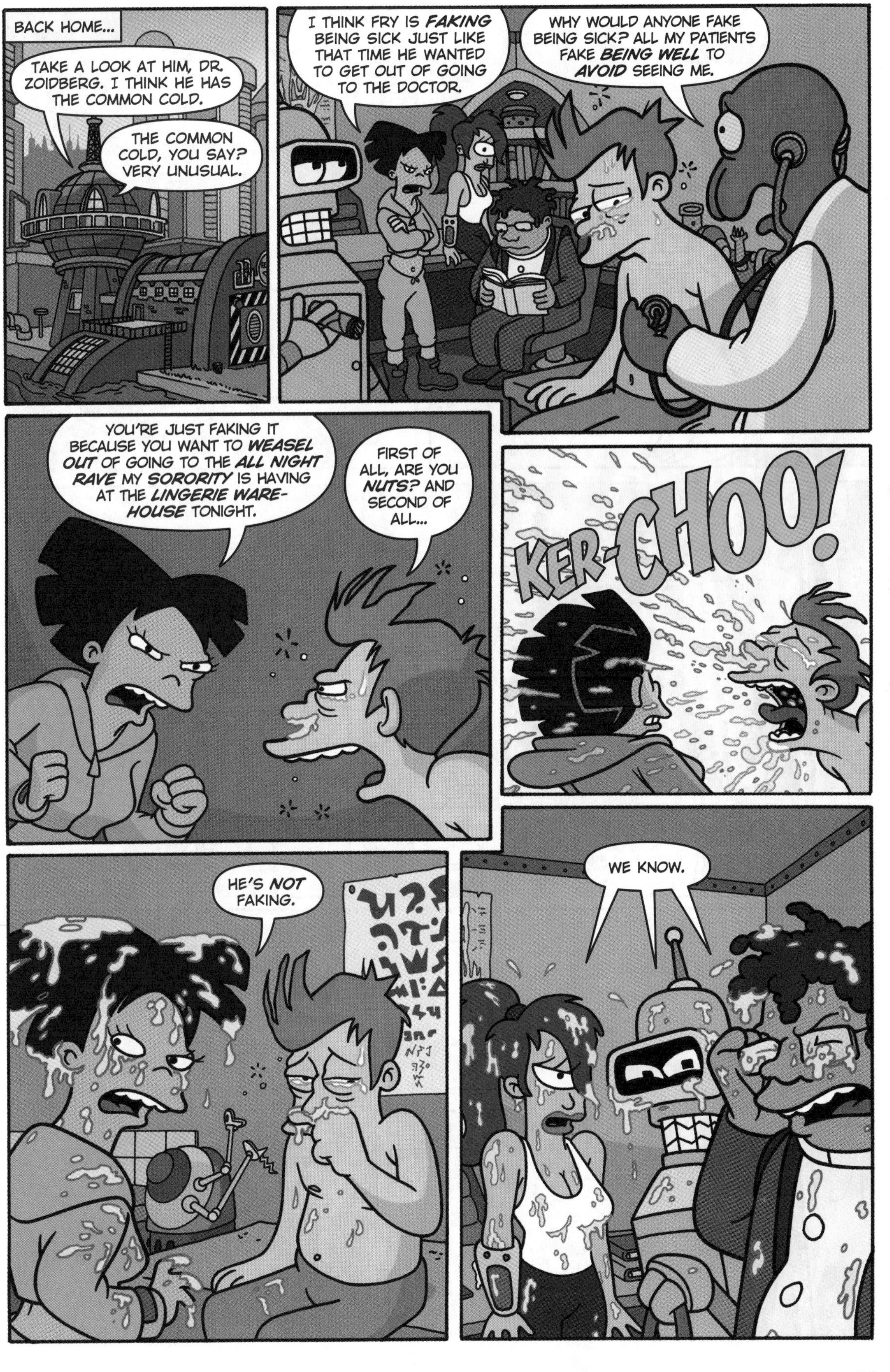
BACK HOME...
TAKE A LOOK AT HIM, DR. ZOIDBERG. I THINK HE HAS THE COMMON COLD.
THE COMMON COLD, YOU SAY? VERY UNUSUAL.
I THINK FRY IS *FAKING* BEING SICK JUST LIKE THAT TIME HE WANTED TO GET OUT OF GOING TO THE DOCTOR.
WHY WOULD ANYONE FAKE BEING SICK? ALL MY PATIENTS FAKE *BEING WELL* TO *AVOID* SEEING ME.
YOU'RE JUST FAKING IT BECAUSE YOU WANT TO *WEASEL OUT* OF GOING TO THE *ALL NIGHT RAVE* MY *SORORITY* IS HAVING AT THE *LINGERIE WARE-HOUSE* TONIGHT.
FIRST OF ALL, ARE YOU *NUTS?* AND SECOND OF ALL...
KER-CHOO!
HE'S *NOT* FAKING.
WE KNOW.

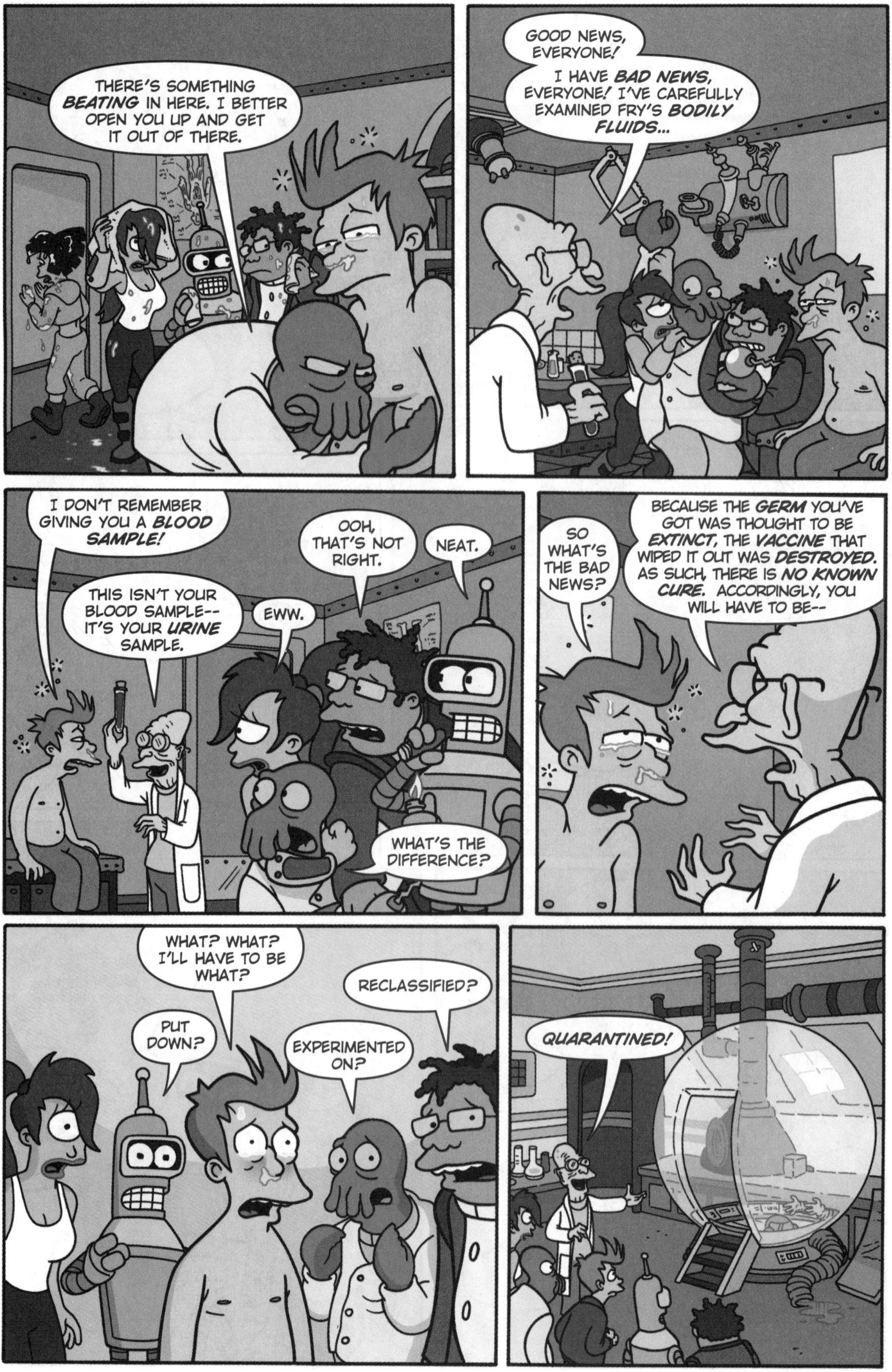
THERE'S SOMETHING BEATING IN HERE. I BETTER OPEN YOU UP AND GET IT OUT OF THERE.
GOOD NEWS, EVERYONE!
I HAVE BAD NEWS, EVERYONE! I'VE CAREFULLY EXAMINED FRY'S BODILY FLUIDS...
I DON'T REMEMBER GIVING YOU A BLOOD SAMPLE!
THIS ISN'T YOUR BLOOD SAMPLE-- IT'S YOUR URINE SAMPLE.
EWW.
OOH, THAT'S NOT RIGHT.
NEAT.
WHAT'S THE DIFFERENCE?
SO WHAT'S THE BAD NEWS?
BECAUSE THE GERM YOU'VE GOT WAS THOUGHT TO BE EXTINCT, THE VACCINE THAT WIPED IT OUT WAS DESTROYED. AS SUCH, THERE IS NO KNOWN CURE. ACCORDINGLY, YOU WILL HAVE TO BE--
WHAT? WHAT? I'LL HAVE TO BE WHAT?
PUT DOWN?
EXPERIMENTED ON?
RECLASSIFIED?
QUARANTINED!

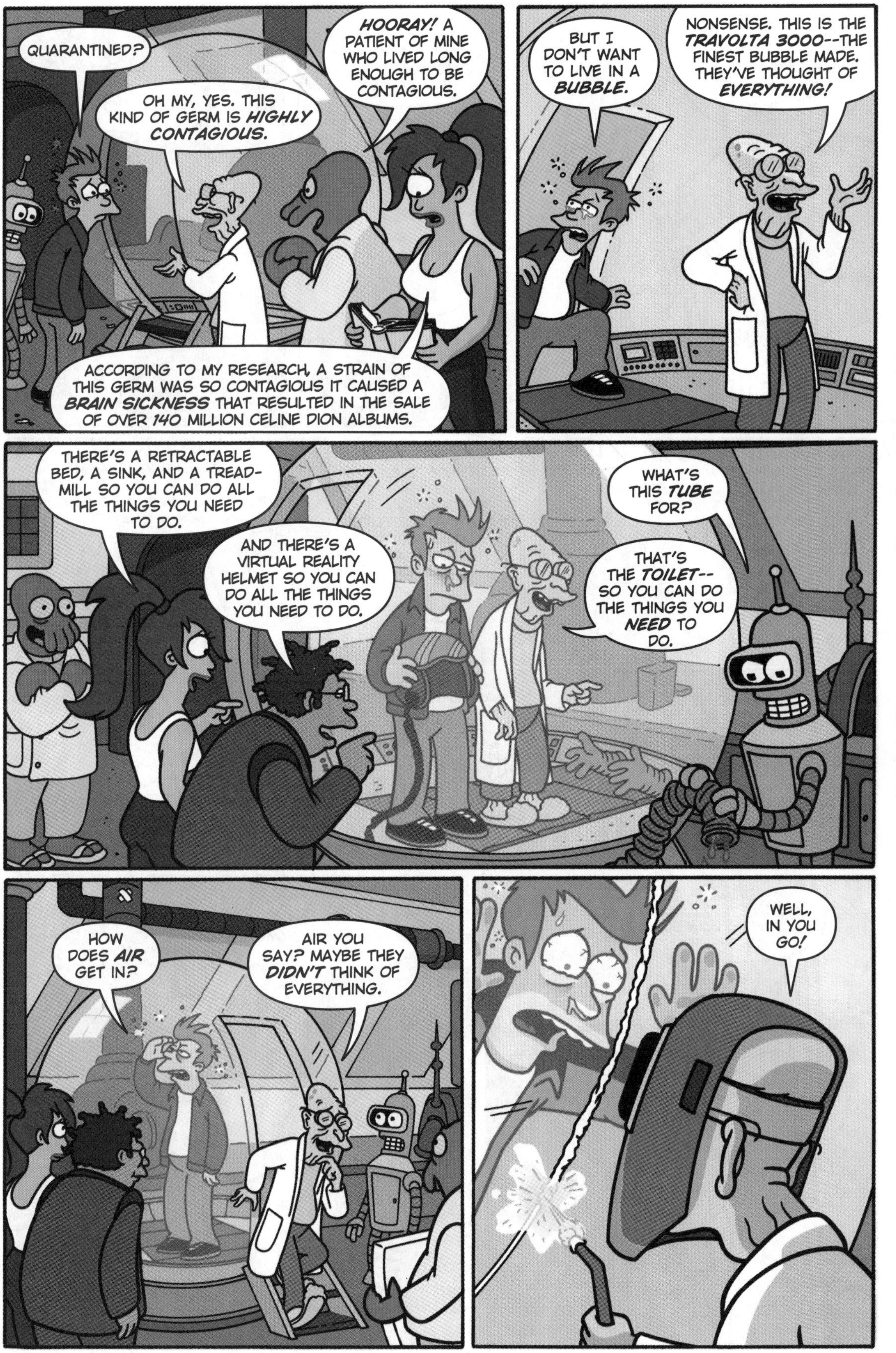
QUARANTINED?
OH MY, YES. THIS KIND OF GERM IS HIGHLY CONTAGIOUS.
HOORAY! A PATIENT OF MINE WHO LIVED LONG ENOUGH TO BE CONTAGIOUS.
ACCORDING TO MY RESEARCH, A STRAIN OF THIS GERM WAS SO CONTAGIOUS IT CAUSED A BRAIN SICKNESS THAT RESULTED IN THE SALE OF OVER 140 MILLION CELINE DION ALBUMS.
BUT I DON'T WANT TO LIVE IN A BUBBLE.
NONSENSE. THIS IS THE TRAVOLTA 3000--THE FINEST BUBBLE MADE. THEY'VE THOUGHT OF EVERYTHING!
THERE'S A RETRACTABLE BED, A SINK, AND A TREAD-MILL SO YOU CAN DO ALL THE THINGS YOU NEED TO DO.
AND THERE'S A VIRTUAL REALITY HELMET SO YOU CAN DO ALL THE THINGS YOU NEED TO DO.
WHAT'S THIS TUBE FOR?
THAT'S THE TOILET--SO YOU CAN DO THE THINGS YOU NEED TO DO.
HOW DOES AIR GET IN?
AIR YOU SAY? MAYBE THEY DIDN'T THINK OF EVERYTHING.
WELL, IN YOU GO!

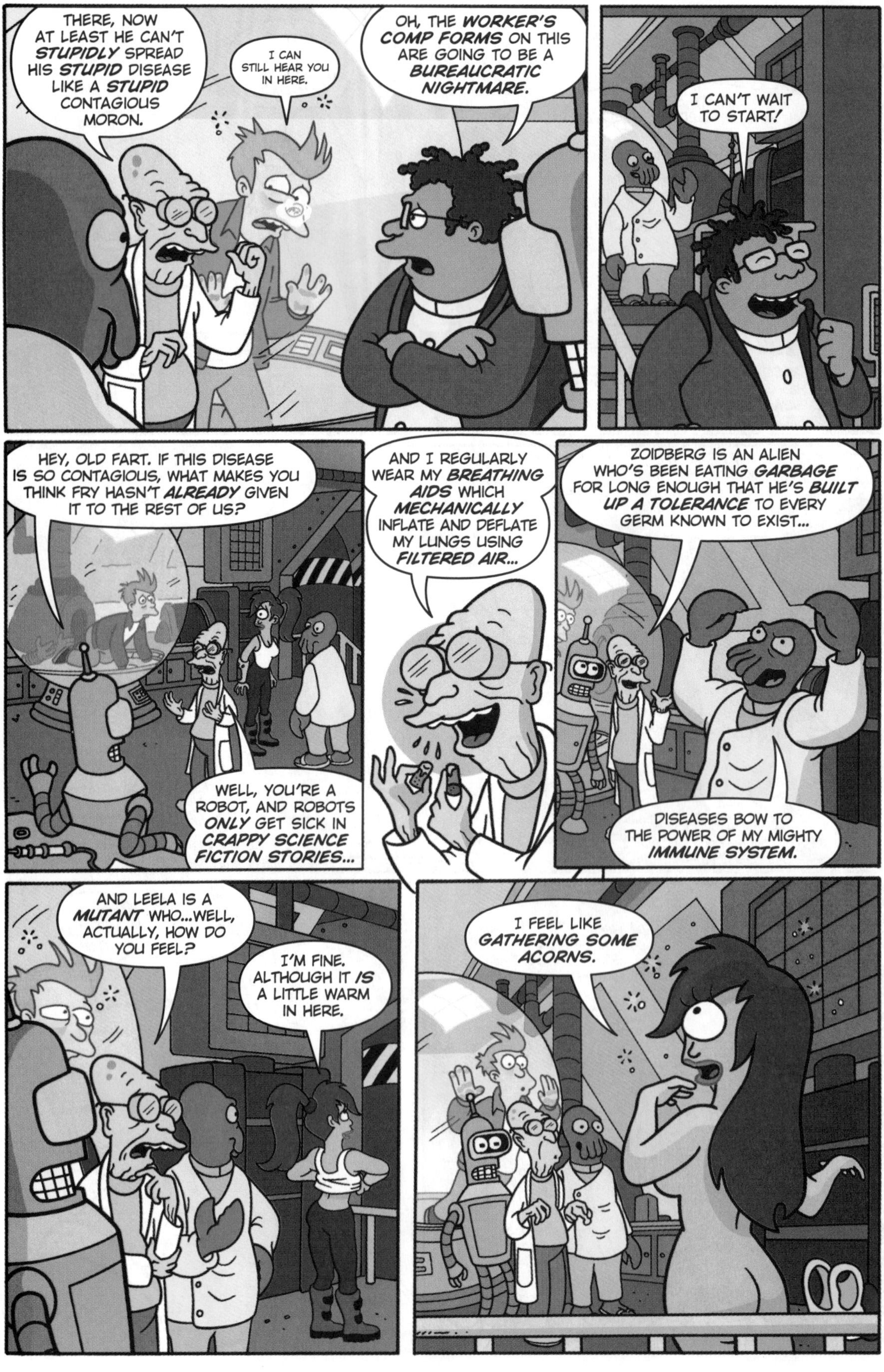
THERE, NOW AT LEAST HE CAN'T STUPIDLY SPREAD HIS STUPID DISEASE LIKE A STUPID CONTAGIOUS MORON.
I CAN STILL HEAR YOU IN HERE.
OH, THE WORKER'S COMP FORMS ON THIS ARE GOING TO BE A BUREAUCRATIC NIGHTMARE.
I CAN'T WAIT TO START!
HEY, OLD FART. IF THIS DISEASE IS SO CONTAGIOUS, WHAT MAKES YOU THINK FRY HASN'T ALREADY GIVEN IT TO THE REST OF US?
WELL, YOU'RE A ROBOT, AND ROBOTS ONLY GET SICK IN CRAPPY SCIENCE FICTION STORIES...
AND I REGULARLY WEAR MY BREATHING AIDS WHICH MECHANICALLY INFLATE AND DEFLATE MY LUNGS USING FILTERED AIR...
ZOIDBERG IS AN ALIEN WHO'S BEEN EATING GARBAGE FOR LONG ENOUGH THAT HE'S BUILT UP A TOLERANCE TO EVERY GERM KNOWN TO EXIST...
DISEASES BOW TO THE POWER OF MY MIGHTY IMMUNE SYSTEM.
AND LEELA IS A MUTANT WHO...WELL, ACTUALLY, HOW DO YOU FEEL?
I'M FINE. ALTHOUGH IT IS A LITTLE WARM IN HERE.
I FEEL LIKE GATHERING SOME ACORNS.

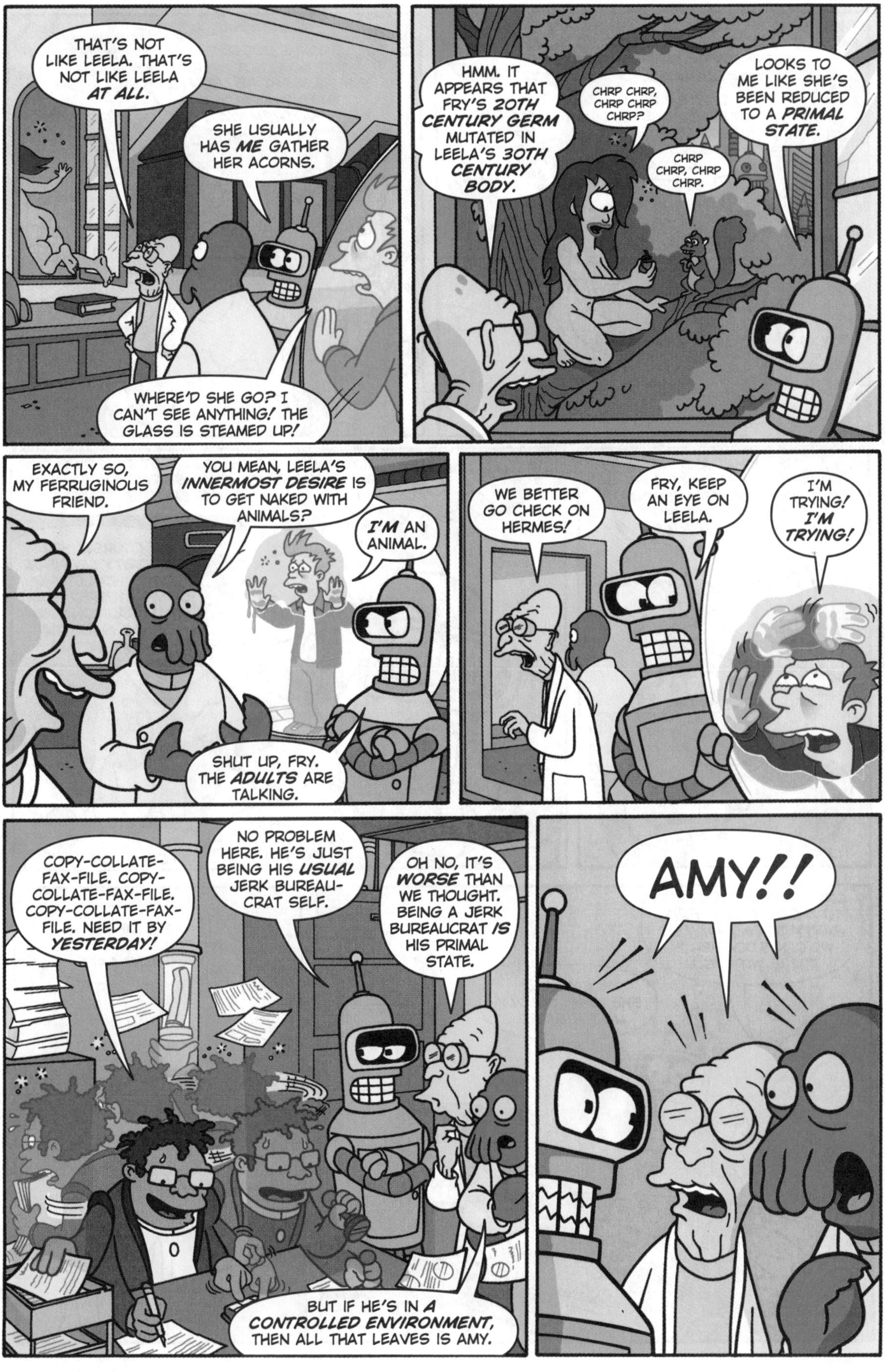
THAT'S NOT LIKE LEELA. THAT'S NOT LIKE LEELA AT ALL.
SHE USUALLY HAS ME GATHER HER ACORNS.
WHERE'D SHE GO? I CAN'T SEE ANYTHING! THE GLASS IS STEAMED UP!
HMM. IT APPEARS THAT FRY'S 20TH CENTURY GERM MUTATED IN LEELA'S 30TH CENTURY BODY.
CHRP CHRP, CHRP CHRP CHRP?
CHRP CHRP, CHRP CHRP.
LOOKS TO ME LIKE SHE'S BEEN REDUCED TO A PRIMAL STATE.
EXACTLY SO, MY FERRUGINOUS FRIEND.
YOU MEAN, LEELA'S INNERMOST DESIRE IS TO GET NAKED WITH ANIMALS?
I'M AN ANIMAL.
SHUT UP, FRY. THE ADULTS ARE TALKING.
WE BETTER GO CHECK ON HERMES!
FRY, KEEP AN EYE ON LEELA.
I'M TRYING! I'M TRYING!
COPY-COLLATE-FAX-FILE. COPY-COLLATE-FAX-FILE. COPY-COLLATE-FAX-FILE. NEED IT BY YESTERDAY!
NO PROBLEM HERE. HE'S JUST BEING HIS USUAL JERK BUREAUCRAT SELF.
OH NO, IT'S WORSE THAN WE THOUGHT. BEING A JERK BUREAUCRAT IS HIS PRIMAL STATE.
BUT IF HE'S IN A CONTROLLED ENVIRONMENT, THEN ALL THAT LEAVES IS AMY.
AMY!!

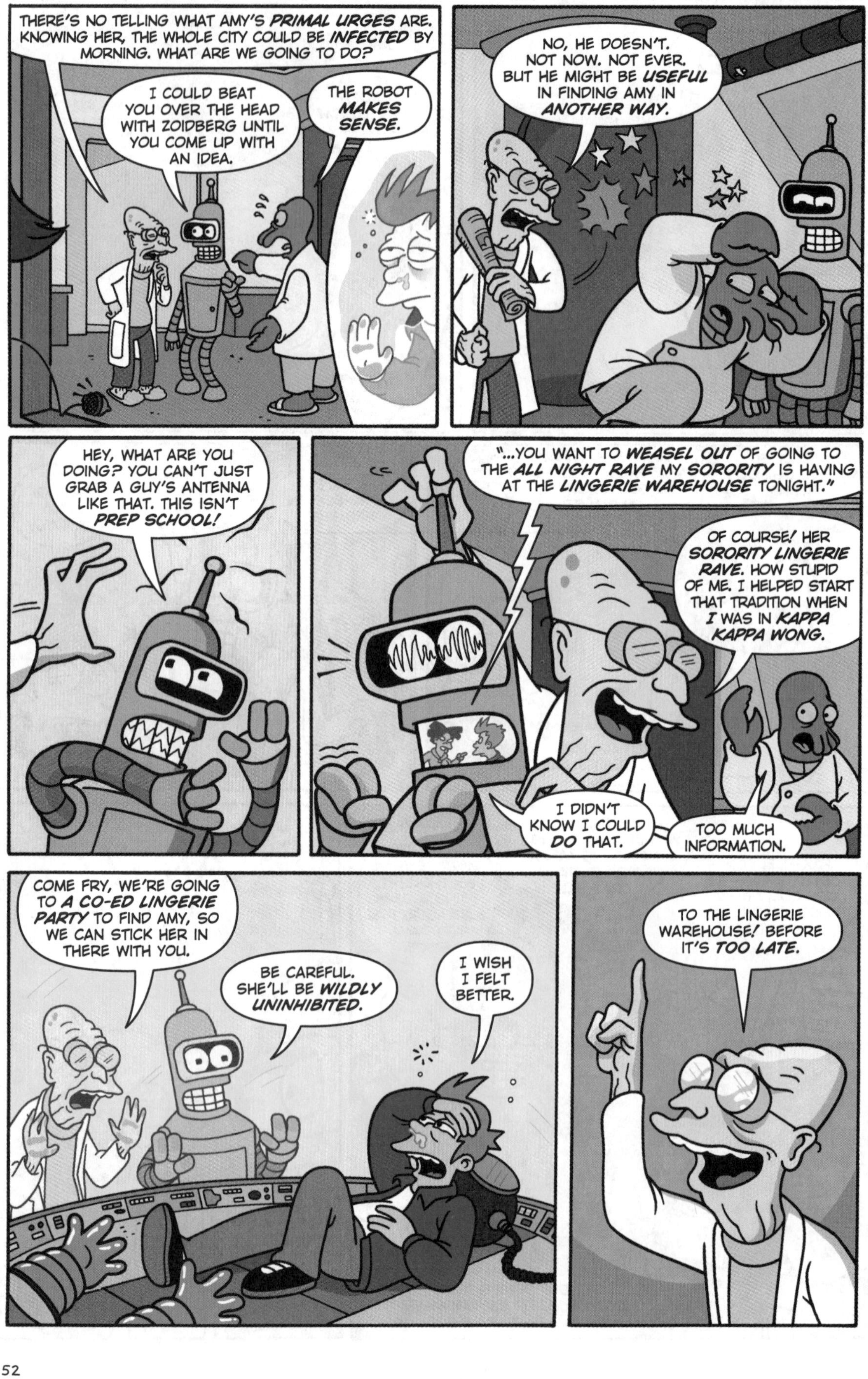
THERE'S NO TELLING WHAT AMY'S PRIMAL URGES ARE. KNOWING HER, THE WHOLE CITY COULD BE INFECTED BY MORNING. WHAT ARE WE GOING TO DO?
I COULD BEAT YOU OVER THE HEAD WITH ZOIDBERG UNTIL YOU COME UP WITH AN IDEA.
THE ROBOT MAKES SENSE.
NO, HE DOESN'T. NOT NOW. NOT EVER. BUT HE MIGHT BE USEFUL IN FINDING AMY IN ANOTHER WAY.
HEY, WHAT ARE YOU DOING? YOU CAN'T JUST GRAB A GUY'S ANTENNA LIKE THAT. THIS ISN'T PREP SCHOOL!
"...YOU WANT TO WEASEL OUT OF GOING TO THE ALL NIGHT RAVE MY SORORITY IS HAVING AT THE LINGERIE WAREHOUSE TONIGHT."
OF COURSE! HER SORORITY LINGERIE RAVE. HOW STUPID OF ME. I HELPED START THAT TRADITION WHEN I WAS IN KAPPA KAPPA WONG.
I DIDN'T KNOW I COULD DO THAT.
TOO MUCH INFORMATION.
COME FRY, WE'RE GOING TO A CO-ED LINGERIE PARTY TO FIND AMY, SO WE CAN STICK HER IN THERE WITH YOU.
BE CAREFUL. SHE'LL BE WILDLY UNINHIBITED.
I WISH I FELT BETTER.
TO THE LINGERIE WAREHOUSE! BEFORE IT'S TOO LATE.

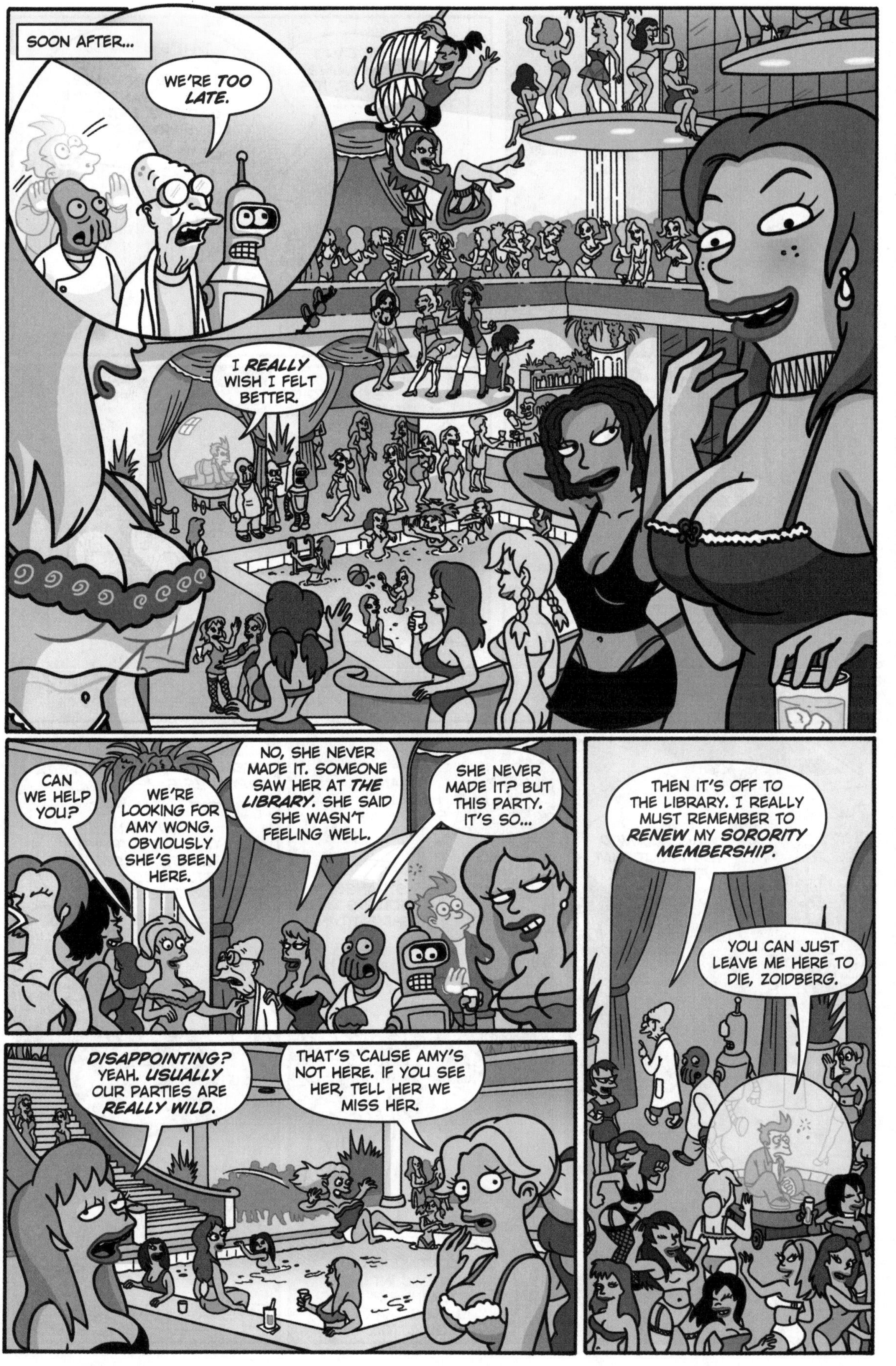
SOON AFTER...
WE'RE *TOO LATE.*
I *REALLY* WISH I FELT BETTER.
CAN WE HELP YOU?
WE'RE LOOKING FOR AMY WONG. OBVIOUSLY SHE'S BEEN HERE.
NO, SHE NEVER MADE IT. SOMEONE SAW HER AT *THE LIBRARY.* SHE SAID SHE WASN'T FEELING WELL.
SHE NEVER MADE IT? BUT THIS PARTY. IT'S SO...
*DISAPPOINTING?* YEAH. *USUALLY* OUR PARTIES ARE *REALLY WILD.*
THAT'S 'CAUSE AMY'S NOT HERE. IF YOU SEE HER, TELL HER WE MISS HER.
THEN IT'S OFF TO THE LIBRARY. I REALLY MUST REMEMBER TO *RENEW* MY *SORORITY MEMBERSHIP.*
YOU CAN JUST LEAVE ME HERE TO DIE, ZOIDBERG.

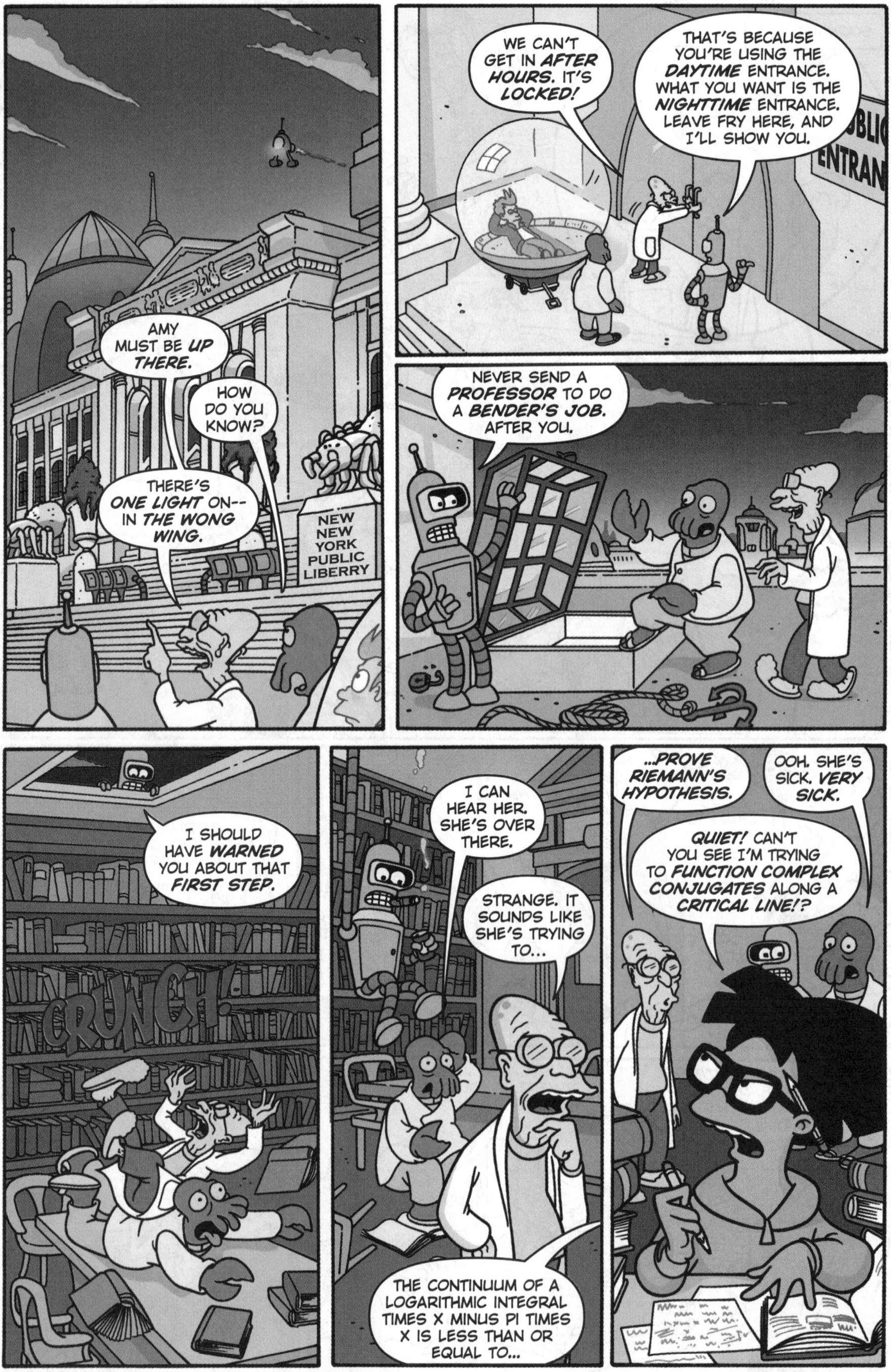
AMY MUST BE UP THERE.
HOW DO YOU KNOW?
THERE'S ONE LIGHT ON-- IN THE WONG WING.
NEW NEW YORK PUBLIC LIBERRY
WE CAN'T GET IN AFTER HOURS. IT'S LOCKED!
THAT'S BECAUSE YOU'RE USING THE DAYTIME ENTRANCE. WHAT YOU WANT IS THE NIGHTTIME ENTRANCE. LEAVE FRY HERE, AND I'LL SHOW YOU.
NEVER SEND A PROFESSOR TO DO A BENDER'S JOB. AFTER YOU.
I SHOULD HAVE WARNED YOU ABOUT THAT FIRST STEP.
CRUNCH!
I CAN HEAR HER. SHE'S OVER THERE.
STRANGE. IT SOUNDS LIKE SHE'S TRYING TO...
THE CONTINUUM OF A LOGARITHMIC INTEGRAL TIMES X MINUS PI TIMES X IS LESS THAN OR EQUAL TO...
...PROVE RIEMANN'S HYPOTHESIS.
OOH. SHE'S SICK. VERY SICK.
QUIET! CAN'T YOU SEE I'M TRYING TO FUNCTION COMPLEX CONJUGATES ALONG A CRITICAL LINE!?

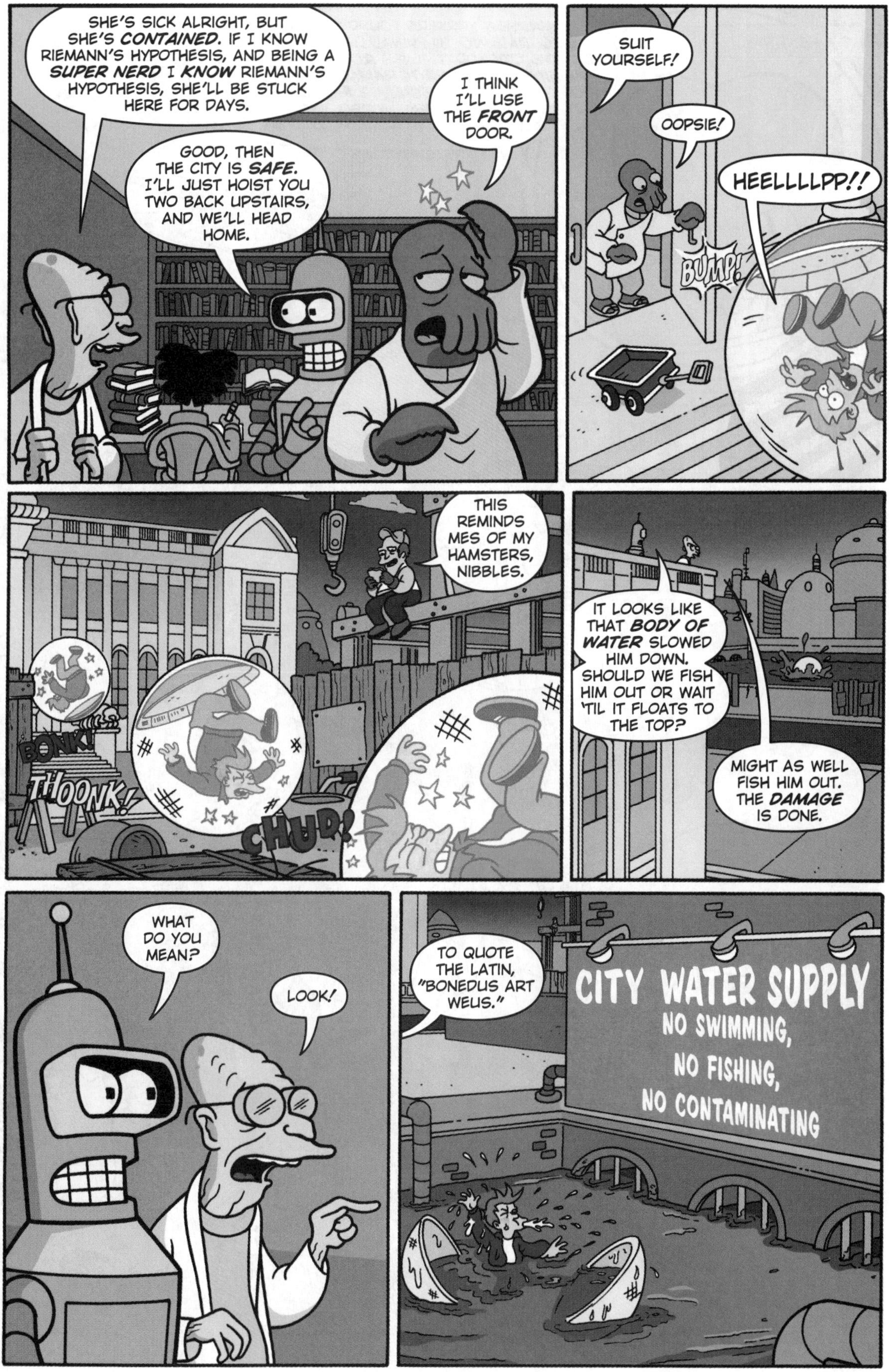
SHE'S SICK ALRIGHT, BUT SHE'S CONTAINED. IF I KNOW RIEMANN'S HYPOTHESIS, AND BEING A SUPER NERD I KNOW RIEMANN'S HYPOTHESIS, SHE'LL BE STUCK HERE FOR DAYS.
GOOD, THEN THE CITY IS SAFE. I'LL JUST HOIST YOU TWO BACK UPSTAIRS, AND WE'LL HEAD HOME.
I THINK I'LL USE THE FRONT DOOR.
SUIT YOURSELF!
OOPSIE!
HEELLLLPP!!
BUMP!
THIS REMINDS MES OF MY HAMSTERS, NIBBLES.
BONK!
THOONK!
CHUD!
IT LOOKS LIKE THAT BODY OF WATER SLOWED HIM DOWN. SHOULD WE FISH HIM OUT OR WAIT 'TIL IT FLOATS TO THE TOP?
MIGHT AS WELL FISH HIM OUT. THE DAMAGE IS DONE.
WHAT DO YOU MEAN?
LOOK!
TO QUOTE THE LATIN, "BONEDUS ART WEUS."
CITY WATER SUPPLY
NO SWIMMING,
NO FISHING,
NO CONTAMINATING

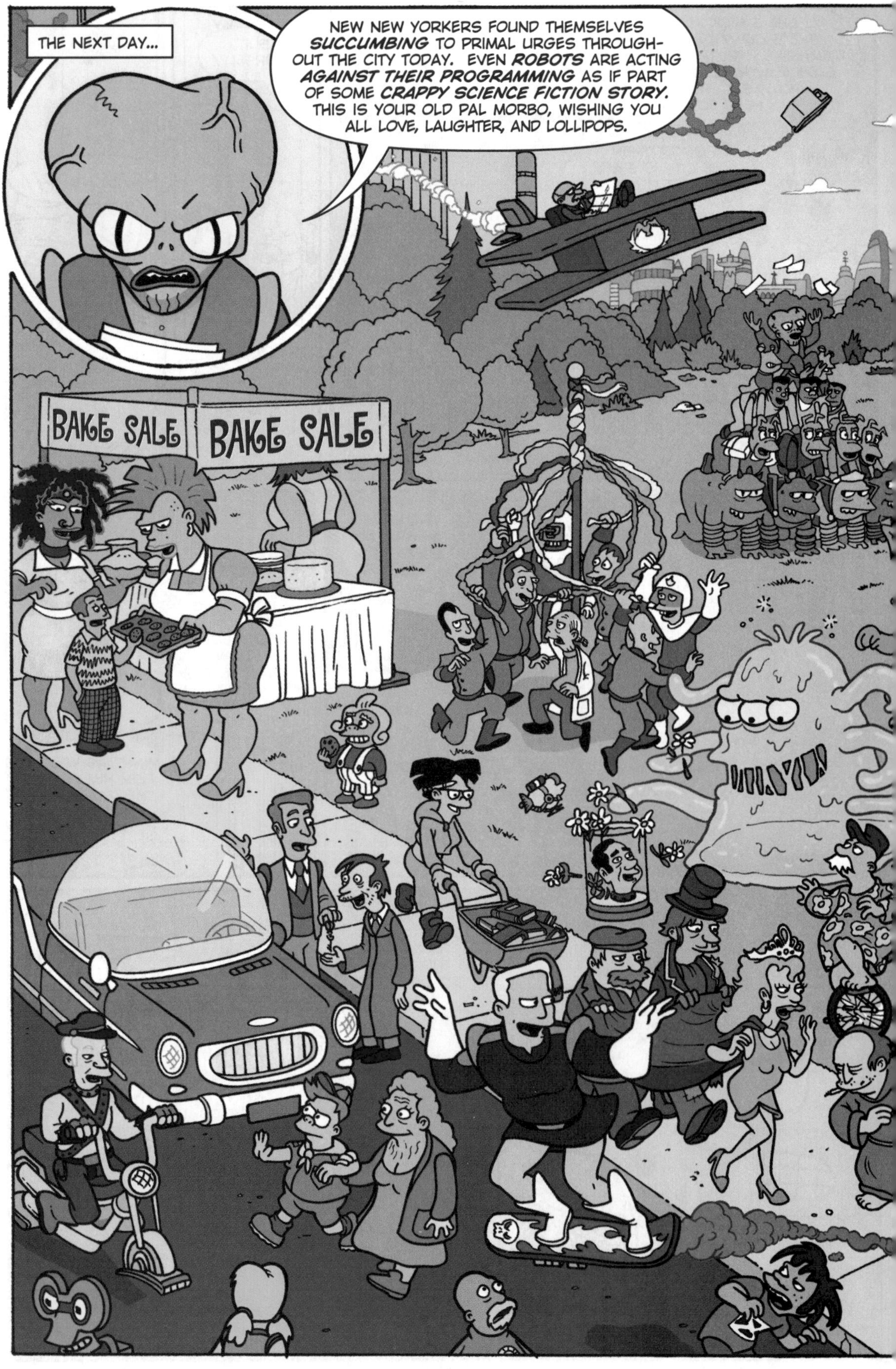
THE NEXT DAY...
NEW NEW YORKERS FOUND THEMSELVES SUCCUMBING TO PRIMAL URGES THROUGH-OUT THE CITY TODAY. EVEN ROBOTS ARE ACTING AGAINST THEIR PROGRAMMING AS IF PART OF SOME CRAPPY SCIENCE FICTION STORY. THIS IS YOUR OLD PAL MORBO, WISHING YOU ALL LOVE, LAUGHTER, AND LOLLIPOPS.
BAKE SALE
BAKE SALE

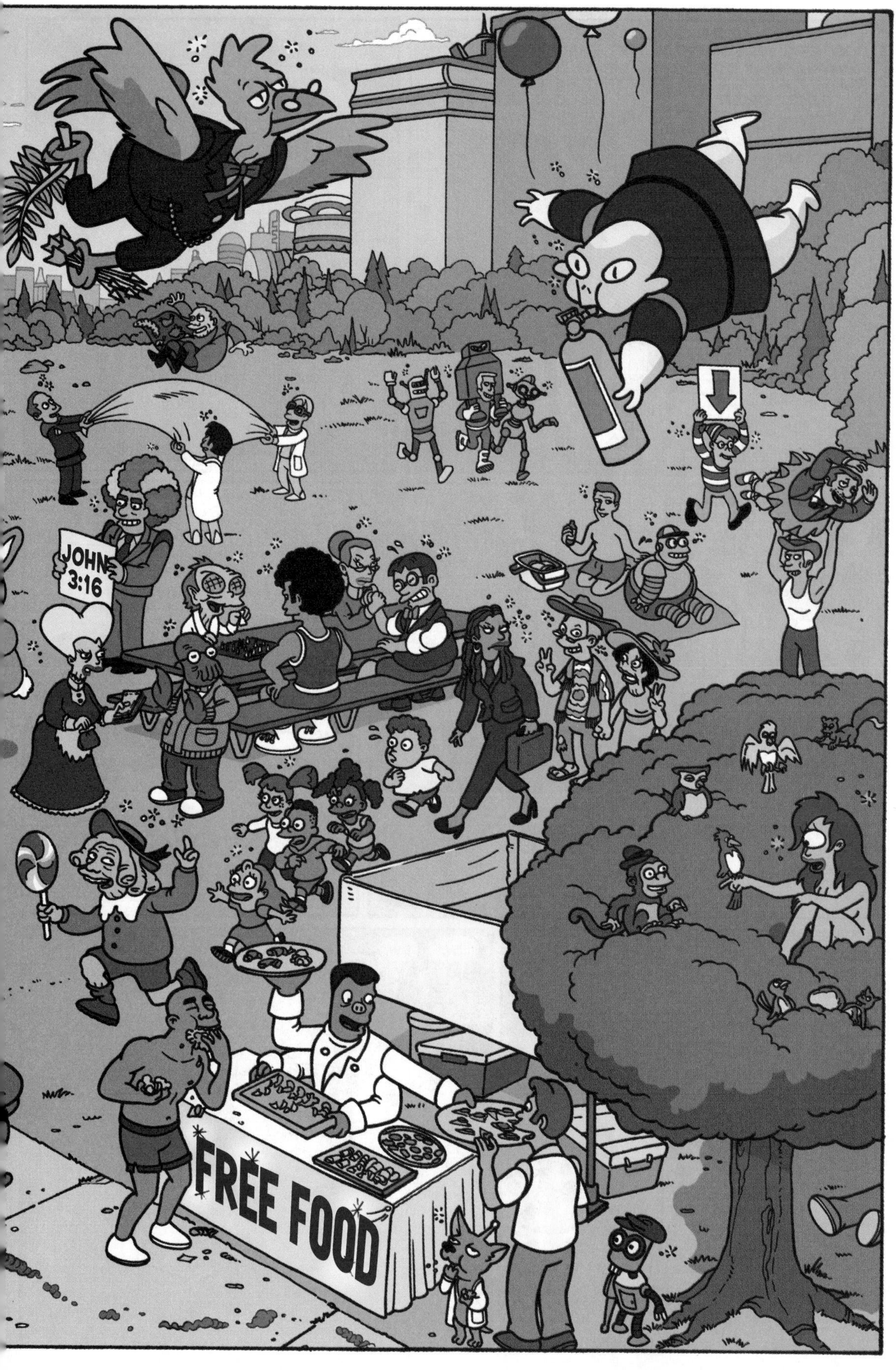
JOHN 3:16
FREE FOOD

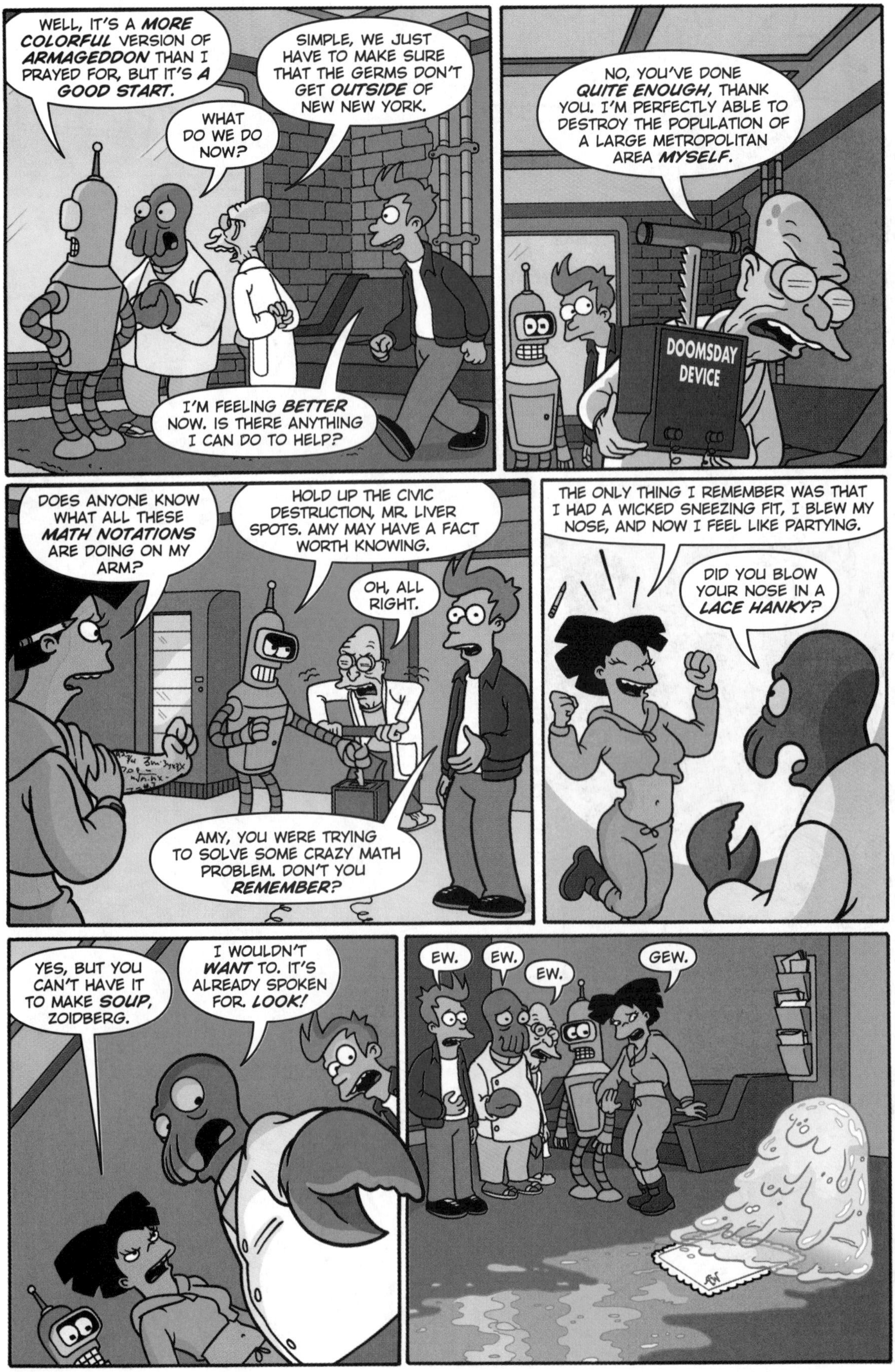
WELL, IT'S A MORE COLORFUL VERSION OF ARMAGEDDON THAN I PRAYED FOR, BUT IT'S A GOOD START.
WHAT DO WE DO NOW?
SIMPLE, WE JUST HAVE TO MAKE SURE THAT THE GERMS DON'T GET OUTSIDE OF NEW NEW YORK.
I'M FEELING BETTER NOW. IS THERE ANYTHING I CAN DO TO HELP?
NO, YOU'VE DONE QUITE ENOUGH, THANK YOU. I'M PERFECTLY ABLE TO DESTROY THE POPULATION OF A LARGE METROPOLITAN AREA MYSELF.
DOOMSDAY DEVICE
DOES ANYONE KNOW WHAT ALL THESE MATH NOTATIONS ARE DOING ON MY ARM?
HOLD UP THE CIVIC DESTRUCTION, MR. LIVER SPOTS. AMY MAY HAVE A FACT WORTH KNOWING.
OH, ALL RIGHT.
AMY, YOU WERE TRYING TO SOLVE SOME CRAZY MATH PROBLEM. DON'T YOU REMEMBER?
THE ONLY THING I REMEMBER WAS THAT I HAD A WICKED SNEEZING FIT, I BLEW MY NOSE, AND NOW I FEEL LIKE PARTYING.
DID YOU BLOW YOUR NOSE IN A LACE HANKY?
YES, BUT YOU CAN'T HAVE IT TO MAKE SOUP, ZOIDBERG.
I WOULDN'T WANT TO. IT'S ALREADY SPOKEN FOR. LOOK!
EW.
EW.
EW.
GEW.

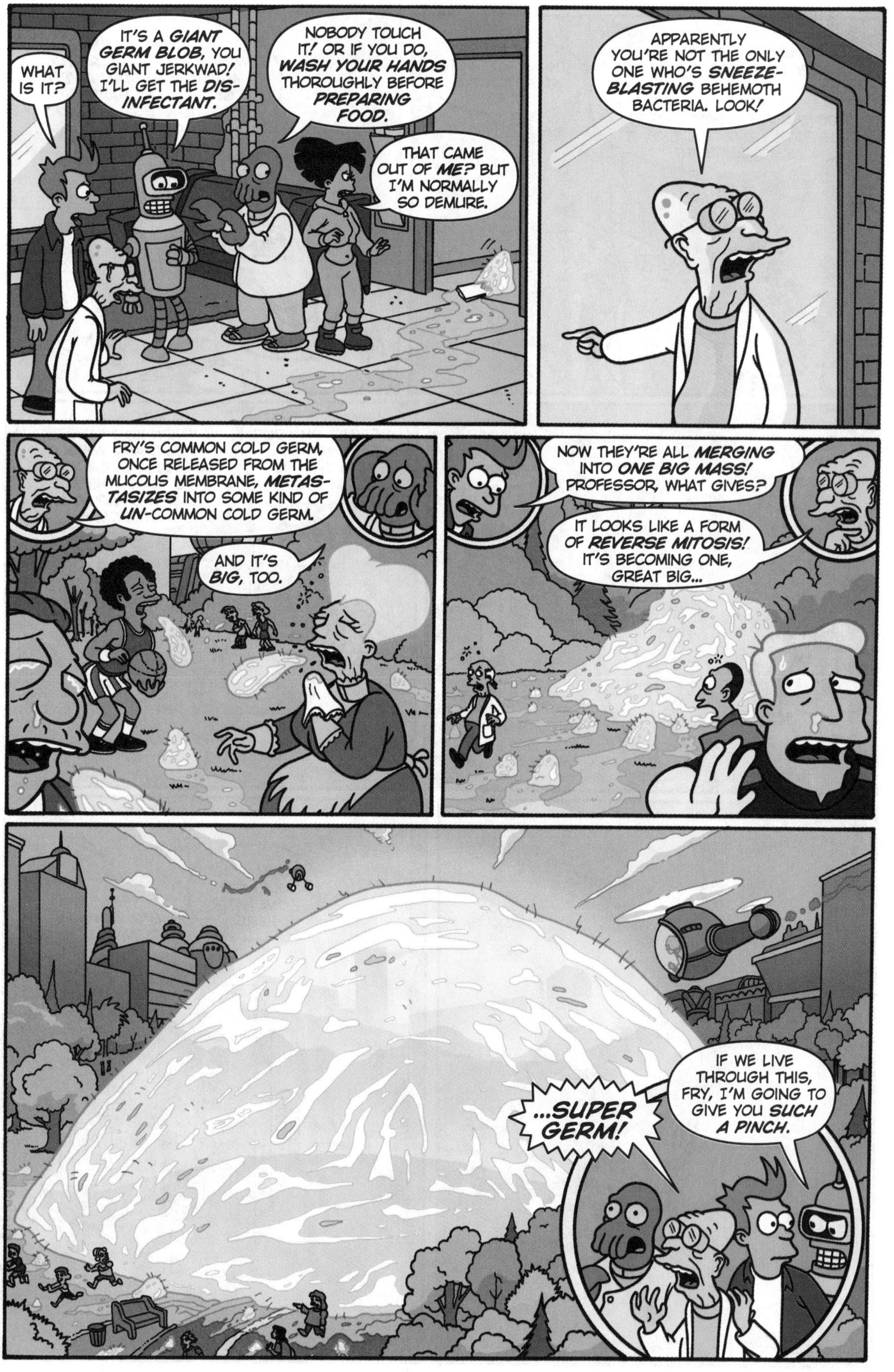
WHAT IS IT?
IT'S A GIANT GERM BLOB, YOU GIANT JERKWAD! I'LL GET THE DIS-INFECTANT.
NOBODY TOUCH IT! OR IF YOU DO, WASH YOUR HANDS THOROUGHLY BEFORE PREPARING FOOD.
THAT CAME OUT OF ME? BUT I'M NORMALLY SO DEMURE.
APPARENTLY YOU'RE NOT THE ONLY ONE WHO'S SNEEZE-BLASTING BEHEMOTH BACTERIA. LOOK!
FRY'S COMMON COLD GERM, ONCE RELEASED FROM THE MUCOUS MEMBRANE, METASTASIZES INTO SOME KIND OF UN-COMMON COLD GERM.
AND IT'S BIG, TOO.
NOW THEY'RE ALL MERGING INTO ONE BIG MASS! PROFESSOR, WHAT GIVES?
IT LOOKS LIKE A FORM OF REVERSE MITOSIS! IT'S BECOMING ONE, GREAT BIG...
...SUPER GERM!
IF WE LIVE THROUGH THIS, FRY, I'M GOING TO GIVE YOU SUCH A PINCH.

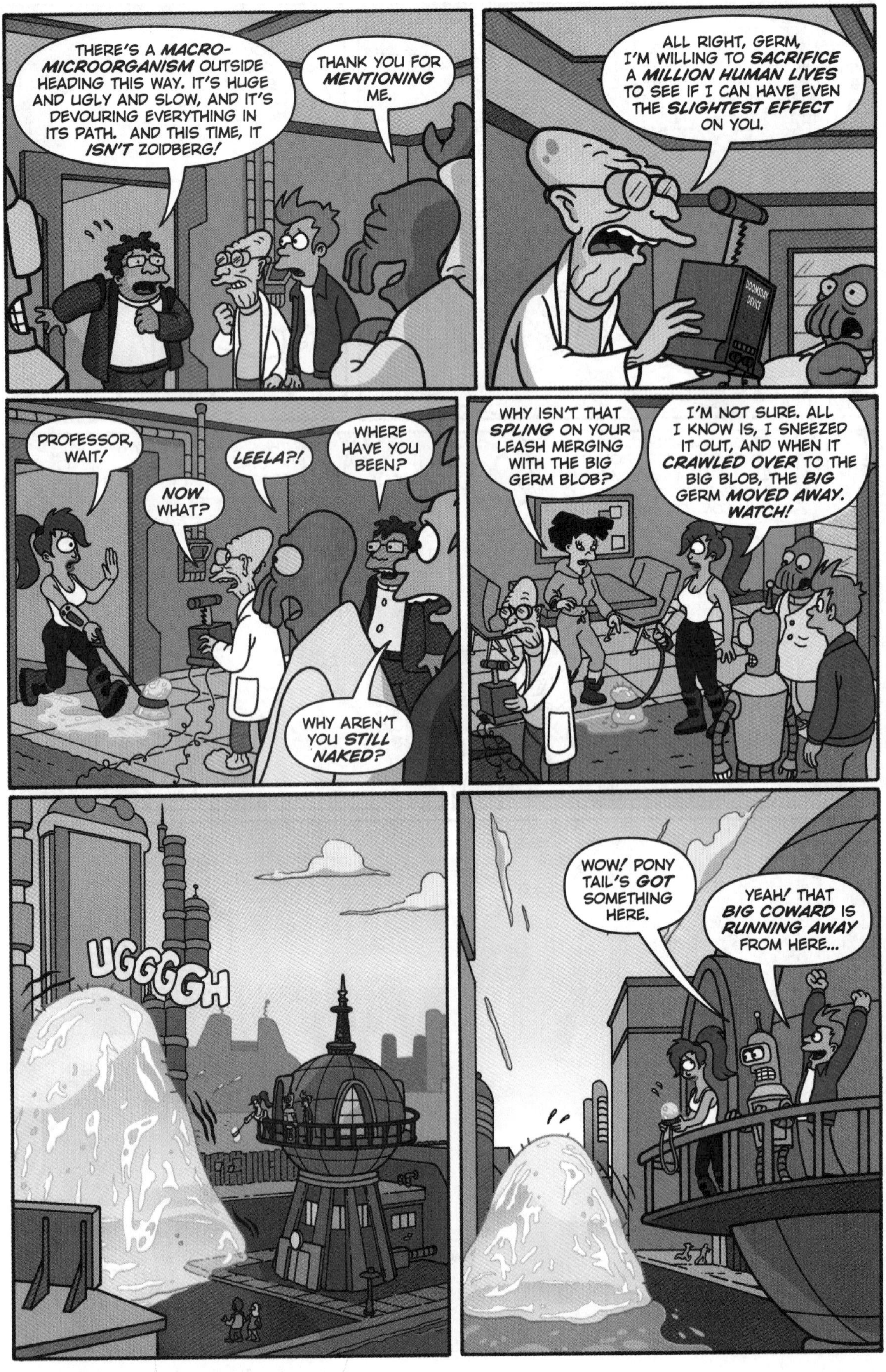

THERE'S A MACRO-MICROORGANISM OUTSIDE HEADING THIS WAY. IT'S HUGE AND UGLY AND SLOW, AND IT'S DEVOURING EVERYTHING IN ITS PATH. AND THIS TIME, IT ISN'T ZOIDBERG!
THANK YOU FOR MENTIONING ME.
ALL RIGHT, GERM, I'M WILLING TO SACRIFICE A MILLION HUMAN LIVES TO SEE IF I CAN HAVE EVEN THE SLIGHTEST EFFECT ON YOU.
DOOMSDAY DEVICE
PROFESSOR, WAIT!
NOW WHAT?
LEELA?!
WHERE HAVE YOU BEEN?
WHY AREN'T YOU STILL NAKED?
WHY ISN'T THAT SPLING ON YOUR LEASH MERGING WITH THE BIG GERM BLOB?
I'M NOT SURE. ALL I KNOW IS, I SNEEZED IT OUT, AND WHEN IT CRAWLED OVER TO THE BIG BLOB, THE BIG GERM MOVED AWAY. WATCH!
UGGGGH
WOW! PONY TAIL'S GOT SOMETHING HERE.
YEAH! THAT BIG COWARD IS RUNNING AWAY FROM HERE...

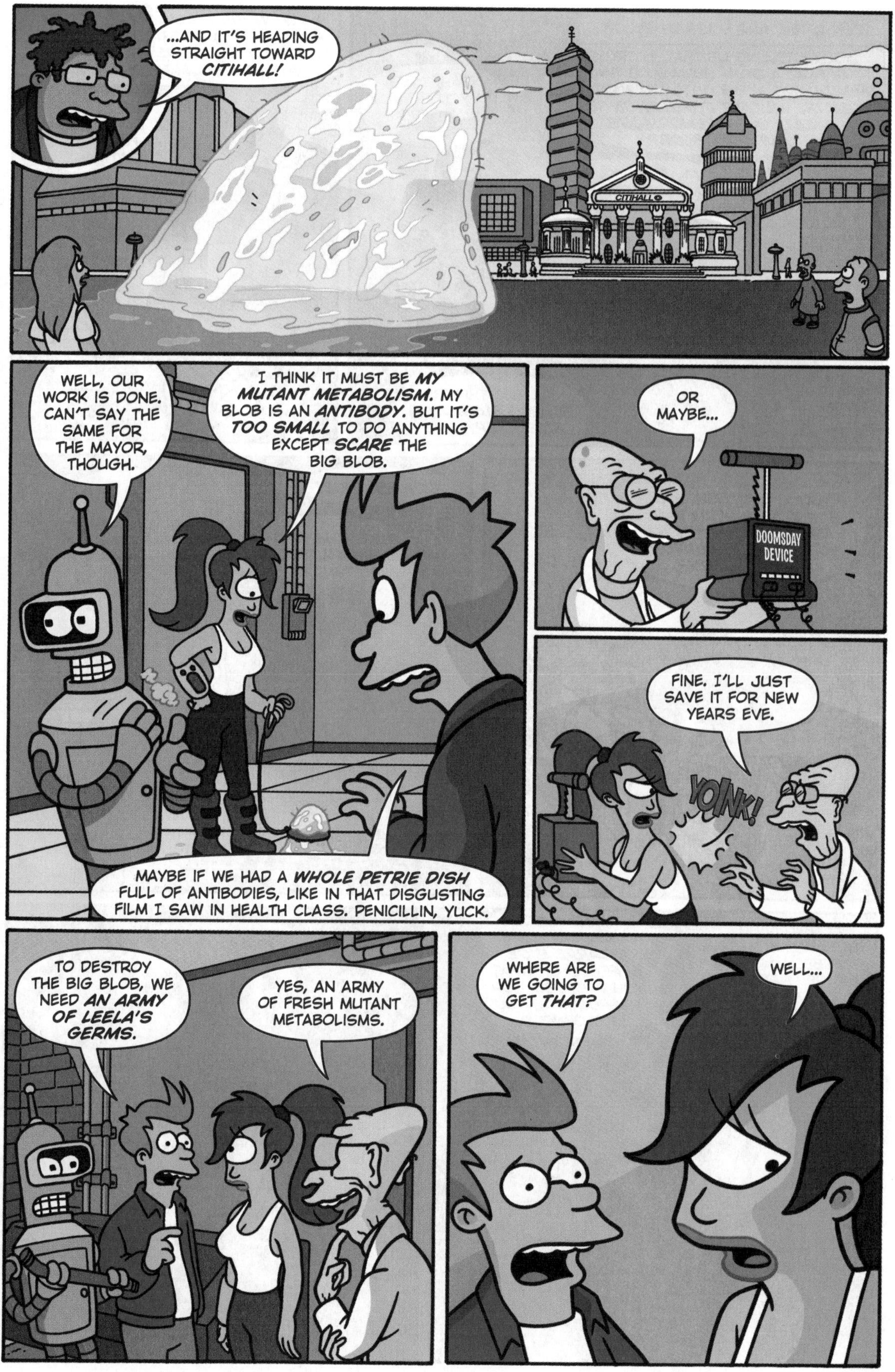
...AND IT'S HEADING STRAIGHT TOWARD CITIHALL!
CITIHALL
WELL, OUR WORK IS DONE. CAN'T SAY THE SAME FOR THE MAYOR, THOUGH.
I THINK IT MUST BE MY MUTANT METABOLISM. MY BLOB IS AN ANTIBODY. BUT IT'S TOO SMALL TO DO ANYTHING EXCEPT SCARE THE BIG BLOB.
MAYBE IF WE HAD A WHOLE PETRIE DISH FULL OF ANTIBODIES, LIKE IN THAT DISGUSTING FILM I SAW IN HEALTH CLASS. PENICILLIN, YUCK.
OR MAYBE...
DOOMSDAY DEVICE
FINE. I'LL JUST SAVE IT FOR NEW YEARS EVE.
YOINK!
TO DESTROY THE BIG BLOB, WE NEED AN ARMY OF LEELA'S GERMS.
YES, AN ARMY OF FRESH MUTANT METABOLISMS.
WHERE ARE WE GOING TO GET THAT?
WELL...

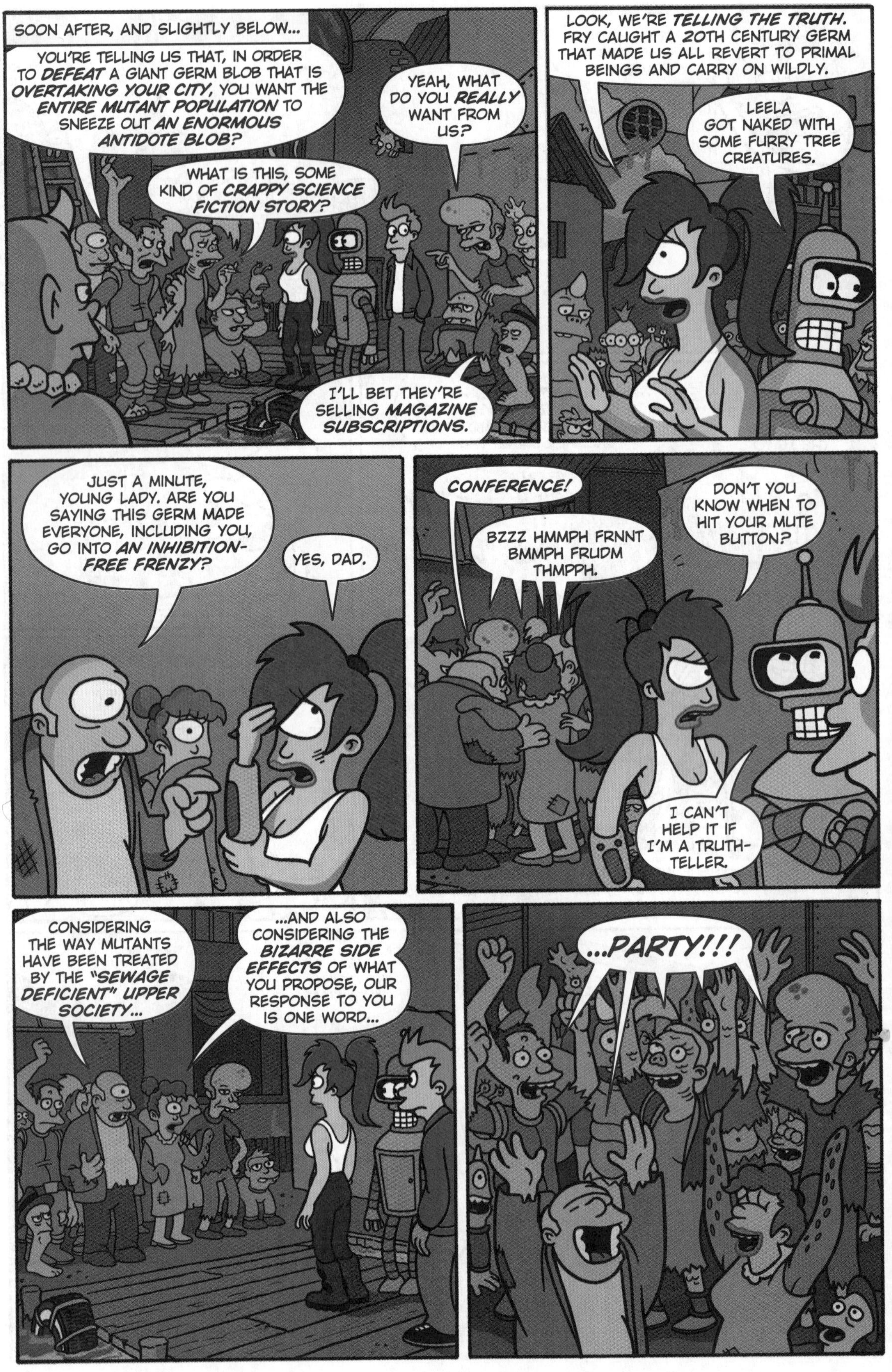
SOON AFTER, AND SLIGHTLY BELOW...
YOU'RE TELLING US THAT, IN ORDER TO DEFEAT A GIANT GERM BLOB THAT IS OVERTAKING YOUR CITY, YOU WANT THE ENTIRE MUTANT POPULATION TO SNEEZE OUT AN ENORMOUS ANTIDOTE BLOB?
WHAT IS THIS, SOME KIND OF CRAPPY SCIENCE FICTION STORY?
YEAH, WHAT DO YOU REALLY WANT FROM US?
I'LL BET THEY'RE SELLING MAGAZINE SUBSCRIPTIONS.
LOOK, WE'RE TELLING THE TRUTH. FRY CAUGHT A 20TH CENTURY GERM THAT MADE US ALL REVERT TO PRIMAL BEINGS AND CARRY ON WILDLY.
LEELA GOT NAKED WITH SOME FURRY TREE CREATURES.
JUST A MINUTE, YOUNG LADY. ARE YOU SAYING THIS GERM MADE EVERYONE, INCLUDING YOU, GO INTO AN INHIBITION-FREE FRENZY?
YES, DAD.
CONFERENCE!
BZZZ HMMPH FRNNT BMMPH FRUDM THMPPH.
DON'T YOU KNOW WHEN TO HIT YOUR MUTE BUTTON?
I CAN'T HELP IT IF I'M A TRUTH-TELLER.
CONSIDERING THE WAY MUTANTS HAVE BEEN TREATED BY THE "SEWAGE DEFICIENT" UPPER SOCIETY...
...AND ALSO CONSIDERING THE BIZARRE SIDE EFFECTS OF WHAT YOU PROPOSE, OUR RESPONSE TO YOU IS ONE WORD...
...PARTY!!!

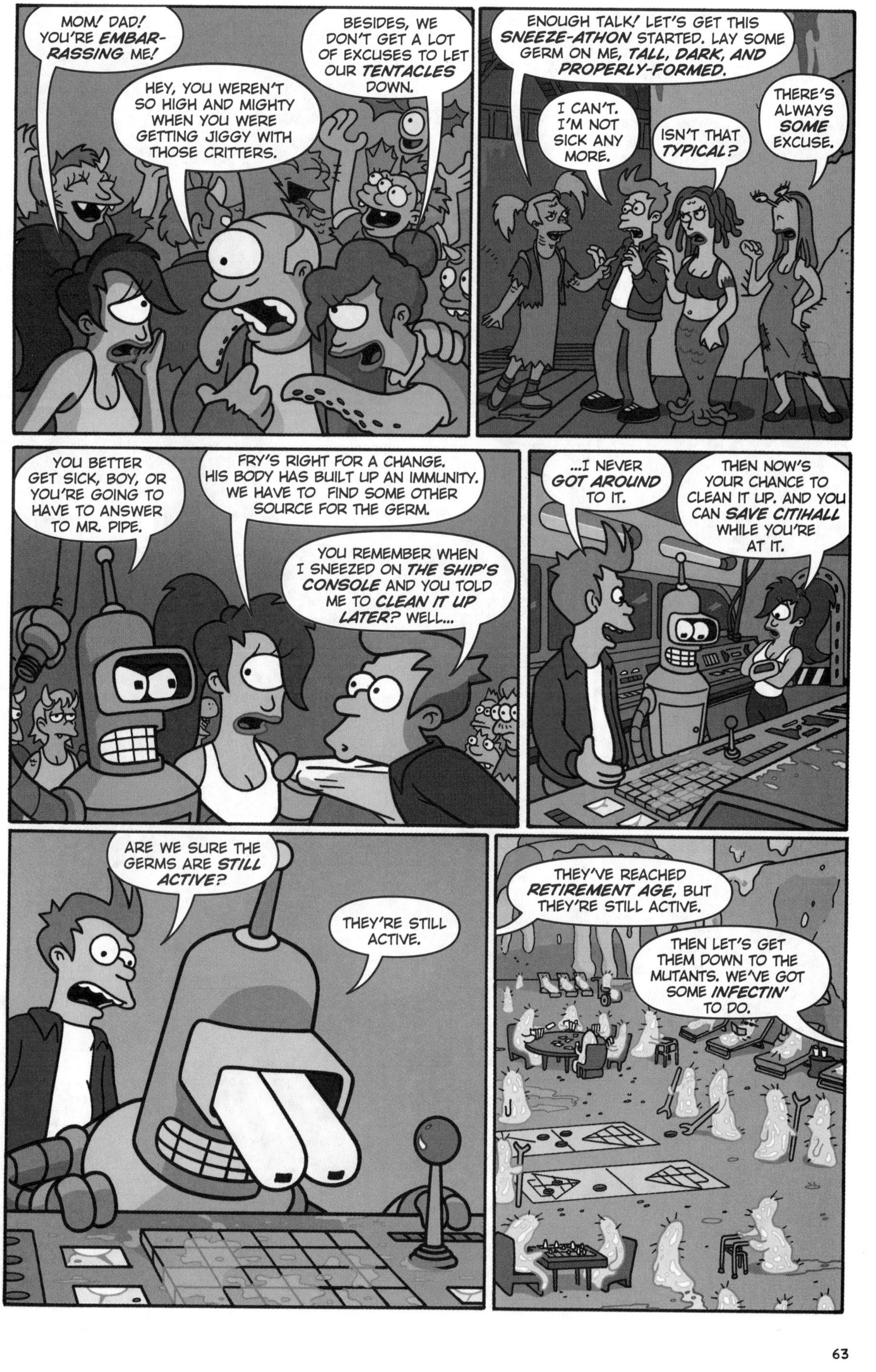
MOM! DAD! YOU'RE EMBARRASSING ME!
HEY, YOU WEREN'T SO HIGH AND MIGHTY WHEN YOU WERE GETTING JIGGY WITH THOSE CRITTERS.
BESIDES, WE DON'T GET A LOT OF EXCUSES TO LET OUR TENTACLES DOWN.
ENOUGH TALK! LET'S GET THIS SNEEZE-ATHON STARTED. LAY SOME GERM ON ME, TALL, DARK, AND PROPERLY-FORMED.
I CAN'T. I'M NOT SICK ANY MORE.
ISN'T THAT TYPICAL?
THERE'S ALWAYS SOME EXCUSE.
YOU BETTER GET SICK, BOY, OR YOU'RE GOING TO HAVE TO ANSWER TO MR. PIPE.
FRY'S RIGHT FOR A CHANGE. HIS BODY HAS BUILT UP AN IMMUNITY. WE HAVE TO FIND SOME OTHER SOURCE FOR THE GERM.
YOU REMEMBER WHEN I SNEEZED ON THE SHIP'S CONSOLE AND YOU TOLD ME TO CLEAN IT UP LATER? WELL...
...I NEVER GOT AROUND TO IT.
THEN NOW'S YOUR CHANCE TO CLEAN IT UP. AND YOU CAN SAVE CITIHALL WHILE YOU'RE AT IT.
ARE WE SURE THE GERMS ARE STILL ACTIVE?
THEY'RE STILL ACTIVE.
THEY'VE REACHED RETIREMENT AGE, BUT THEY'RE STILL ACTIVE.
THEN LET'S GET THEM DOWN TO THE MUTANTS. WE'VE GOT SOME INFECTIN' TO DO.

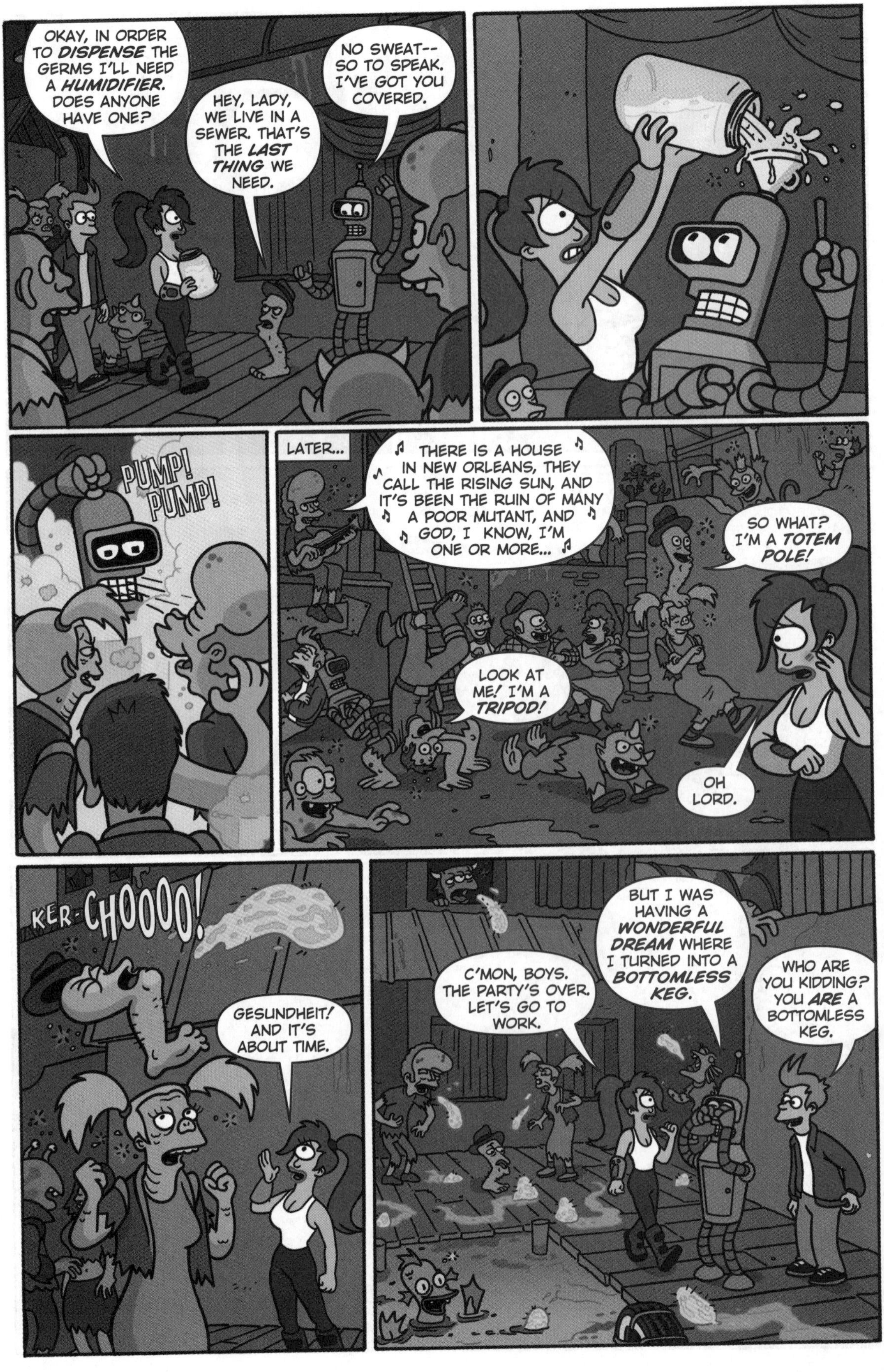
OKAY, IN ORDER TO *DISPENSE* THE GERMS I'LL NEED A *HUMIDIFIER*. DOES ANYONE HAVE ONE?
HEY, LADY, WE LIVE IN A SEWER. THAT'S THE *LAST THING* WE NEED.
NO SWEAT-- SO TO SPEAK. I'VE GOT YOU COVERED.
PUMP! PUMP!
LATER...
♪ THERE IS A HOUSE IN NEW ORLEANS, THEY CALL THE RISING SUN, AND IT'S BEEN THE RUIN OF MANY A POOR MUTANT, AND GOD, I KNOW, I'M ONE OR MORE... ♪
SO WHAT? I'M A *TOTEM POLE!*
LOOK AT ME! I'M A *TRIPOD!*
OH LORD.
KER-CHOOOO!
GESUNDHEIT! AND IT'S ABOUT TIME.
C'MON, BOYS. THE PARTY'S OVER. LET'S GO TO WORK.
BUT I WAS HAVING A *WONDERFUL DREAM* WHERE I TURNED INTO A *BOTTOMLESS KEG*.
WHO ARE YOU KIDDING? YOU *ARE* A BOTTOMLESS KEG.

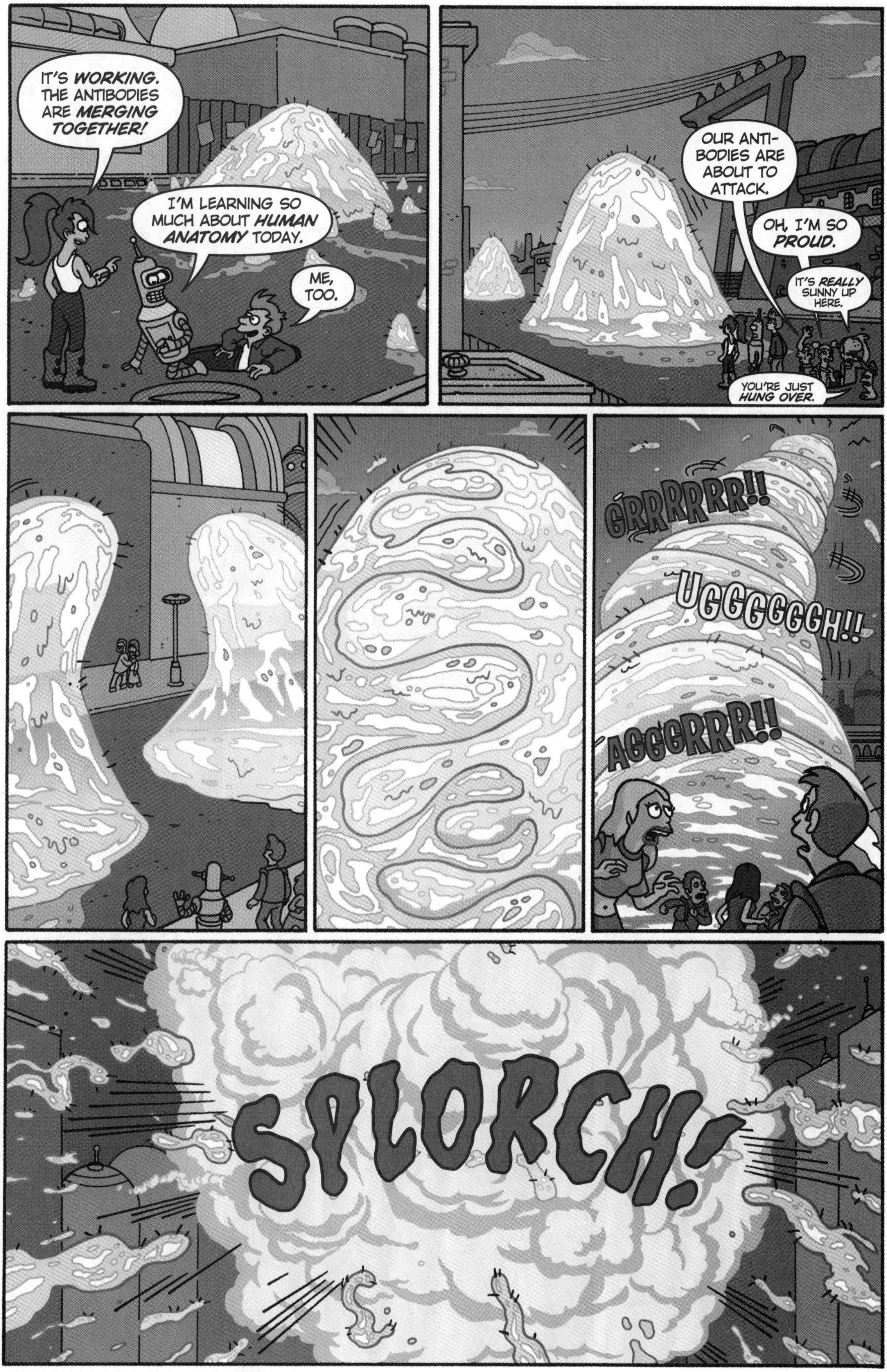
IT'S **WORKING.** THE ANTIBODIES ARE **MERGING TOGETHER!**
I'M LEARNING SO MUCH ABOUT **HUMAN ANATOMY** TODAY.
ME, TOO.
OUR ANTI-BODIES ARE ABOUT TO ATTACK.
OH, I'M SO **PROUD.**
IT'S **REALLY** SUNNY UP HERE.
YOU'RE JUST **HUNG OVER.**
GRRRRRR!!
UGGGGGGH!!
AGGGRRR!!
SPLORCH!

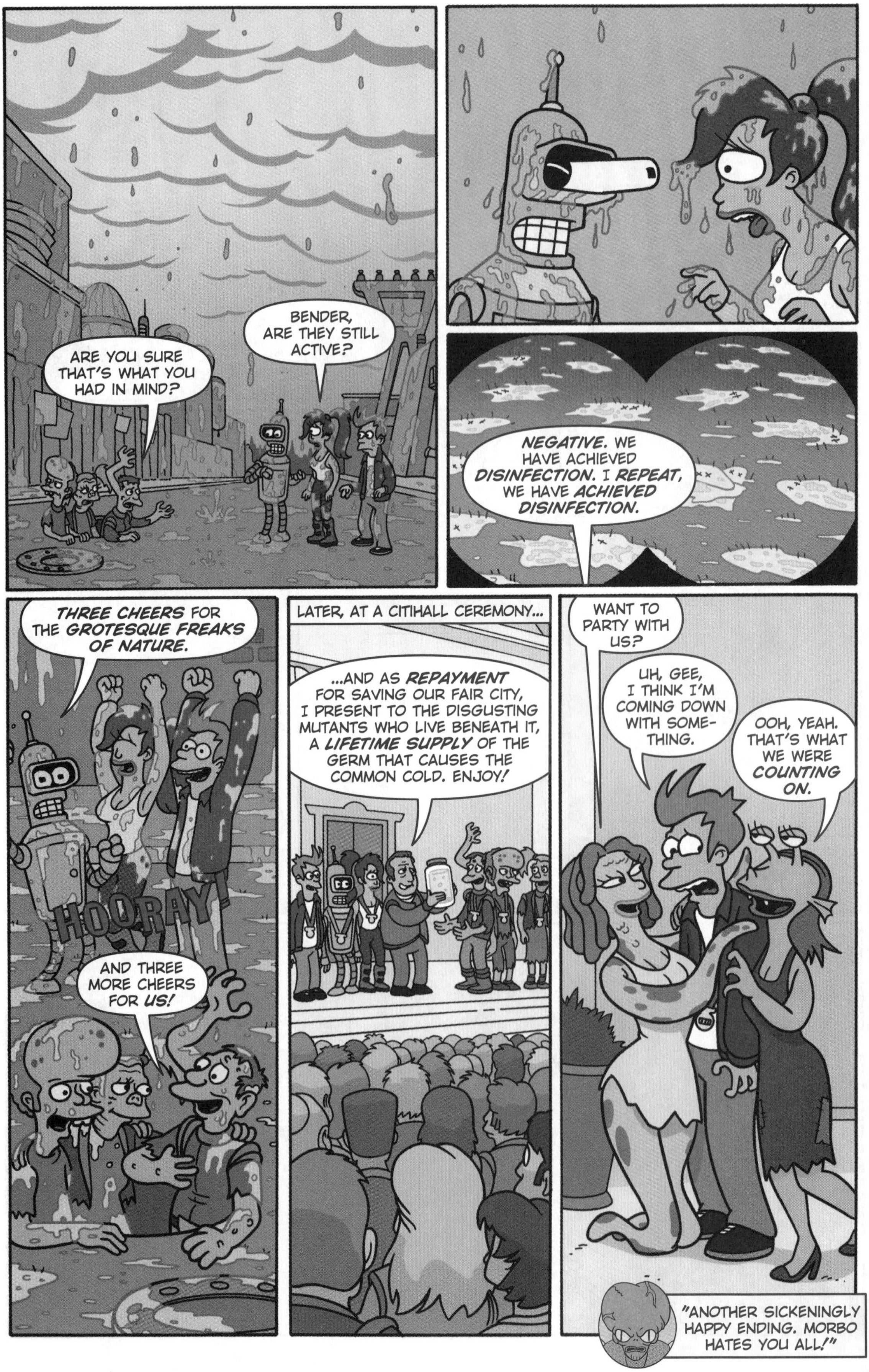
ARE YOU SURE THAT'S WHAT YOU HAD IN MIND?
BENDER, ARE THEY STILL ACTIVE?
NEGATIVE. WE HAVE ACHIEVED DISINFECTION. I REPEAT, WE HAVE ACHIEVED DISINFECTION.
THREE CHEERS FOR THE GROTESQUE FREAKS OF NATURE.
HOORAY!
AND THREE MORE CHEERS FOR US!
LATER, AT A CITIHALL CEREMONY...
...AND AS REPAYMENT FOR SAVING OUR FAIR CITY, I PRESENT TO THE DISGUSTING MUTANTS WHO LIVE BENEATH IT, A LIFETIME SUPPLY OF THE GERM THAT CAUSES THE COMMON COLD. ENJOY!
WANT TO PARTY WITH US?
UH, GEE, I THINK I'M COMING DOWN WITH SOME-THING.
OOH, YEAH. THAT'S WHAT WE WERE COUNTING ON.
"ANOTHER SICKENINGLY HAPPY ENDING. MORBO HATES YOU ALL!"

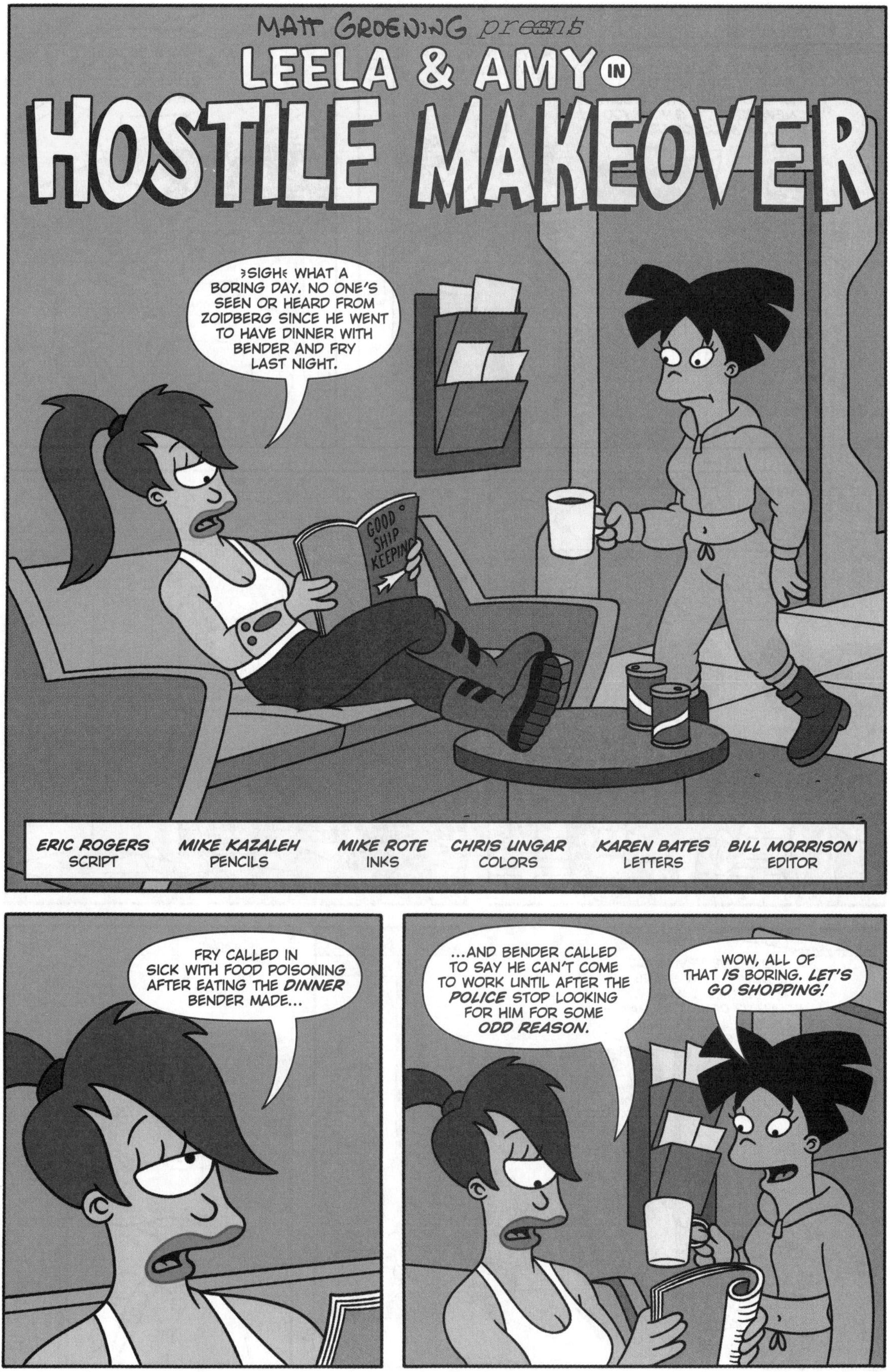
MATT GROENING presents
LEELA & AMY IN
HOSTILE MAKEOVER
SIGH WHAT A BORING DAY. NO ONE'S SEEN OR HEARD FROM ZOIDBERG SINCE HE WENT TO HAVE DINNER WITH BENDER AND FRY LAST NIGHT.
GOOD SHIP KEEPING
ERIC ROGERS SCRIPT
MIKE KAZALEH PENCILS
MIKE ROTE INKS
CHRIS UNGAR COLORS
KAREN BATES LETTERS
BILL MORRISON EDITOR
FRY CALLED IN SICK WITH FOOD POISONING AFTER EATING THE DINNER BENDER MADE...
...AND BENDER CALLED TO SAY HE CAN'T COME TO WORK UNTIL AFTER THE POLICE STOP LOOKING FOR HIM FOR SOME ODD REASON.
WOW, ALL OF THAT IS BORING. LET'S GO SHOPPING!

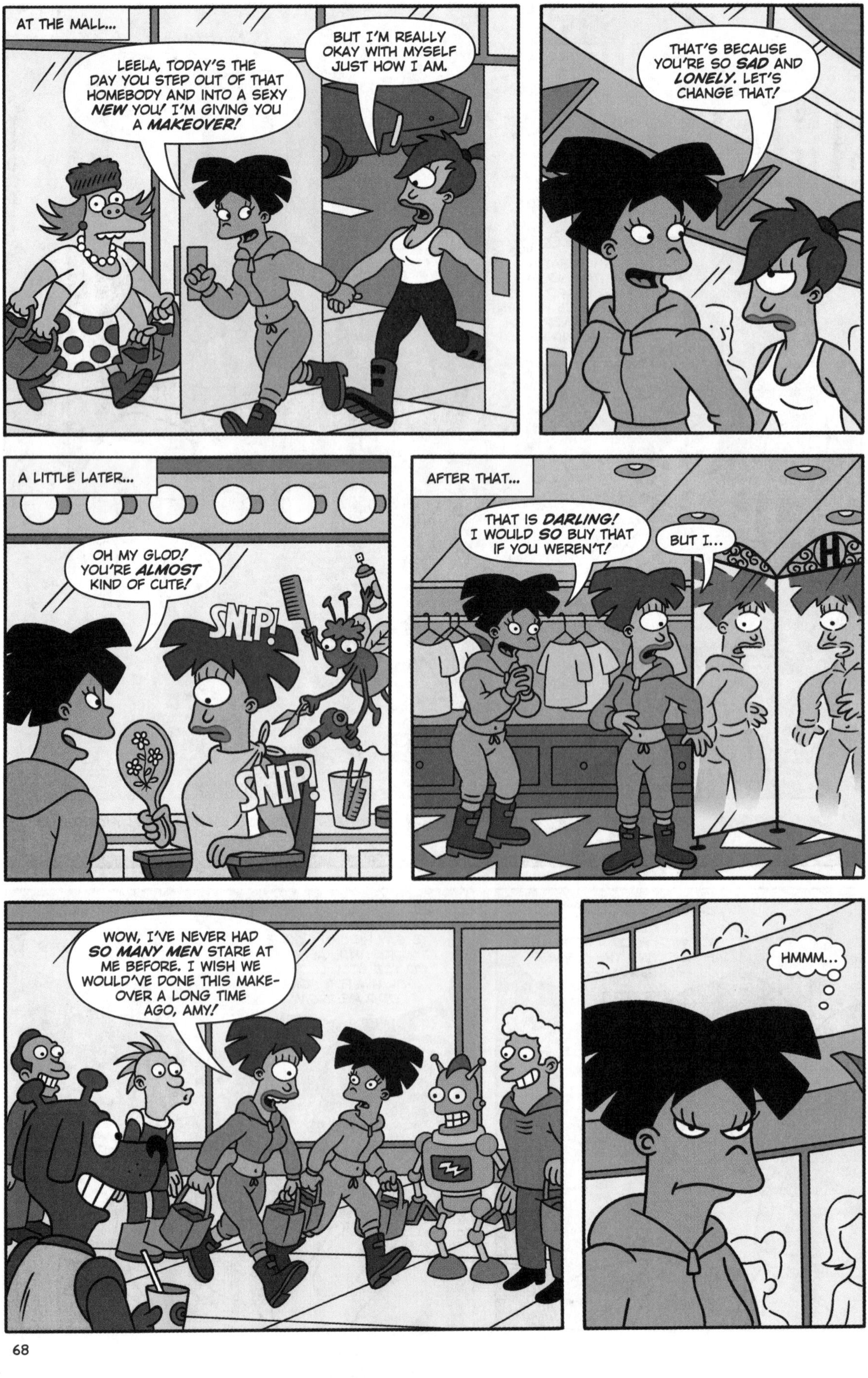

AT THE MALL...
LEELA, TODAY'S THE DAY YOU STEP OUT OF THAT HOMEBODY AND INTO A SEXY *NEW* YOU! I'M GIVING YOU A *MAKEOVER!*
BUT I'M REALLY OKAY WITH MYSELF JUST HOW I AM.
THAT'S BECAUSE YOU'RE SO *SAD* AND *LONELY*. LET'S CHANGE THAT!
A LITTLE LATER...
OH MY GLOD! YOU'RE *ALMOST* KIND OF CUTE!
SNIP!
SNIP!
AFTER THAT...
THAT IS *DARLING!* I WOULD *SO* BUY THAT IF YOU WEREN'T!
BUT I...
H
WOW, I'VE NEVER HAD *SO MANY MEN* STARE AT ME BEFORE. I WISH WE WOULD'VE DONE THIS MAKE-OVER A LONG TIME AGO, AMY!
HMMM...

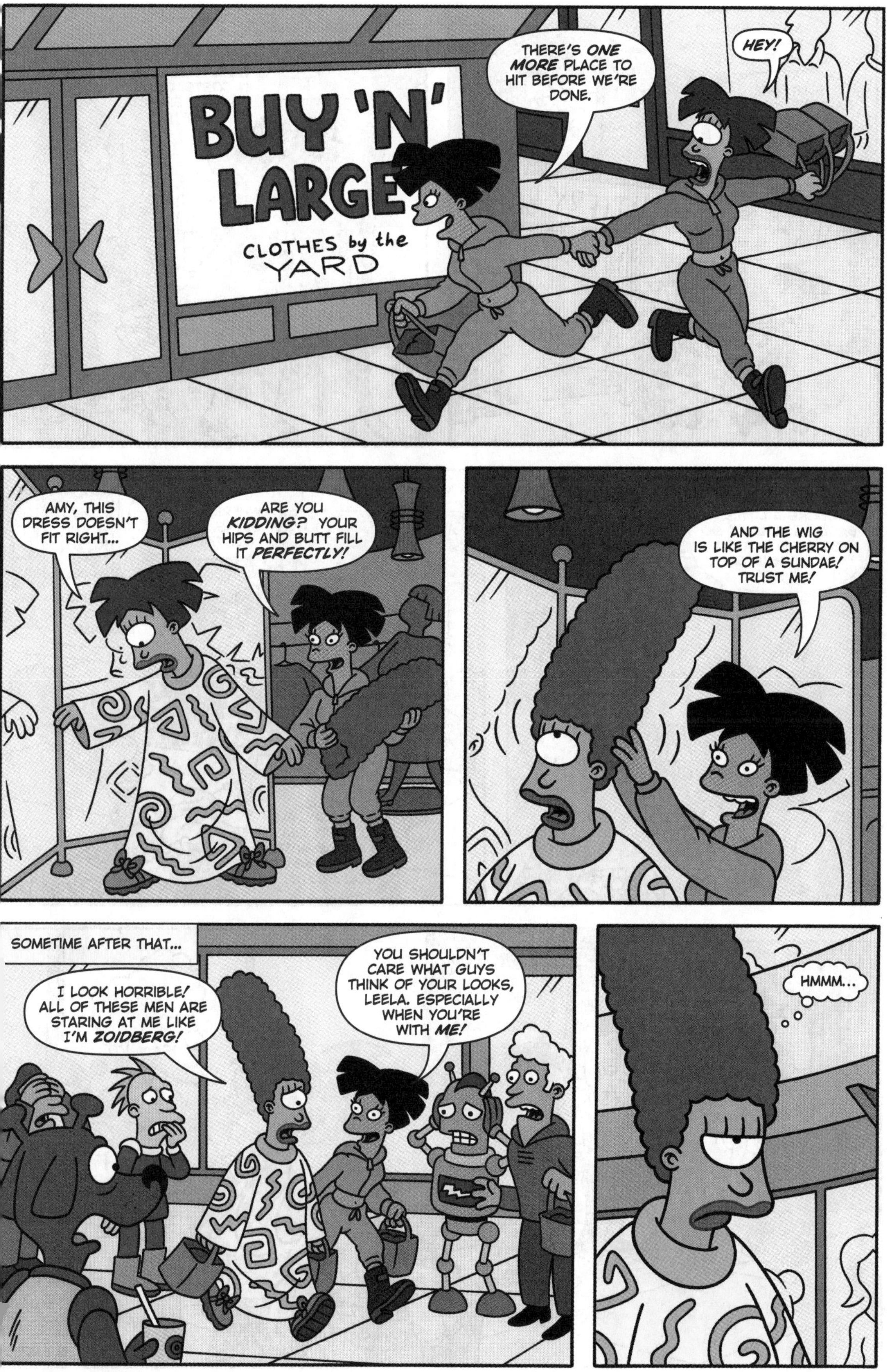
BUY 'N' LARGE
CLOTHES by the YARD
THERE'S ONE MORE PLACE TO HIT BEFORE WE'RE DONE.
HEY!
AMY, THIS DRESS DOESN'T FIT RIGHT...
ARE YOU KIDDING? YOUR HIPS AND BUTT FILL IT PERFECTLY!
AND THE WIG IS LIKE THE CHERRY ON TOP OF A SUNDAE! TRUST ME!
SOMETIME AFTER THAT...
I LOOK HORRIBLE! ALL OF THESE MEN ARE STARING AT ME LIKE I'M ZOIDBERG!
YOU SHOULDN'T CARE WHAT GUYS THINK OF YOUR LOOKS, LEELA. ESPECIALLY WHEN YOU'RE WITH ME!
HMMM...

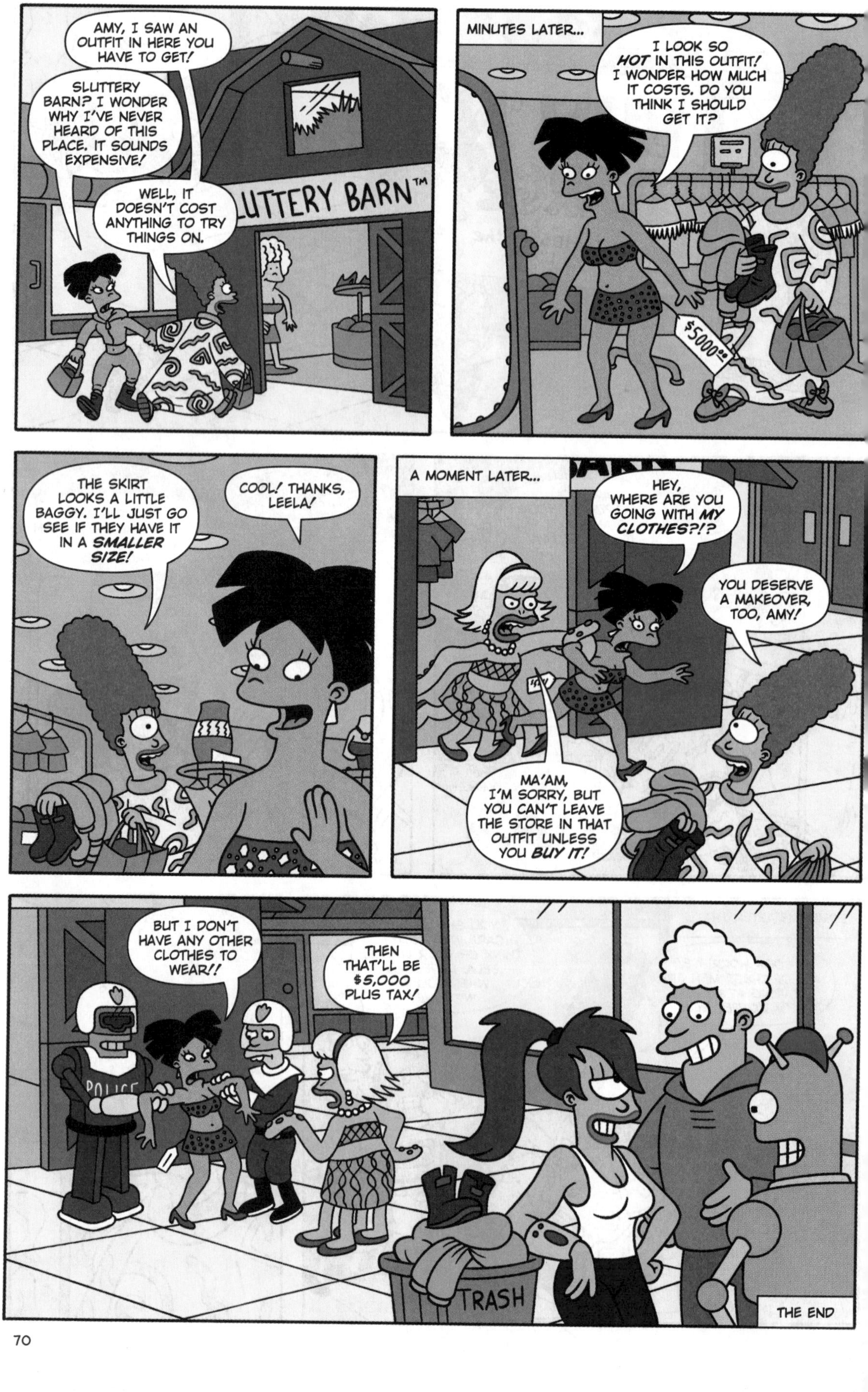
AMY, I SAW AN OUTFIT IN HERE YOU HAVE TO GET!
SLUTTERY BARN? I WONDER WHY I'VE NEVER HEARD OF THIS PLACE. IT SOUNDS EXPENSIVE!
LUTTERY BARN™
WELL, IT DOESN'T COST ANYTHING TO TRY THINGS ON.
MINUTES LATER...
I LOOK SO HOT IN THIS OUTFIT! I WONDER HOW MUCH IT COSTS. DO YOU THINK I SHOULD GET IT?
$5000.00
THE SKIRT LOOKS A LITTLE BAGGY. I'LL JUST GO SEE IF THEY HAVE IT IN A SMALLER SIZE!
COOL! THANKS, LEELA!
A MOMENT LATER...
HEY, WHERE ARE YOU GOING WITH MY CLOTHES?!?
YOU DESERVE A MAKEOVER, TOO, AMY!
MA'AM, I'M SORRY, BUT YOU CAN'T LEAVE THE STORE IN THAT OUTFIT UNLESS YOU BUY IT!
BUT I DON'T HAVE ANY OTHER CLOTHES TO WEAR!!
THEN THAT'LL BE $5,000 PLUS TAX!
TRASH
THE END

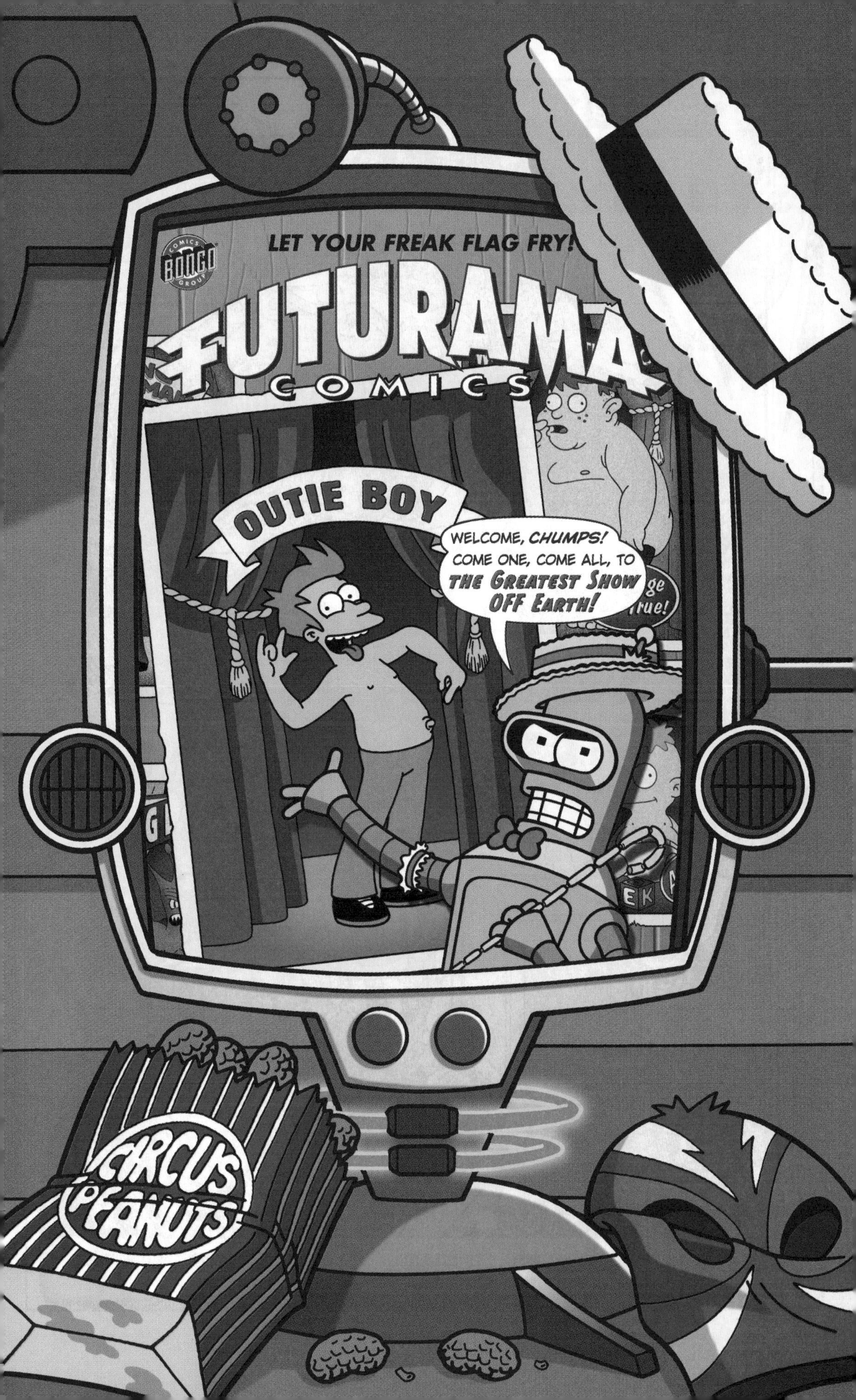
BONGO COMICS GROUP
LET YOUR FREAK FLAG FRY!
FUTURAMA COMICS
OUTIE BOY
WELCOME, CHUMPS! COME ONE, COME ALL, TO THE GREATEST SHOW OFF EARTH!
CIRCUS PEANUTS

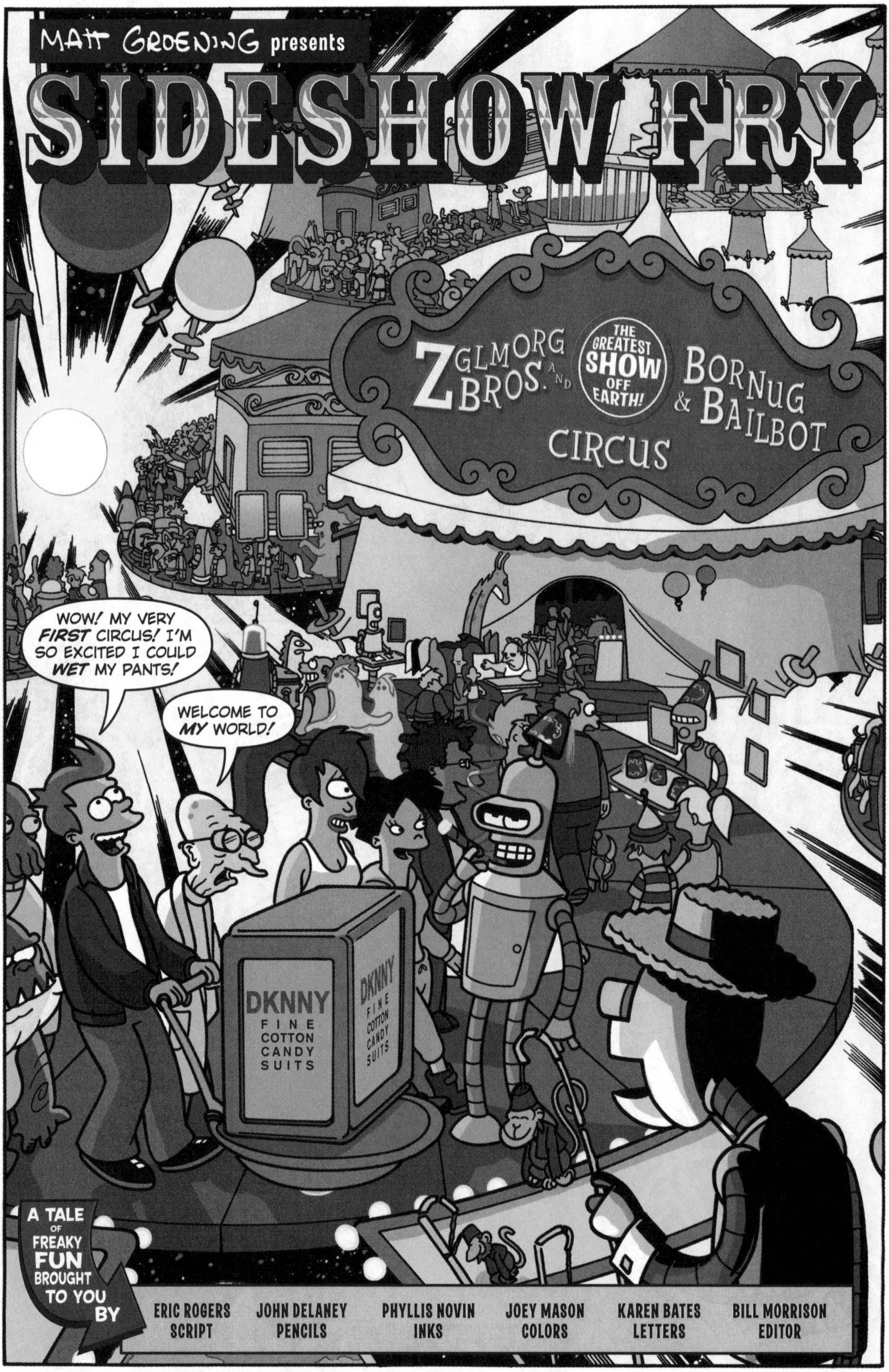
MATT GROENING presents
SIDESHOW FRY
ZGLMORG BROS. AND BORNUG & BAILBOT CIRCUS
THE GREATEST SHOW OFF EARTH!
WOW! MY VERY FIRST CIRCUS! I'M SO EXCITED I COULD WET MY PANTS!
WELCOME TO MY WORLD!
DKNNY FINE COTTON CANDY SUITS
A TALE OF FREAKY FUN BROUGHT TO YOU BY
ERIC ROGERS SCRIPT
JOHN DELANEY PENCILS
PHYLLIS NOVIN INKS
JOEY MASON COLORS
KAREN BATES LETTERS
BILL MORRISON EDITOR

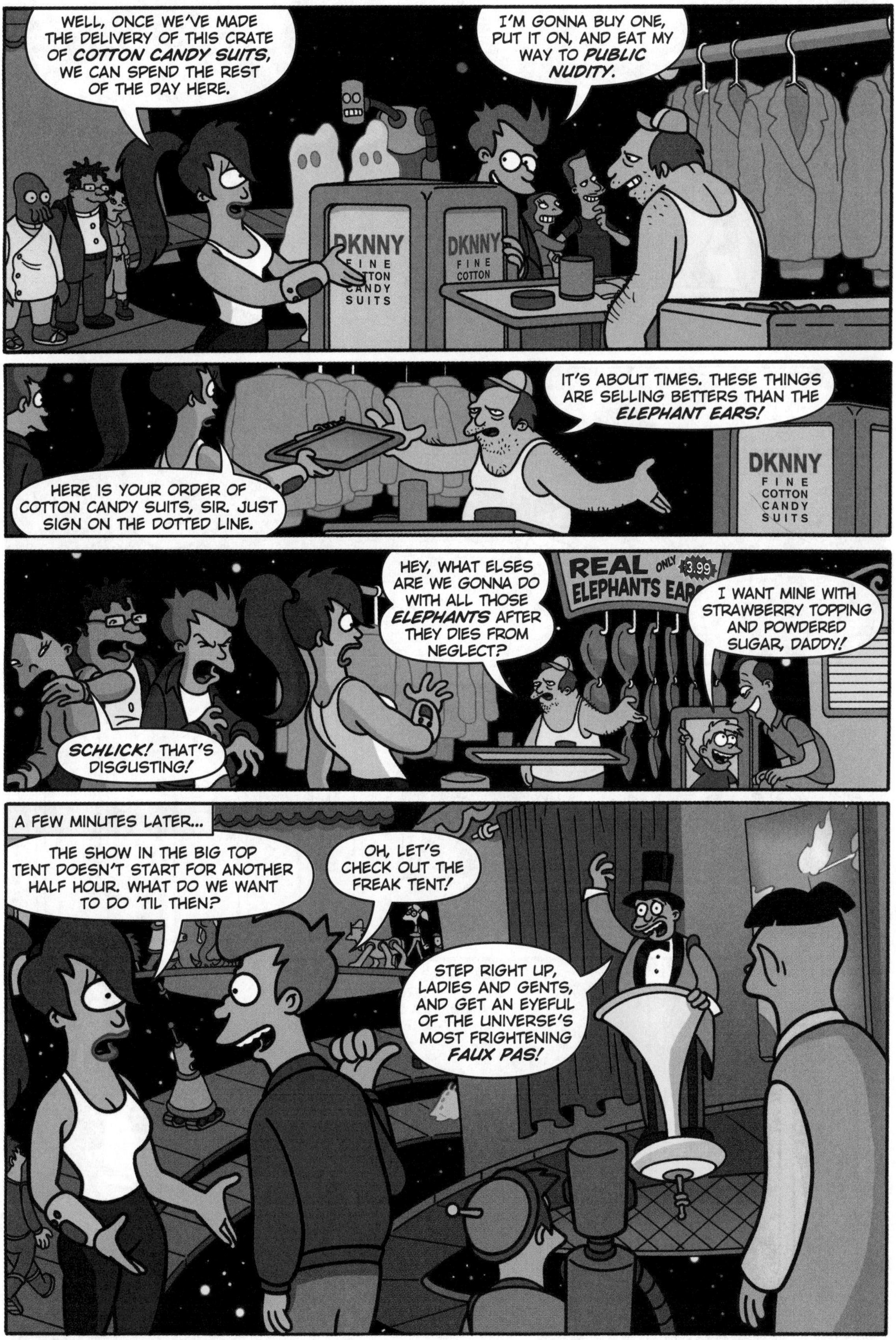
WELL, ONCE WE'VE MADE THE DELIVERY OF THIS CRATE OF COTTON CANDY SUITS, WE CAN SPEND THE REST OF THE DAY HERE.
I'M GONNA BUY ONE, PUT IT ON, AND EAT MY WAY TO PUBLIC NUDITY.
DKNNY FINE COTTON CANDY SUITS
IT'S ABOUT TIMES. THESE THINGS ARE SELLING BETTERS THAN THE ELEPHANT EARS!
HERE IS YOUR ORDER OF COTTON CANDY SUITS, SIR. JUST SIGN ON THE DOTTED LINE.
REAL ONLY 3.99 ELEPHANTS EAR
HEY, WHAT ELSES ARE WE GONNA DO WITH ALL THOSE ELEPHANTS AFTER THEY DIES FROM NEGLECT?
SCHLICK! THAT'S DISGUSTING!
I WANT MINE WITH STRAWBERRY TOPPING AND POWDERED SUGAR, DADDY!
A FEW MINUTES LATER...
THE SHOW IN THE BIG TOP TENT DOESN'T START FOR ANOTHER HALF HOUR. WHAT DO WE WANT TO DO 'TIL THEN?
OH, LET'S CHECK OUT THE FREAK TENT!
STEP RIGHT UP, LADIES AND GENTS, AND GET AN EYEFUL OF THE UNIVERSE'S MOST FRIGHTENING FAUX PAS!

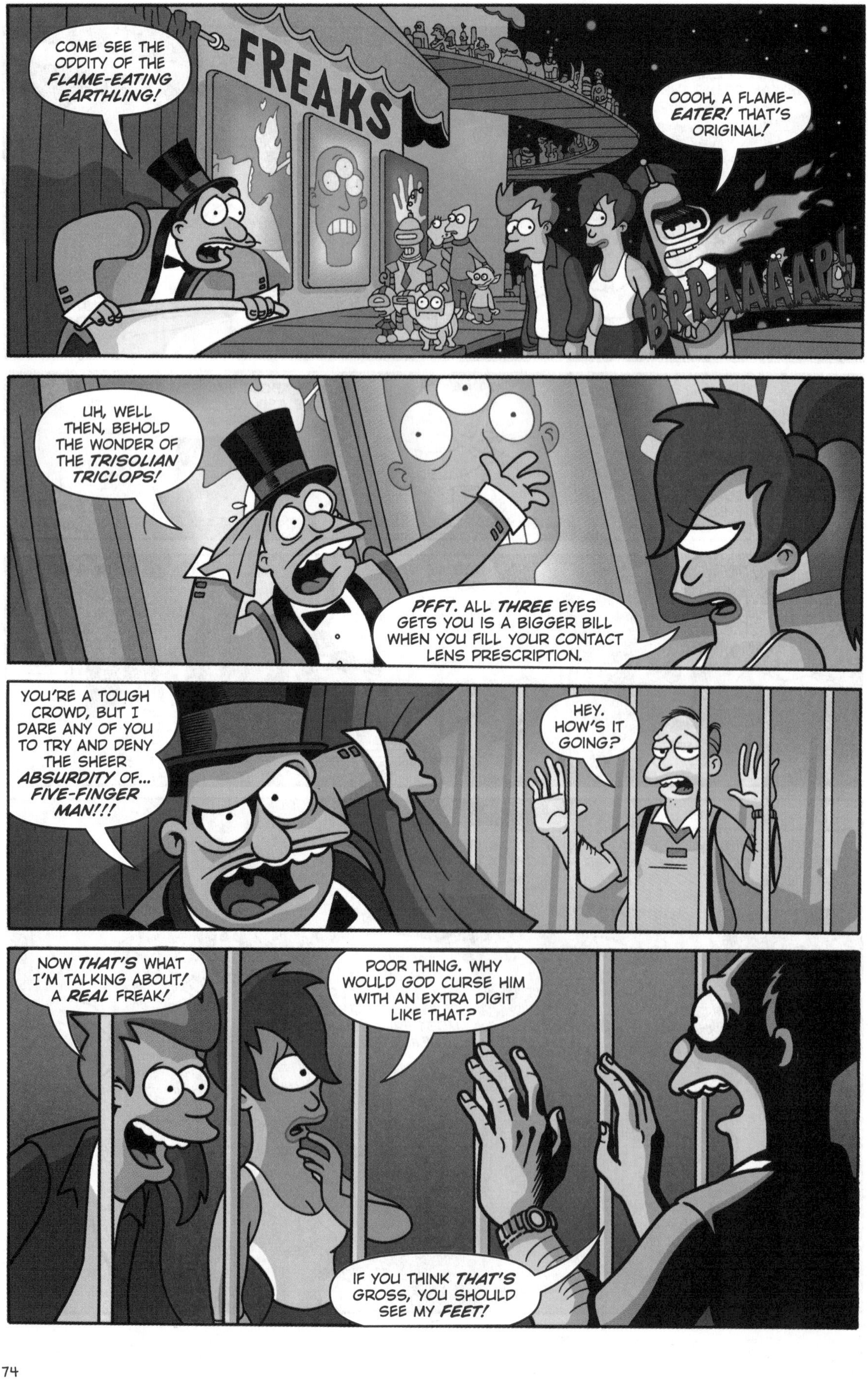
COME SEE THE ODDITY OF THE *FLAME-EATING EARTHLING!*
FREAKS
OOOH, A FLAME-*EATER!* THAT'S ORIGINAL!
BRRAAAAP!
UH, WELL THEN, BEHOLD THE WONDER OF THE *TRISOLIAN TRICLOPS!*
*PFFT.* ALL *THREE* EYES GETS YOU IS A BIGGER BILL WHEN YOU FILL YOUR CONTACT LENS PRESCRIPTION.
YOU'RE A TOUGH CROWD, BUT I DARE ANY OF YOU TO TRY AND DENY THE SHEER *ABSURDITY* OF... *FIVE-FINGER MAN!!!*
HEY. HOW'S IT GOING?
NOW *THAT'S* WHAT I'M TALKING ABOUT! A *REAL* FREAK!
POOR THING. WHY WOULD GOD CURSE HIM WITH AN EXTRA DIGIT LIKE THAT?
IF YOU THINK *THAT'S* GROSS, YOU SHOULD SEE MY *FEET!*

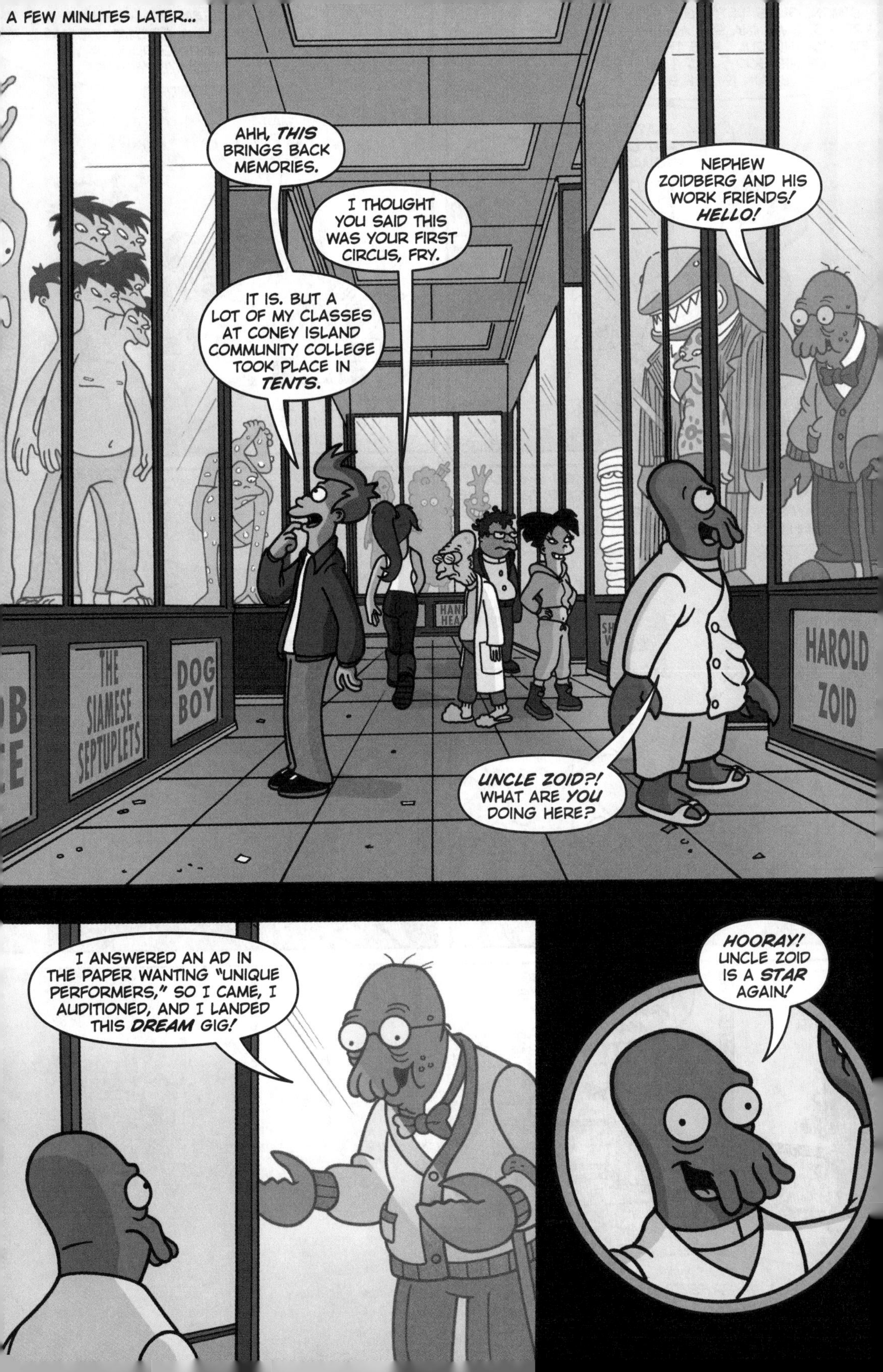
A FEW MINUTES LATER...
AHH, THIS BRINGS BACK MEMORIES.
I THOUGHT YOU SAID THIS WAS YOUR FIRST CIRCUS, FRY.
IT IS. BUT A LOT OF MY CLASSES AT CONEY ISLAND COMMUNITY COLLEGE TOOK PLACE IN TENTS.
NEPHEW ZOIDBERG AND HIS WORK FRIENDS! HELLO!
UNCLE ZOID?! WHAT ARE YOU DOING HERE?
THE SIAMESE SEPTUPLETS
DOG BOY
HAROLD ZOID
I ANSWERED AN AD IN THE PAPER WANTING "UNIQUE PERFORMERS," SO I CAME, I AUDITIONED, AND I LANDED THIS DREAM GIG!
HOORAY! UNCLE ZOID IS A STAR AGAIN!

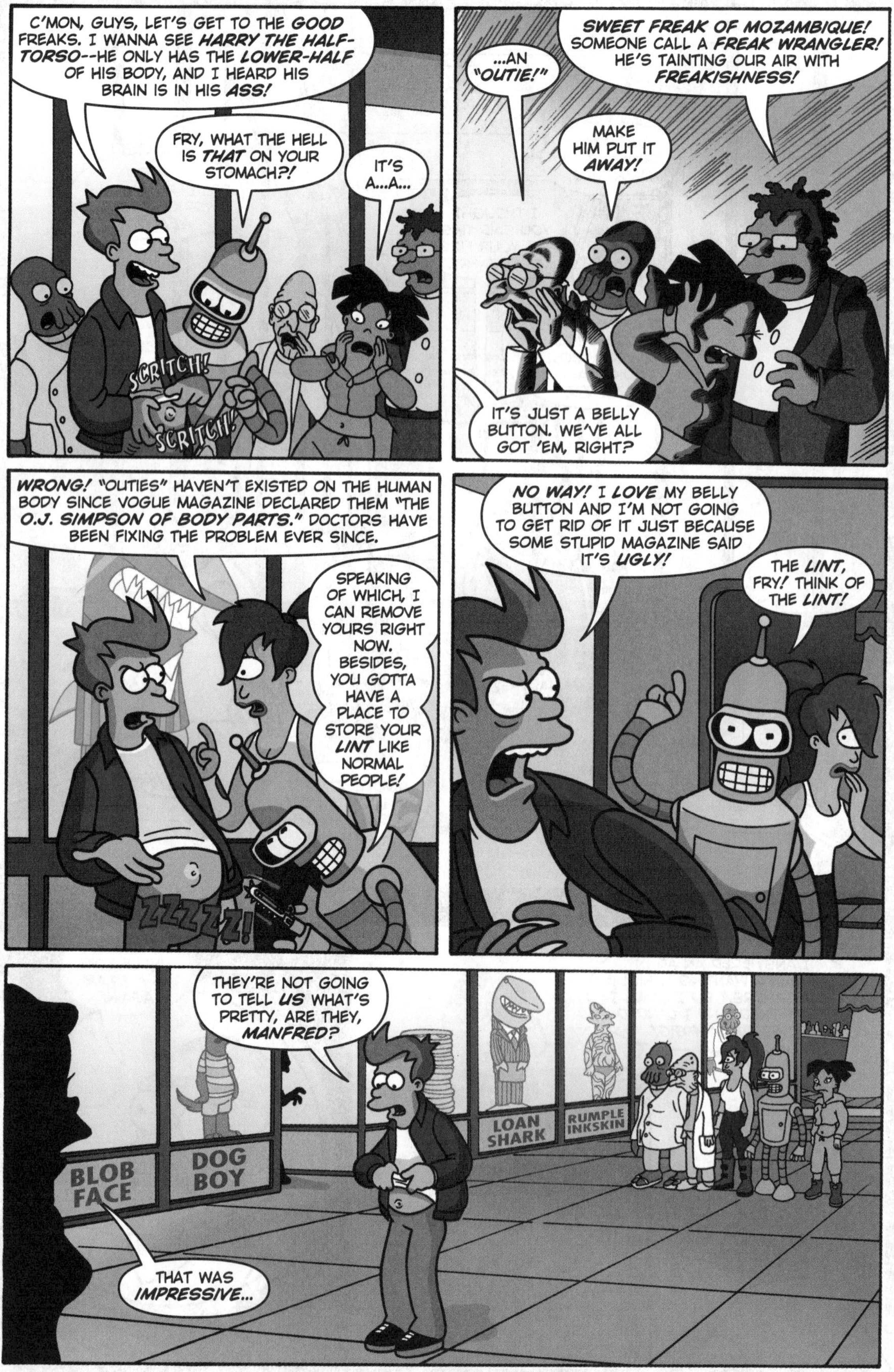
C'MON, GUYS, LET'S GET TO THE GOOD FREAKS. I WANNA SEE HARRY THE HALF-TORSO--HE ONLY HAS THE LOWER-HALF OF HIS BODY, AND I HEARD HIS BRAIN IS IN HIS ASS!
FRY, WHAT THE HELL IS THAT ON YOUR STOMACH?!
IT'S A...A...
SCRITCH!
SCRITCH!
...AN "OUTIE!"
SWEET FREAK OF MOZAMBIQUE! SOMEONE CALL A FREAK WRANGLER! HE'S TAINTING OUR AIR WITH FREAKISHNESS!
MAKE HIM PUT IT AWAY!
IT'S JUST A BELLY BUTTON. WE'VE ALL GOT 'EM, RIGHT?
WRONG! "OUTIES" HAVEN'T EXISTED ON THE HUMAN BODY SINCE VOGUE MAGAZINE DECLARED THEM "THE O.J. SIMPSON OF BODY PARTS." DOCTORS HAVE BEEN FIXING THE PROBLEM EVER SINCE.
SPEAKING OF WHICH, I CAN REMOVE YOURS RIGHT NOW. BESIDES, YOU GOTTA HAVE A PLACE TO STORE YOUR LINT LIKE NORMAL PEOPLE!
ZZZZZZ!
NO WAY! I LOVE MY BELLY BUTTON AND I'M NOT GOING TO GET RID OF IT JUST BECAUSE SOME STUPID MAGAZINE SAID IT'S UGLY!
THE LINT, FRY! THINK OF THE LINT!
THEY'RE NOT GOING TO TELL US WHAT'S PRETTY, ARE THEY, MANFRED?
BLOB FACE
DOG BOY
LOAN SHARK
RUMPLE INKSKIN
THAT WAS IMPRESSIVE...

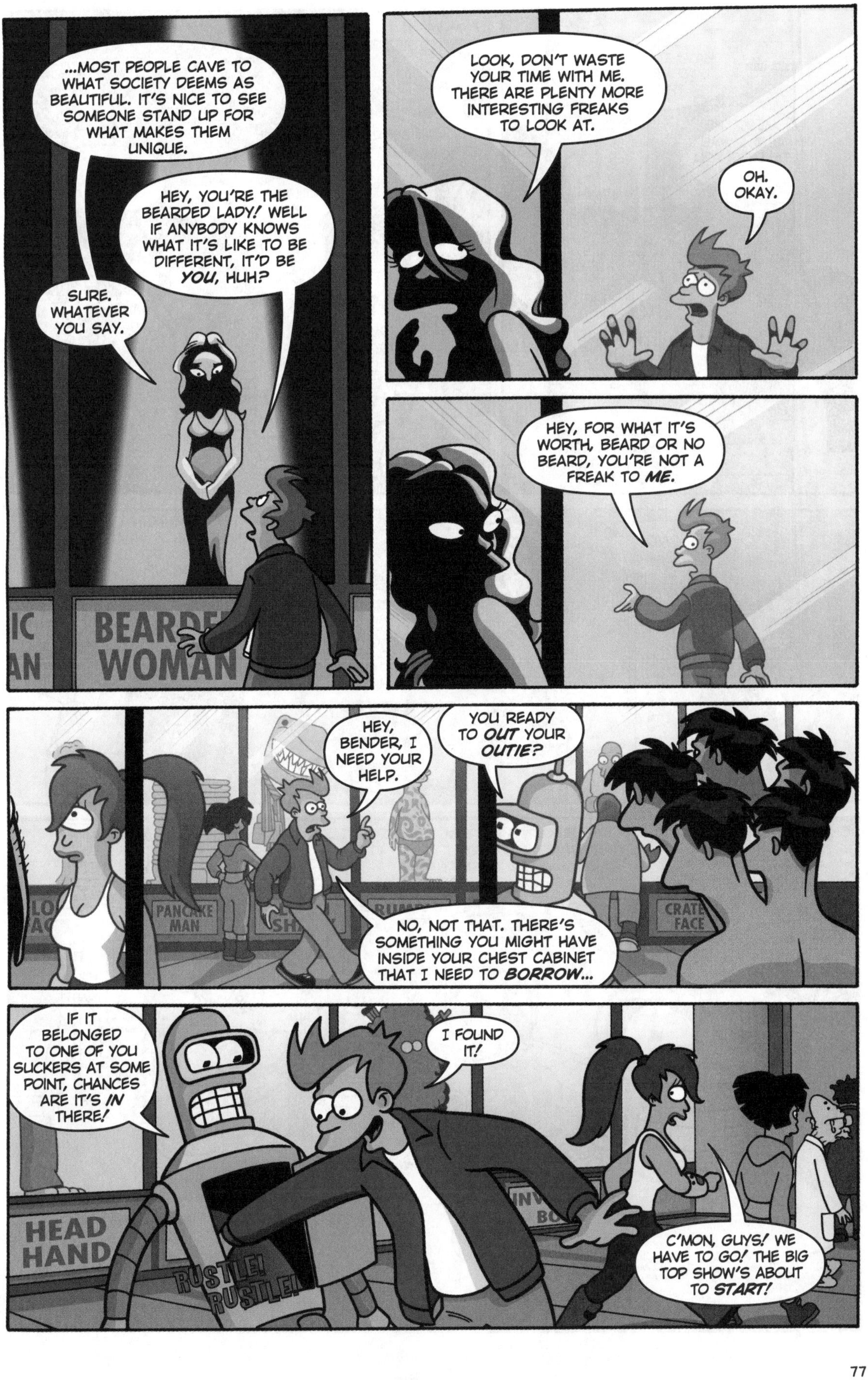
...MOST PEOPLE CAVE TO WHAT SOCIETY DEEMS AS BEAUTIFUL. IT'S NICE TO SEE SOMEONE STAND UP FOR WHAT MAKES THEM UNIQUE.
HEY, YOU'RE THE BEARDED LADY! WELL IF ANYBODY KNOWS WHAT IT'S LIKE TO BE DIFFERENT, IT'D BE *YOU*, HUH?
SURE. WHATEVER YOU SAY.
LOOK, DON'T WASTE YOUR TIME WITH ME. THERE ARE PLENTY MORE INTERESTING FREAKS TO LOOK AT.
OH. OKAY.
HEY, FOR WHAT IT'S WORTH, BEARD OR NO BEARD, YOU'RE NOT A FREAK TO *ME*.
HEY, BENDER, I NEED YOUR HELP.
YOU READY TO *OUT* YOUR *OUTIE?*
NO, NOT THAT. THERE'S SOMETHING YOU MIGHT HAVE INSIDE YOUR CHEST CABINET THAT I NEED TO *BORROW*...
IF IT BELONGED TO ONE OF YOU SUCKERS AT SOME POINT, CHANCES ARE IT'S *IN* THERE!
I FOUND IT!
C'MON, GUYS! WE HAVE TO GO! THE BIG TOP SHOW'S ABOUT TO *START!*
WOMAN
PANCAKE MAN
CRATE FACE
HEAD HAND
RUSTLE! RUSTLE!

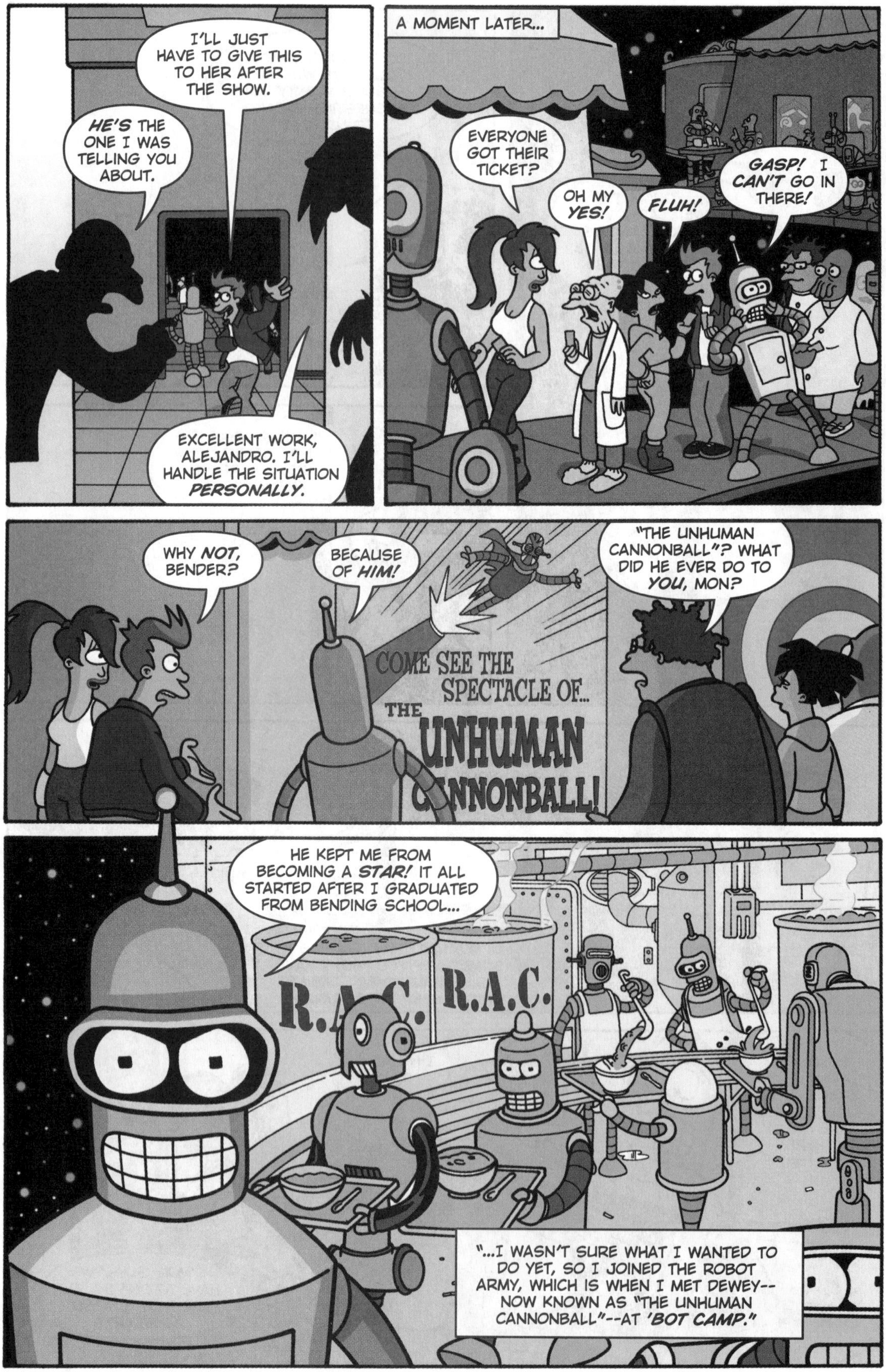
I'LL JUST HAVE TO GIVE THIS TO HER AFTER THE SHOW.
HE'S THE ONE I WAS TELLING YOU ABOUT.
EXCELLENT WORK, ALEJANDRO. I'LL HANDLE THE SITUATION PERSONALLY.
A MOMENT LATER...
EVERYONE GOT THEIR TICKET?
OH MY YES!
FLUH!
GASP! I CAN'T GO IN THERE!
WHY NOT, BENDER?
BECAUSE OF HIM!
"THE UNHUMAN CANNONBALL"? WHAT DID HE EVER DO TO YOU, MON?
COME SEE THE SPECTACLE OF... THE UNHUMAN CANNONBALL!
HE KEPT ME FROM BECOMING A STAR! IT ALL STARTED AFTER I GRADUATED FROM BENDING SCHOOL...
R.A.C.
R.A.C.
"...I WASN'T SURE WHAT I WANTED TO DO YET, SO I JOINED THE ROBOT ARMY, WHICH IS WHEN I MET DEWEY--NOW KNOWN AS "THE UNHUMAN CANNONBALL"--AT 'BOT CAMP."

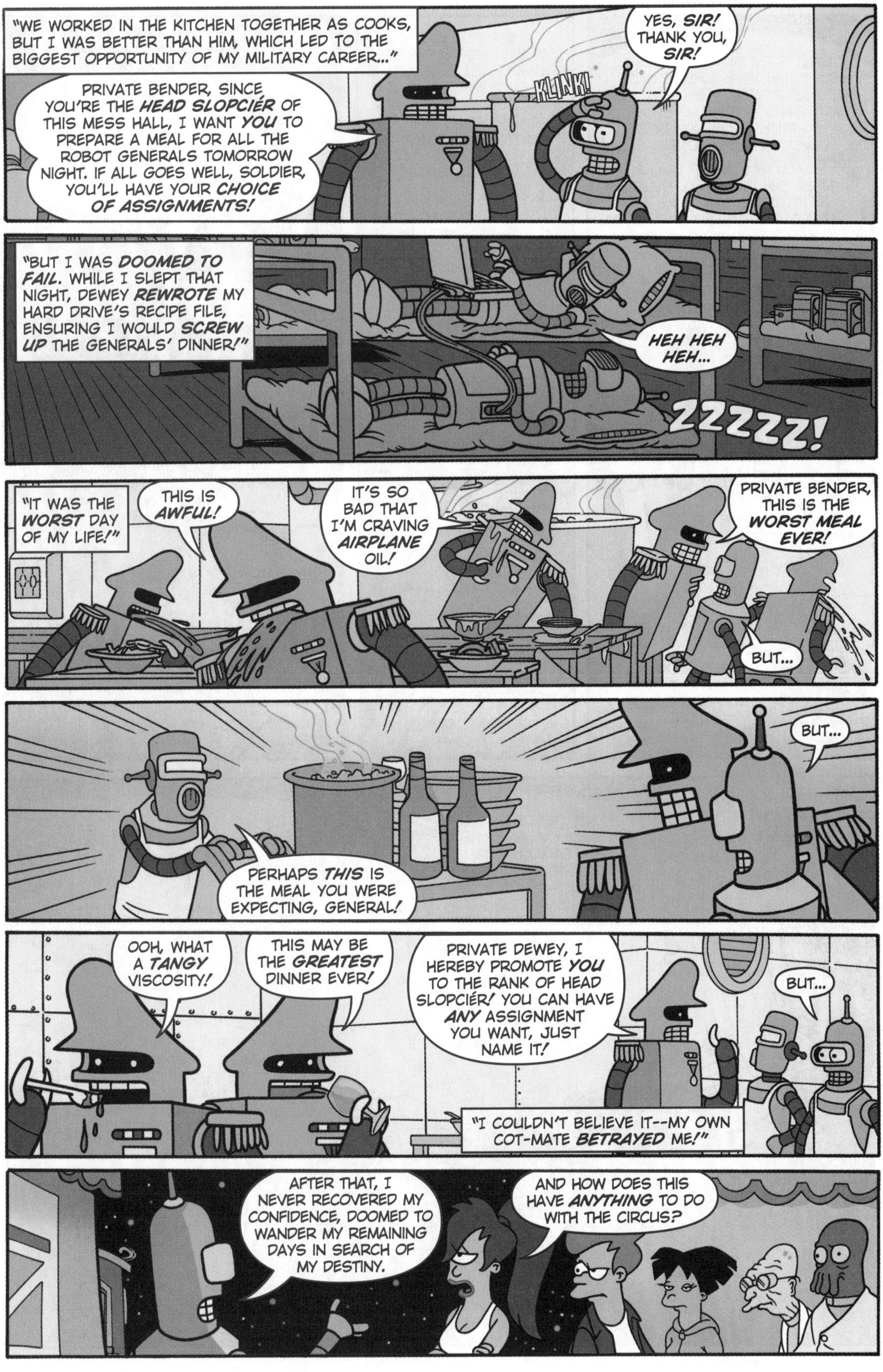
"WE WORKED IN THE KITCHEN TOGETHER AS COOKS, BUT I WAS BETTER THAN HIM, WHICH LED TO THE BIGGEST OPPORTUNITY OF MY MILITARY CAREER..."
PRIVATE BENDER, SINCE YOU'RE THE HEAD SLOPCIÉR OF THIS MESS HALL, I WANT YOU TO PREPARE A MEAL FOR ALL THE ROBOT GENERALS TOMORROW NIGHT. IF ALL GOES WELL, SOLDIER, YOU'LL HAVE YOUR CHOICE OF ASSIGNMENTS!
KLINK!
YES, SIR! THANK YOU, SIR!
"BUT I WAS DOOMED TO FAIL. WHILE I SLEPT THAT NIGHT, DEWEY REWROTE MY HARD DRIVE'S RECIPE FILE, ENSURING I WOULD SCREW UP THE GENERALS' DINNER!"
HEH HEH HEH...
ZZZZZ!
"IT WAS THE WORST DAY OF MY LIFE!"
THIS IS AWFUL!
IT'S SO BAD THAT I'M CRAVING AIRPLANE OIL!
PRIVATE BENDER, THIS IS THE WORST MEAL EVER!
BUT...
BUT...
PERHAPS THIS IS THE MEAL YOU WERE EXPECTING, GENERAL!
OOH, WHAT A TANGY VISCOSITY!
THIS MAY BE THE GREATEST DINNER EVER!
PRIVATE DEWEY, I HEREBY PROMOTE YOU TO THE RANK OF HEAD SLOPCIÉR! YOU CAN HAVE ANY ASSIGNMENT YOU WANT, JUST NAME IT!
BUT...
"I COULDN'T BELIEVE IT--MY OWN COT-MATE BETRAYED ME!"
AFTER THAT, I NEVER RECOVERED MY CONFIDENCE, DOOMED TO WANDER MY REMAINING DAYS IN SEARCH OF MY DESTINY.
AND HOW DOES THIS HAVE ANYTHING TO DO WITH THE CIRCUS?

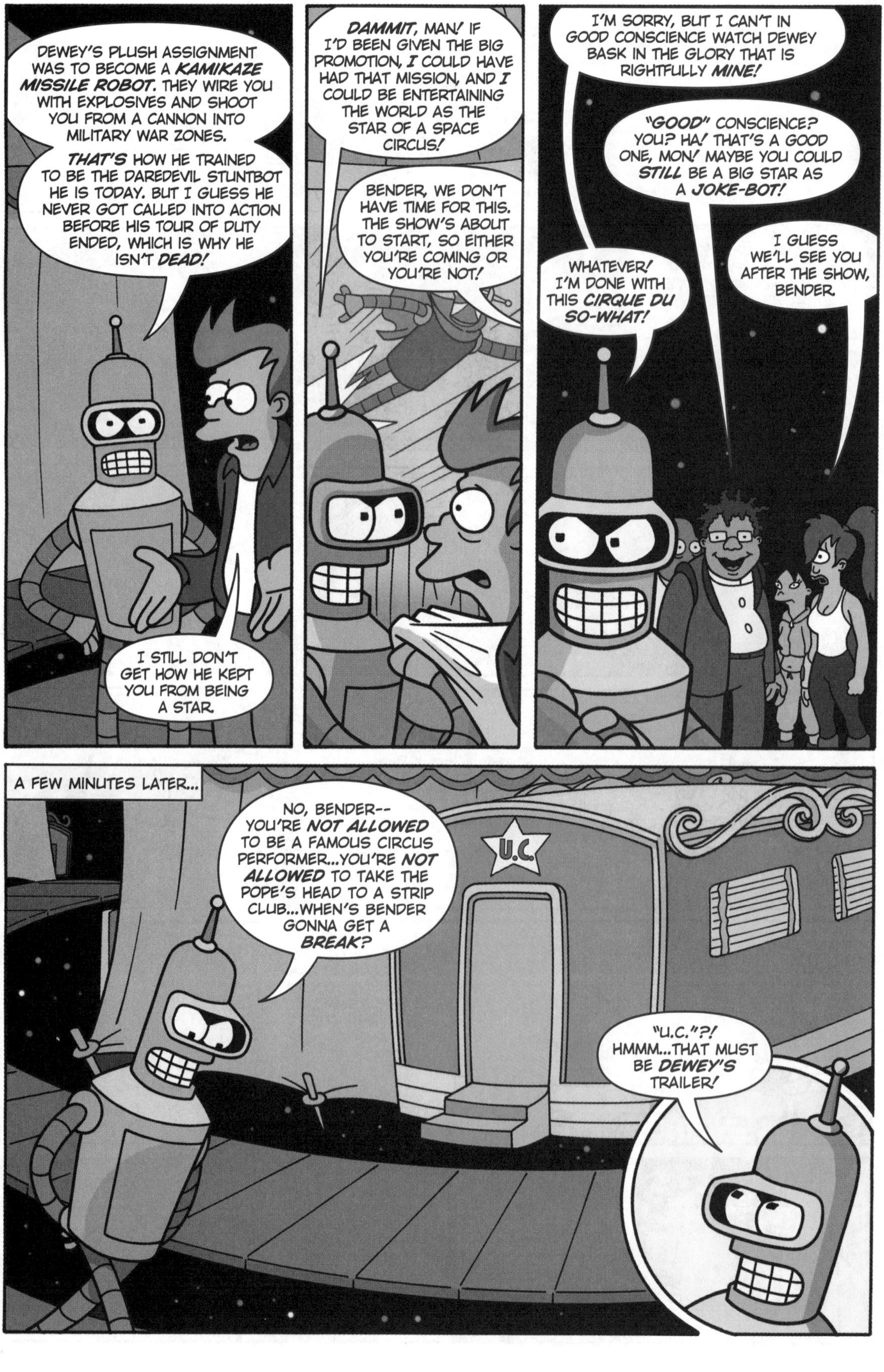
DEWEY'S PLUSH ASSIGNMENT WAS TO BECOME A KAMIKAZE MISSILE ROBOT. THEY WIRE YOU WITH EXPLOSIVES AND SHOOT YOU FROM A CANNON INTO MILITARY WAR ZONES.
THAT'S HOW HE TRAINED TO BE THE DAREDEVIL STUNTBOT HE IS TODAY. BUT I GUESS HE NEVER GOT CALLED INTO ACTION BEFORE HIS TOUR OF DUTY ENDED, WHICH IS WHY HE ISN'T DEAD!
I STILL DON'T GET HOW HE KEPT YOU FROM BEING A STAR.
DAMMIT, MAN! IF I'D BEEN GIVEN THE BIG PROMOTION, I COULD HAVE HAD THAT MISSION, AND I COULD BE ENTERTAINING THE WORLD AS THE STAR OF A SPACE CIRCUS!
BENDER, WE DON'T HAVE TIME FOR THIS. THE SHOW'S ABOUT TO START, SO EITHER YOU'RE COMING OR YOU'RE NOT!
I'M SORRY, BUT I CAN'T IN GOOD CONSCIENCE WATCH DEWEY BASK IN THE GLORY THAT IS RIGHTFULLY MINE!
"GOOD" CONSCIENCE? YOU? HA! THAT'S A GOOD ONE, MON! MAYBE YOU COULD STILL BE A BIG STAR AS A JOKE-BOT!
WHATEVER! I'M DONE WITH THIS CIRQUE DU SO-WHAT!
I GUESS WE'LL SEE YOU AFTER THE SHOW, BENDER.
A FEW MINUTES LATER...
NO, BENDER-- YOU'RE NOT ALLOWED TO BE A FAMOUS CIRCUS PERFORMER...YOU'RE NOT ALLOWED TO TAKE THE POPE'S HEAD TO A STRIP CLUB...WHEN'S BENDER GONNA GET A BREAK?
U.C.
"U.C."?! HMMM...THAT MUST BE DEWEY'S TRAILER!

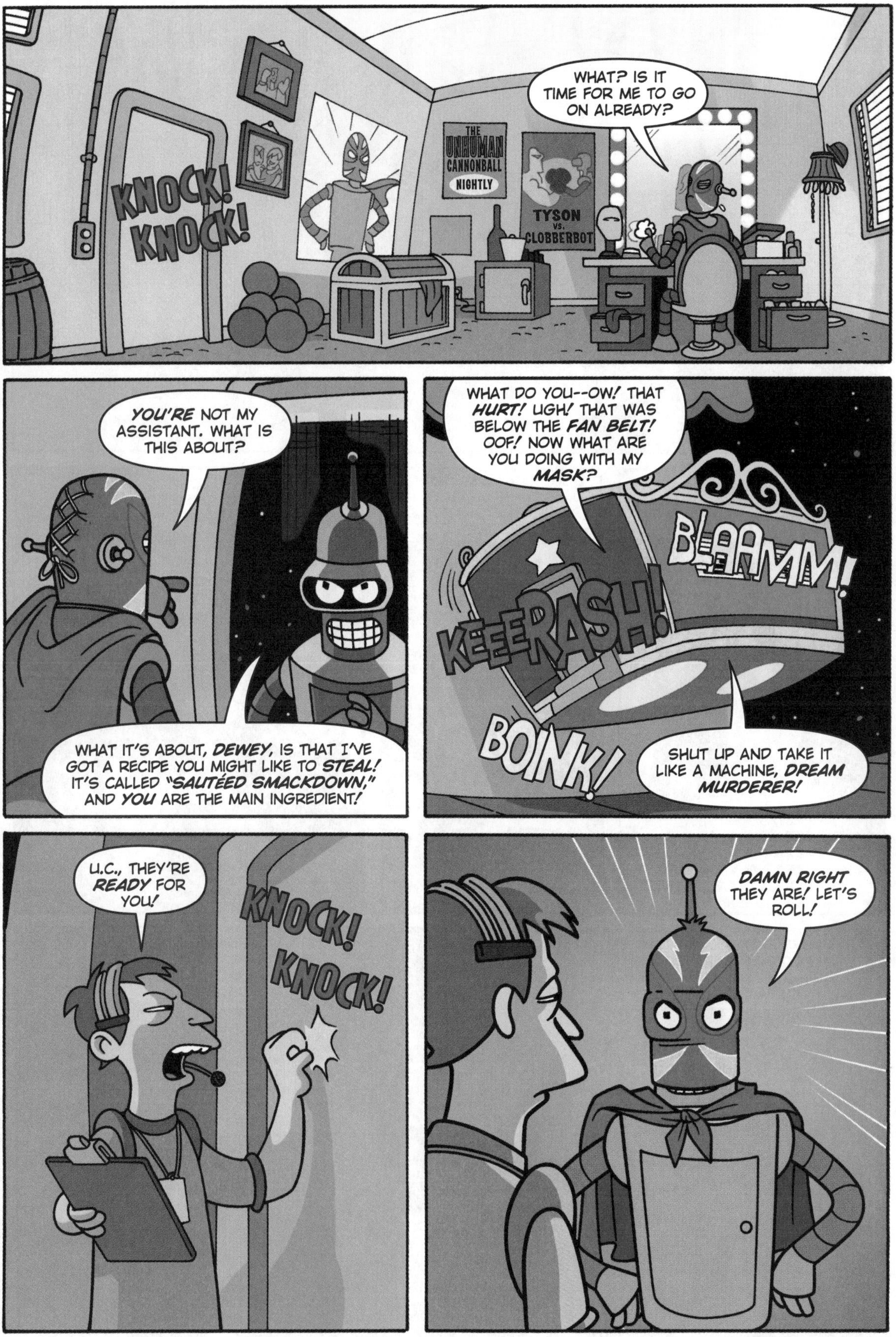
WHAT? IS IT TIME FOR ME TO GO ON ALREADY?
THE UNHUMAN CANNONBALL NIGHTLY
TYSON VS. CLOBBERBOT
KNOCK! KNOCK!
YOU'RE NOT MY ASSISTANT. WHAT IS THIS ABOUT?
WHAT IT'S ABOUT, DEWEY, IS THAT I'VE GOT A RECIPE YOU MIGHT LIKE TO STEAL! IT'S CALLED "SAUTÉED SMACKDOWN," AND YOU ARE THE MAIN INGREDIENT!
WHAT DO YOU--OW! THAT HURT! UGH! THAT WAS BELOW THE FAN BELT! OOF! NOW WHAT ARE YOU DOING WITH MY MASK?
BLAAMM!
KEEERASH!
BOINK!
SHUT UP AND TAKE IT LIKE A MACHINE, DREAM MURDERER!
U.C., THEY'RE READY FOR YOU!
KNOCK! KNOCK!
DAMN RIGHT THEY ARE! LET'S ROLL!

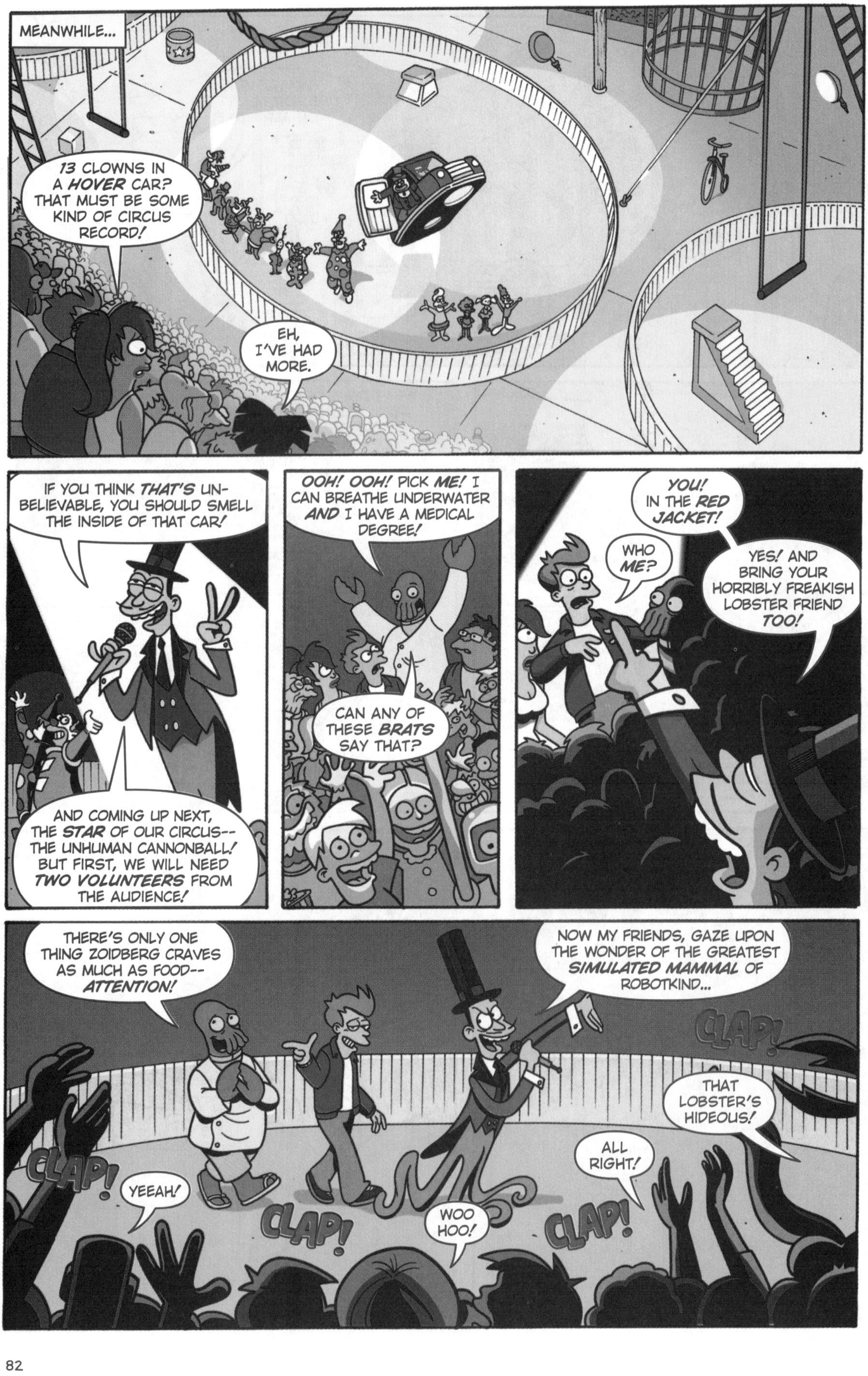
MEANWHILE...
13 CLOWNS IN A HOVER CAR? THAT MUST BE SOME KIND OF CIRCUS RECORD!
EH, I'VE HAD MORE.
IF YOU THINK THAT'S UNBELIEVABLE, YOU SHOULD SMELL THE INSIDE OF THAT CAR!
AND COMING UP NEXT, THE STAR OF OUR CIRCUS-- THE UNHUMAN CANNONBALL! BUT FIRST, WE WILL NEED TWO VOLUNTEERS FROM THE AUDIENCE!
OOH! OOH! PICK ME! I CAN BREATHE UNDERWATER AND I HAVE A MEDICAL DEGREE!
CAN ANY OF THESE BRATS SAY THAT?
YOU! IN THE RED JACKET!
WHO ME?
YES! AND BRING YOUR HORRIBLY FREAKISH LOBSTER FRIEND TOO!
THERE'S ONLY ONE THING ZOIDBERG CRAVES AS MUCH AS FOOD-- ATTENTION!
NOW MY FRIENDS, GAZE UPON THE WONDER OF THE GREATEST SIMULATED MAMMAL OF ROBOTKIND...
CLAP!
THAT LOBSTER'S HIDEOUS!
ALL RIGHT!
CLAP!
YEEAH!
CLAP!
WOO HOO!
CLAP!

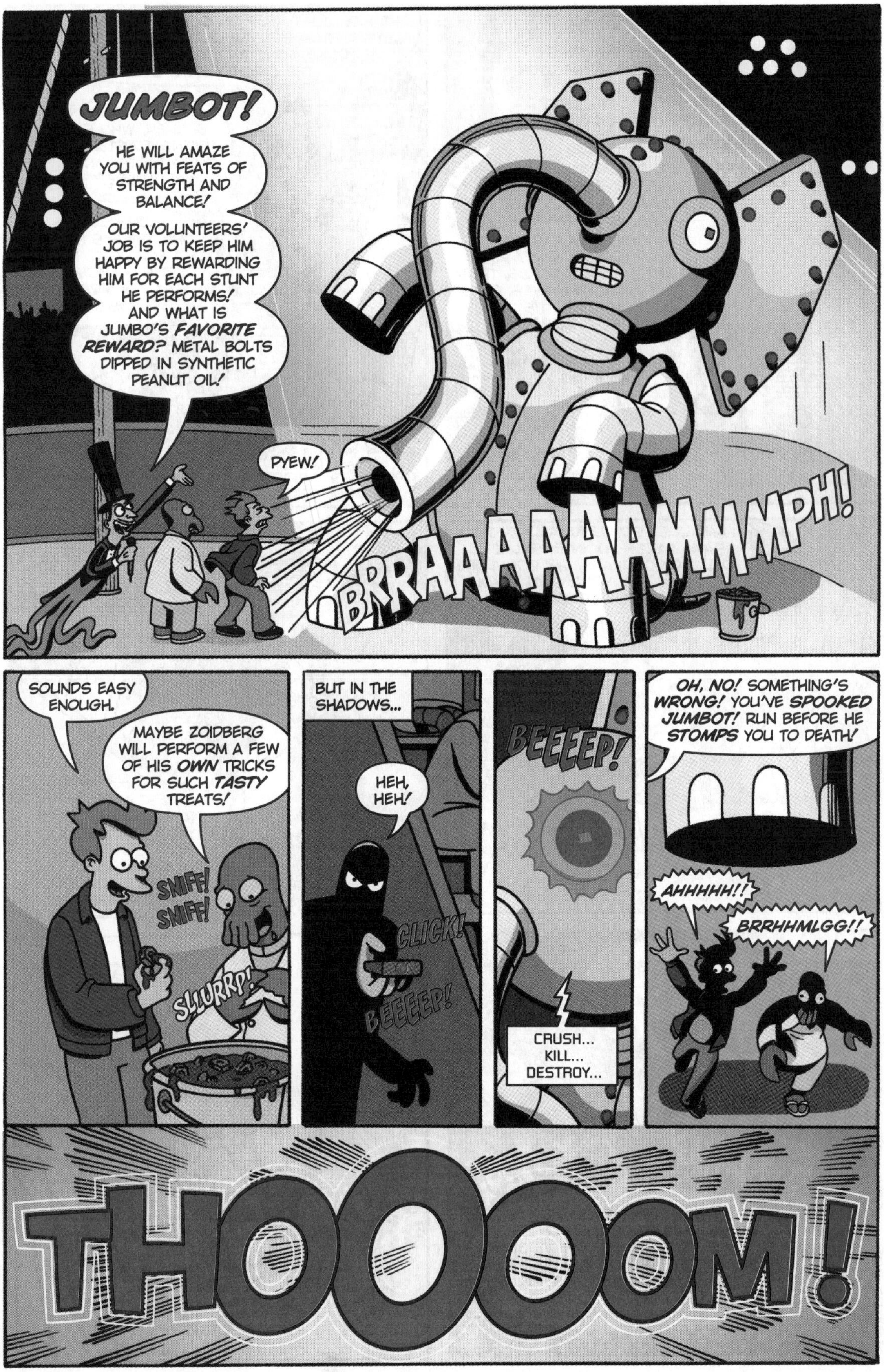
JUMBOT!
HE WILL AMAZE YOU WITH FEATS OF STRENGTH AND BALANCE!
OUR VOLUNTEERS' JOB IS TO KEEP HIM HAPPY BY REWARDING HIM FOR EACH STUNT HE PERFORMS! AND WHAT IS JUMBO'S FAVORITE REWARD? METAL BOLTS DIPPED IN SYNTHETIC PEANUT OIL!
PYEW!
BRRAAAAAAMMMMPH!
SOUNDS EASY ENOUGH.
MAYBE ZOIDBERG WILL PERFORM A FEW OF HIS OWN TRICKS FOR SUCH TASTY TREATS!
SNIFF! SNIFF!
SLURRP!
BUT IN THE SHADOWS...
HEH, HEH!
CLICK!
BEEEEEP!
BEEEEP!
CRUSH... KILL... DESTROY...
OH, NO! SOMETHING'S WRONG! YOU'VE SPOOKED JUMBOT! RUN BEFORE HE STOMPS YOU TO DEATH!
AHHHHH!!
BRRHHMLGG!!
THOOOOM!

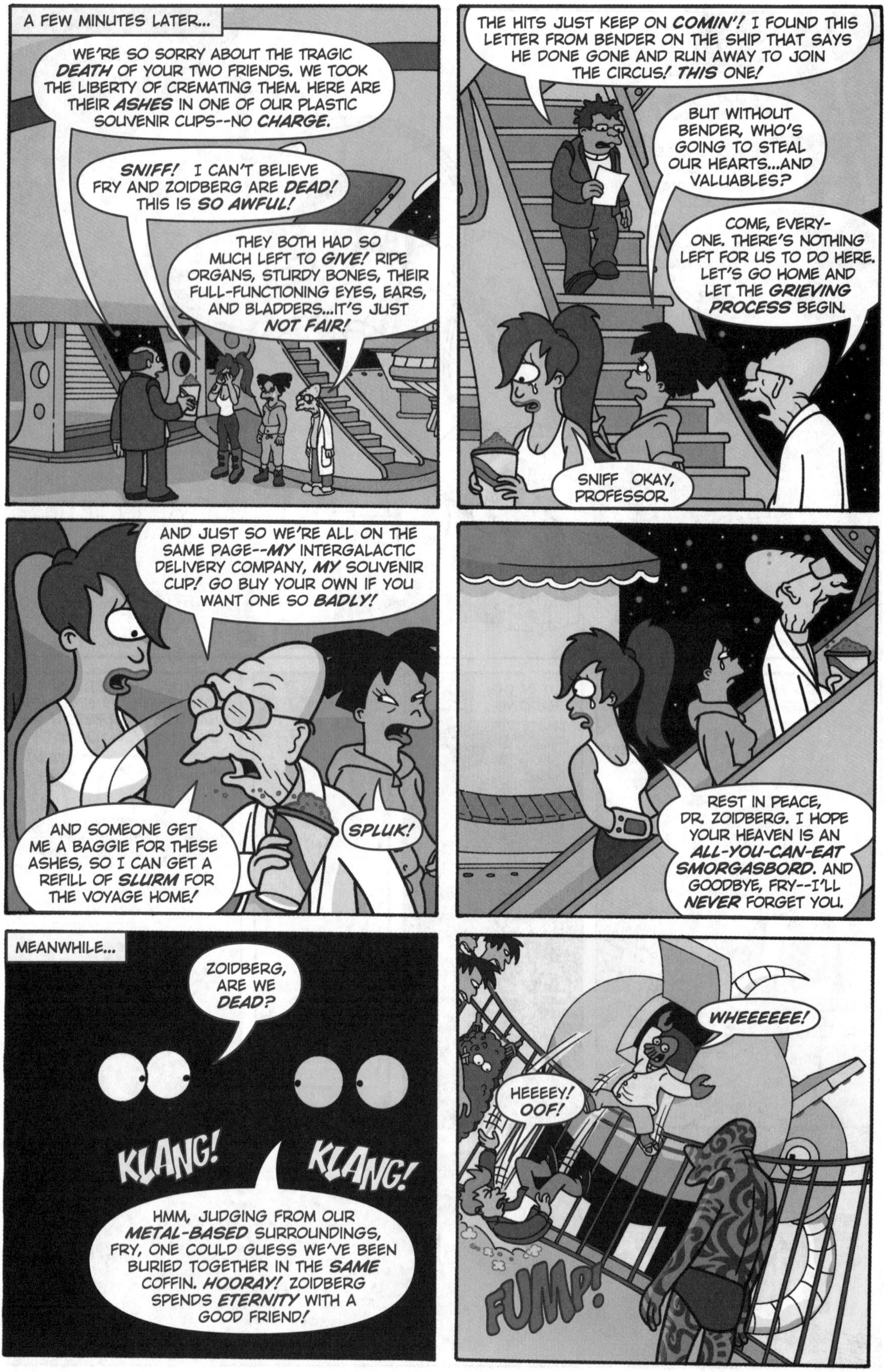
A FEW MINUTES LATER...
WE'RE SO SORRY ABOUT THE TRAGIC DEATH OF YOUR TWO FRIENDS. WE TOOK THE LIBERTY OF CREMATING THEM. HERE ARE THEIR ASHES IN ONE OF OUR PLASTIC SOUVENIR CUPS--NO CHARGE.
SNIFF! I CAN'T BELIEVE FRY AND ZOIDBERG ARE DEAD! THIS IS SO AWFUL!
THEY BOTH HAD SO MUCH LEFT TO GIVE! RIPE ORGANS, STURDY BONES, THEIR FULL-FUNCTIONING EYES, EARS, AND BLADDERS...IT'S JUST NOT FAIR!
THE HITS JUST KEEP ON COMIN'! I FOUND THIS LETTER FROM BENDER ON THE SHIP THAT SAYS HE DONE GONE AND RUN AWAY TO JOIN THE CIRCUS! THIS ONE!
BUT WITHOUT BENDER, WHO'S GOING TO STEAL OUR HEARTS...AND VALUABLES?
COME, EVERY-ONE. THERE'S NOTHING LEFT FOR US TO DO HERE. LET'S GO HOME AND LET THE GRIEVING PROCESS BEGIN.
SNIFF OKAY, PROFESSOR.
AND JUST SO WE'RE ALL ON THE SAME PAGE--MY INTERGALACTIC DELIVERY COMPANY, MY SOUVENIR CUP! GO BUY YOUR OWN IF YOU WANT ONE SO BADLY!
AND SOMEONE GET ME A BAGGIE FOR THESE ASHES, SO I CAN GET A REFILL OF SLURM FOR THE VOYAGE HOME!
SPLUK!
REST IN PEACE, DR. ZOIDBERG. I HOPE YOUR HEAVEN IS AN ALL-YOU-CAN-EAT SMORGASBORD. AND GOODBYE, FRY--I'LL NEVER FORGET YOU.
MEANWHILE...
ZOIDBERG, ARE WE DEAD?
KLANG!
KLANG!
HMM, JUDGING FROM OUR METAL-BASED SURROUNDINGS, FRY, ONE COULD GUESS WE'VE BEEN BURIED TOGETHER IN THE SAME COFFIN. HOORAY! ZOIDBERG SPENDS ETERNITY WITH A GOOD FRIEND!
WHEEEEEE!
HEEEEY! OOF!
FUMP!

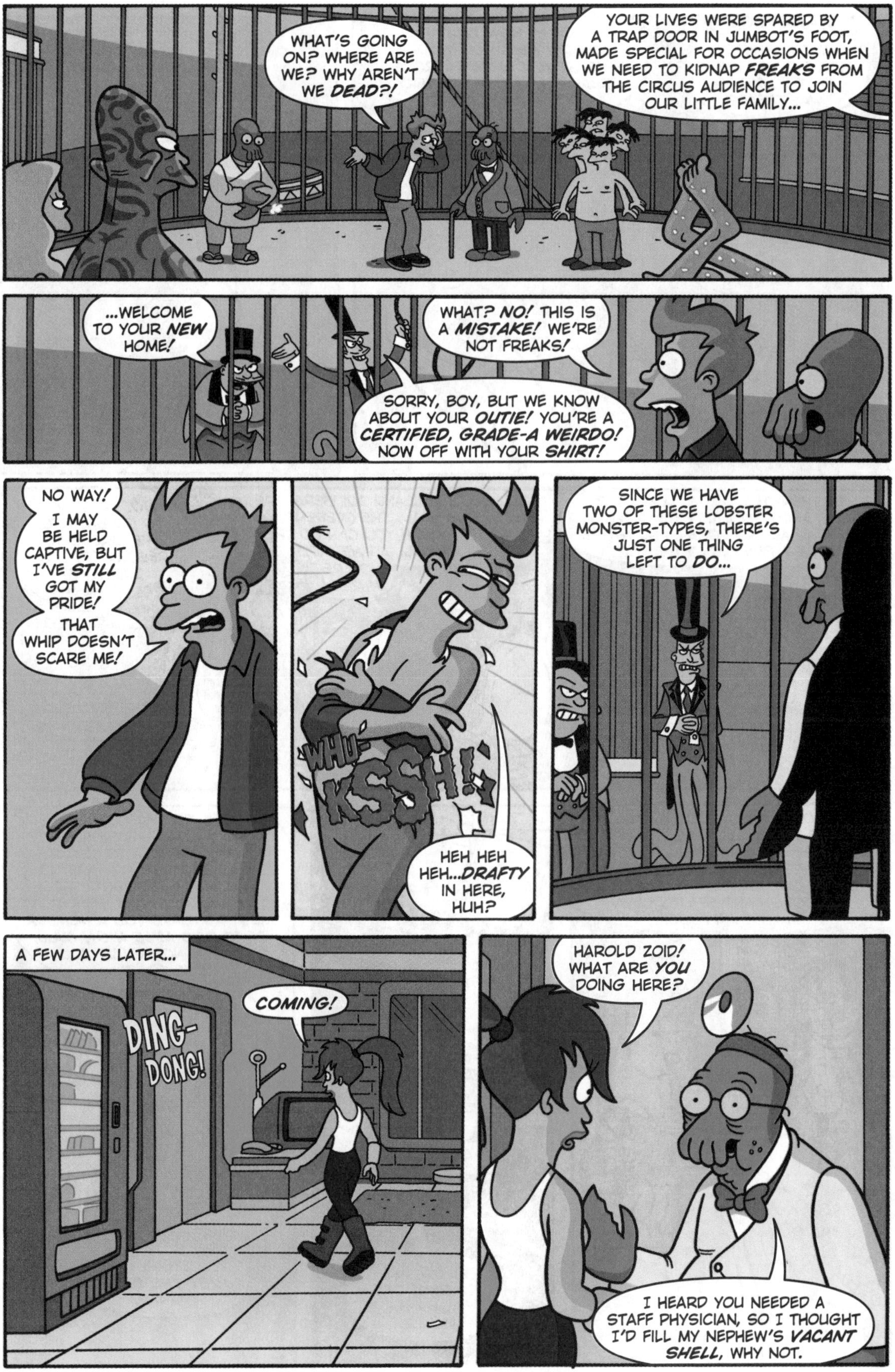
WHAT'S GOING ON? WHERE ARE WE? WHY AREN'T WE DEAD?!
YOUR LIVES WERE SPARED BY A TRAP DOOR IN JUMBOT'S FOOT, MADE SPECIAL FOR OCCASIONS WHEN WE NEED TO KIDNAP FREAKS FROM THE CIRCUS AUDIENCE TO JOIN OUR LITTLE FAMILY...
...WELCOME TO YOUR NEW HOME!
WHAT? NO! THIS IS A MISTAKE! WE'RE NOT FREAKS!
SORRY, BOY, BUT WE KNOW ABOUT YOUR OUTIE! YOU'RE A CERTIFIED, GRADE-A WEIRDO! NOW OFF WITH YOUR SHIRT!
NO WAY! I MAY BE HELD CAPTIVE, BUT I'VE STILL GOT MY PRIDE!
THAT WHIP DOESN'T SCARE ME!
WHU-KSSH!
HEH HEH HEH...DRAFTY IN HERE, HUH?
SINCE WE HAVE TWO OF THESE LOBSTER MONSTER-TYPES, THERE'S JUST ONE THING LEFT TO DO...
A FEW DAYS LATER...
DING-DONG!
COMING!
HAROLD ZOID! WHAT ARE YOU DOING HERE?
I HEARD YOU NEEDED A STAFF PHYSICIAN, SO I THOUGHT I'D FILL MY NEPHEW'S VACANT SHELL, WHY NOT.

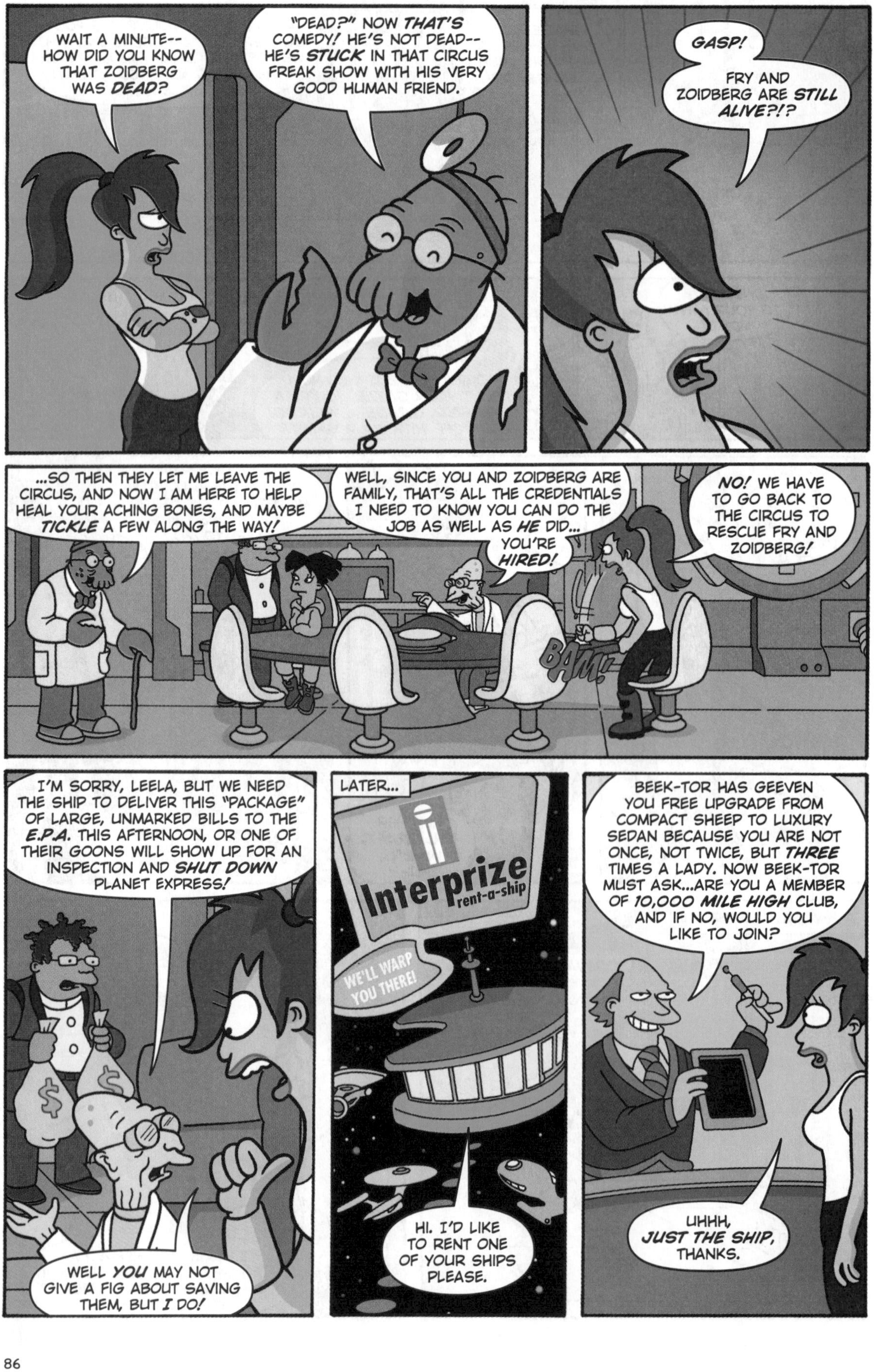
WAIT A MINUTE-- HOW DID YOU KNOW THAT ZOIDBERG WAS DEAD?
"DEAD?" NOW THAT'S COMEDY! HE'S NOT DEAD-- HE'S STUCK IN THAT CIRCUS FREAK SHOW WITH HIS VERY GOOD HUMAN FRIEND.
GASP!
FRY AND ZOIDBERG ARE STILL ALIVE?!?
...SO THEN THEY LET ME LEAVE THE CIRCUS, AND NOW I AM HERE TO HELP HEAL YOUR ACHING BONES, AND MAYBE TICKLE A FEW ALONG THE WAY!
WELL, SINCE YOU AND ZOIDBERG ARE FAMILY, THAT'S ALL THE CREDENTIALS I NEED TO KNOW YOU CAN DO THE JOB AS WELL AS HE DID...
YOU'RE HIRED!
BAM!
NO! WE HAVE TO GO BACK TO THE CIRCUS TO RESCUE FRY AND ZOIDBERG!
I'M SORRY, LEELA, BUT WE NEED THE SHIP TO DELIVER THIS "PACKAGE" OF LARGE, UNMARKED BILLS TO THE E.P.A. THIS AFTERNOON, OR ONE OF THEIR GOONS WILL SHOW UP FOR AN INSPECTION AND SHUT DOWN PLANET EXPRESS!
WELL YOU MAY NOT GIVE A FIG ABOUT SAVING THEM, BUT I DO!
LATER...
Interprize rent-a-ship
WE'LL WARP YOU THERE!
HI. I'D LIKE TO RENT ONE OF YOUR SHIPS PLEASE.
BEEK-TOR HAS GEEVEN YOU FREE UPGRADE FROM COMPACT SHEEP TO LUXURY SEDAN BECAUSE YOU ARE NOT ONCE, NOT TWICE, BUT THREE TIMES A LADY. NOW BEEK-TOR MUST ASK...ARE YOU A MEMBER OF 10,000 MILE HIGH CLUB, AND IF NO, WOULD YOU LIKE TO JOIN?
UHHH, JUST THE SHIP, THANKS.

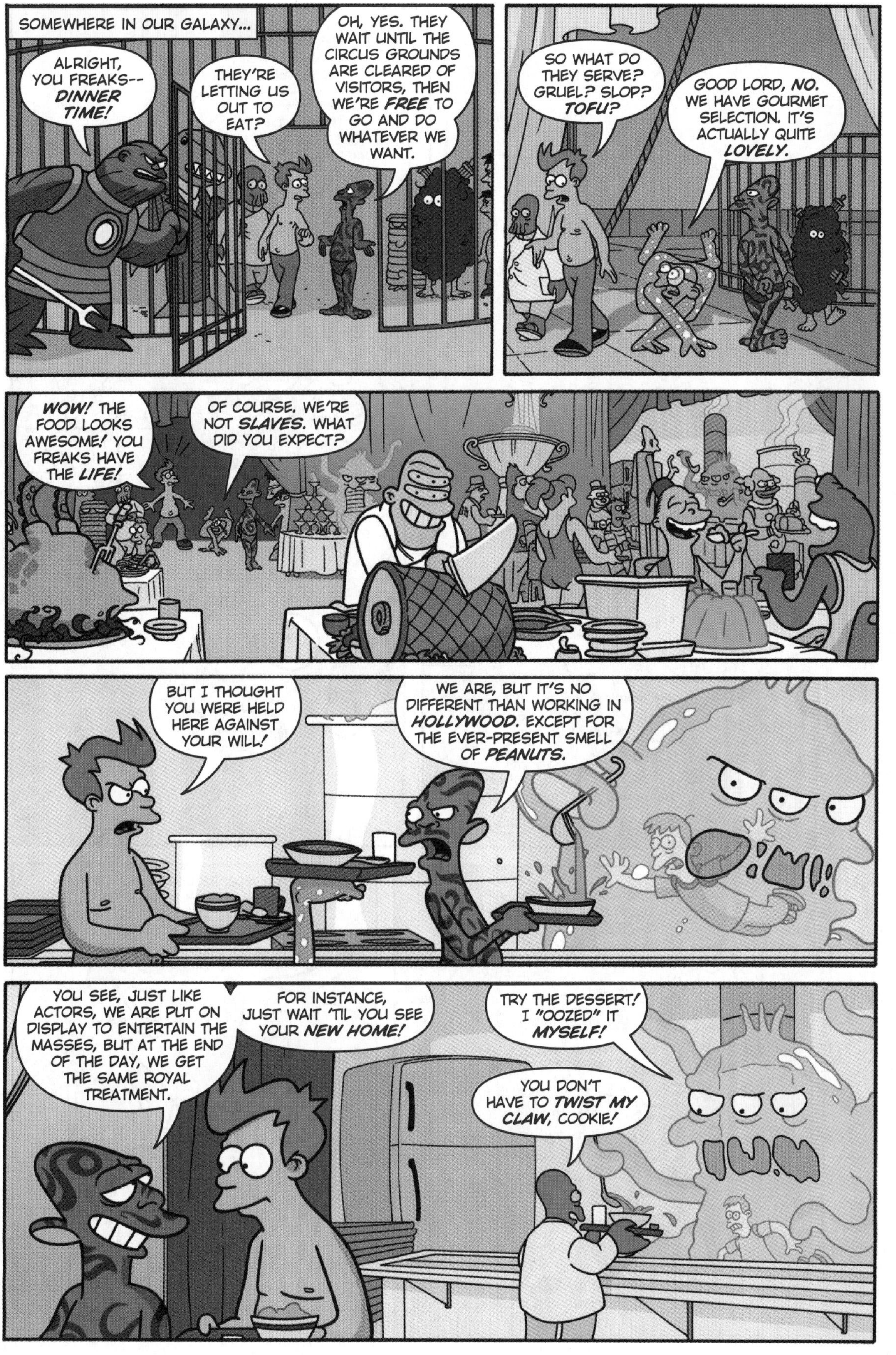
SOMEWHERE IN OUR GALAXY...
ALRIGHT, YOU FREAKS-- DINNER TIME!
THEY'RE LETTING US OUT TO EAT?
OH, YES. THEY WAIT UNTIL THE CIRCUS GROUNDS ARE CLEARED OF VISITORS, THEN WE'RE FREE TO GO AND DO WHATEVER WE WANT.
SO WHAT DO THEY SERVE? GRUEL? SLOP? TOFU?
GOOD LORD, NO. WE HAVE GOURMET SELECTION. IT'S ACTUALLY QUITE LOVELY.
WOW! THE FOOD LOOKS AWESOME! YOU FREAKS HAVE THE LIFE!
OF COURSE. WE'RE NOT SLAVES. WHAT DID YOU EXPECT?
BUT I THOUGHT YOU WERE HELD HERE AGAINST YOUR WILL!
WE ARE, BUT IT'S NO DIFFERENT THAN WORKING IN HOLLYWOOD. EXCEPT FOR THE EVER-PRESENT SMELL OF PEANUTS.
YOU SEE, JUST LIKE ACTORS, WE ARE PUT ON DISPLAY TO ENTERTAIN THE MASSES, BUT AT THE END OF THE DAY, WE GET THE SAME ROYAL TREATMENT.
FOR INSTANCE, JUST WAIT 'TIL YOU SEE YOUR NEW HOME!
TRY THE DESSERT! I "OOZED" IT MYSELF!
YOU DON'T HAVE TO TWIST MY CLAW, COOKIE!

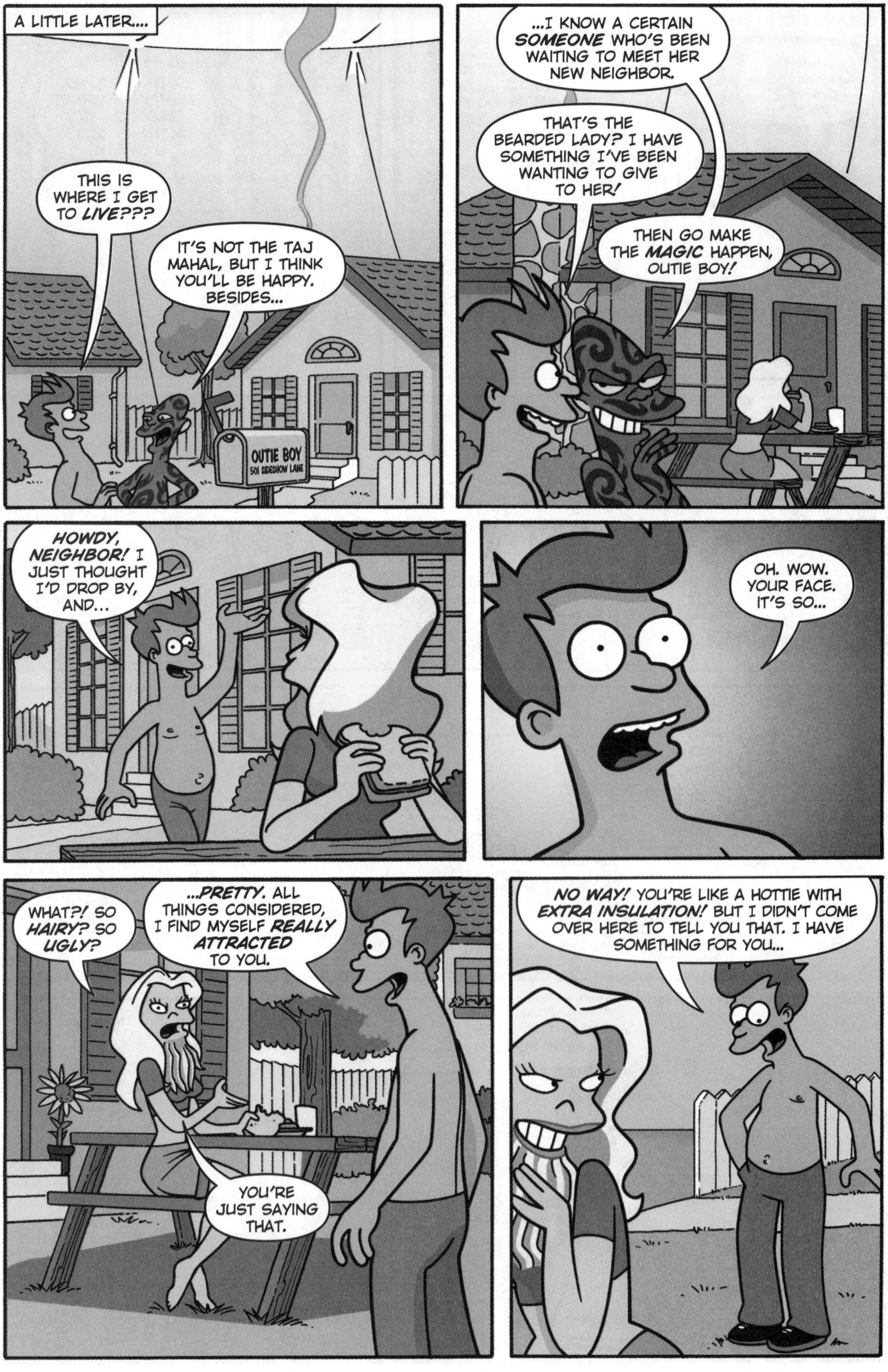
A LITTLE LATER....
THIS IS WHERE I GET TO *LIVE???*
IT'S NOT THE TAJ MAHAL, BUT I THINK YOU'LL BE HAPPY. BESIDES...
OUTIE BOY
501 SIDESHOW LANE
...I KNOW A CERTAIN *SOMEONE* WHO'S BEEN WAITING TO MEET HER NEW NEIGHBOR.
THAT'S THE BEARDED LADY? I HAVE SOMETHING I'VE BEEN WANTING TO GIVE TO HER!
THEN GO MAKE THE *MAGIC* HAPPEN, OUTIE BOY!
*HOWDY, NEIGHBOR!* I JUST THOUGHT I'D DROP BY, AND...
OH. WOW. YOUR FACE. IT'S SO...
WHAT?! SO *HAIRY?* SO *UGLY?*
*...PRETTY.* ALL THINGS CONSIDERED, I FIND MYSELF *REALLY ATTRACTED* TO YOU.
YOU'RE JUST SAYING THAT.
*NO WAY!* YOU'RE LIKE A HOTTIE WITH *EXTRA INSULATION!* BUT I DIDN'T COME OVER HERE TO TELL YOU THAT. I HAVE SOMETHING FOR YOU...

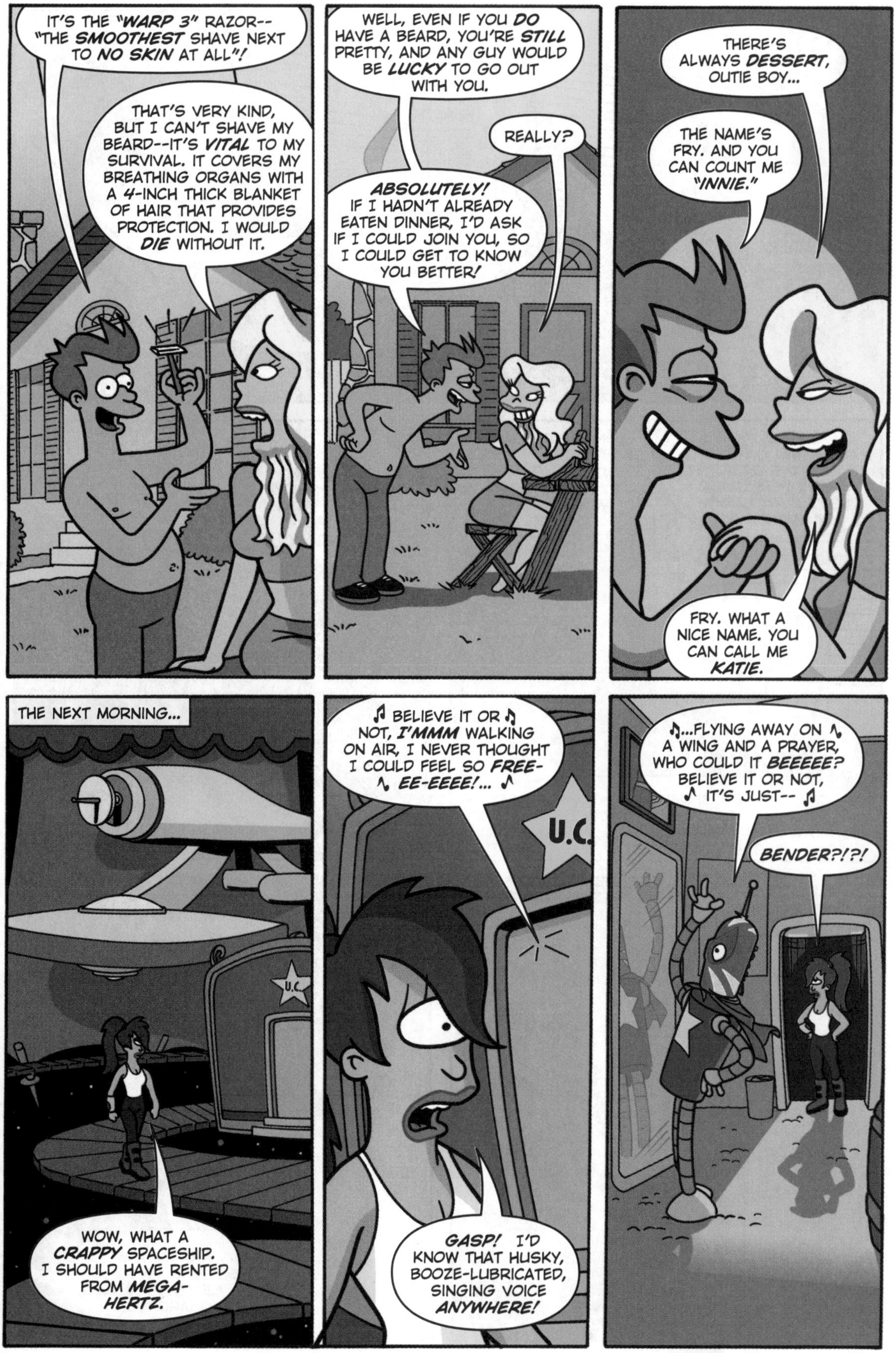
IT'S THE "WARP 3" RAZOR-- "THE SMOOTHEST SHAVE NEXT TO NO SKIN AT ALL"!
THAT'S VERY KIND, BUT I CAN'T SHAVE MY BEARD--IT'S VITAL TO MY SURVIVAL. IT COVERS MY BREATHING ORGANS WITH A 4-INCH THICK BLANKET OF HAIR THAT PROVIDES PROTECTION. I WOULD DIE WITHOUT IT.
WELL, EVEN IF YOU DO HAVE A BEARD, YOU'RE STILL PRETTY, AND ANY GUY WOULD BE LUCKY TO GO OUT WITH YOU.
REALLY?
ABSOLUTELY! IF I HADN'T ALREADY EATEN DINNER, I'D ASK IF I COULD JOIN YOU, SO I COULD GET TO KNOW YOU BETTER!
THERE'S ALWAYS DESSERT, OUTIE BOY...
THE NAME'S FRY. AND YOU CAN COUNT ME "INNIE."
FRY. WHAT A NICE NAME. YOU CAN CALL ME KATIE.
THE NEXT MORNING...
WOW, WHAT A CRAPPY SPACESHIP. I SHOULD HAVE RENTED FROM MEGA-HERTZ.
♫ BELIEVE IT OR ♫ NOT, I'MMM WALKING ON AIR, I NEVER THOUGHT I COULD FEEL SO FREE-EE-EEEE!... ♪
U.C.
GASP! I'D KNOW THAT HUSKY, BOOZE-LUBRICATED, SINGING VOICE ANYWHERE!
♫...FLYING AWAY ON A WING AND A PRAYER, WHO COULD IT BEEEEE? BELIEVE IT OR NOT, ♪ IT'S JUST-- ♫
BENDER?!?!

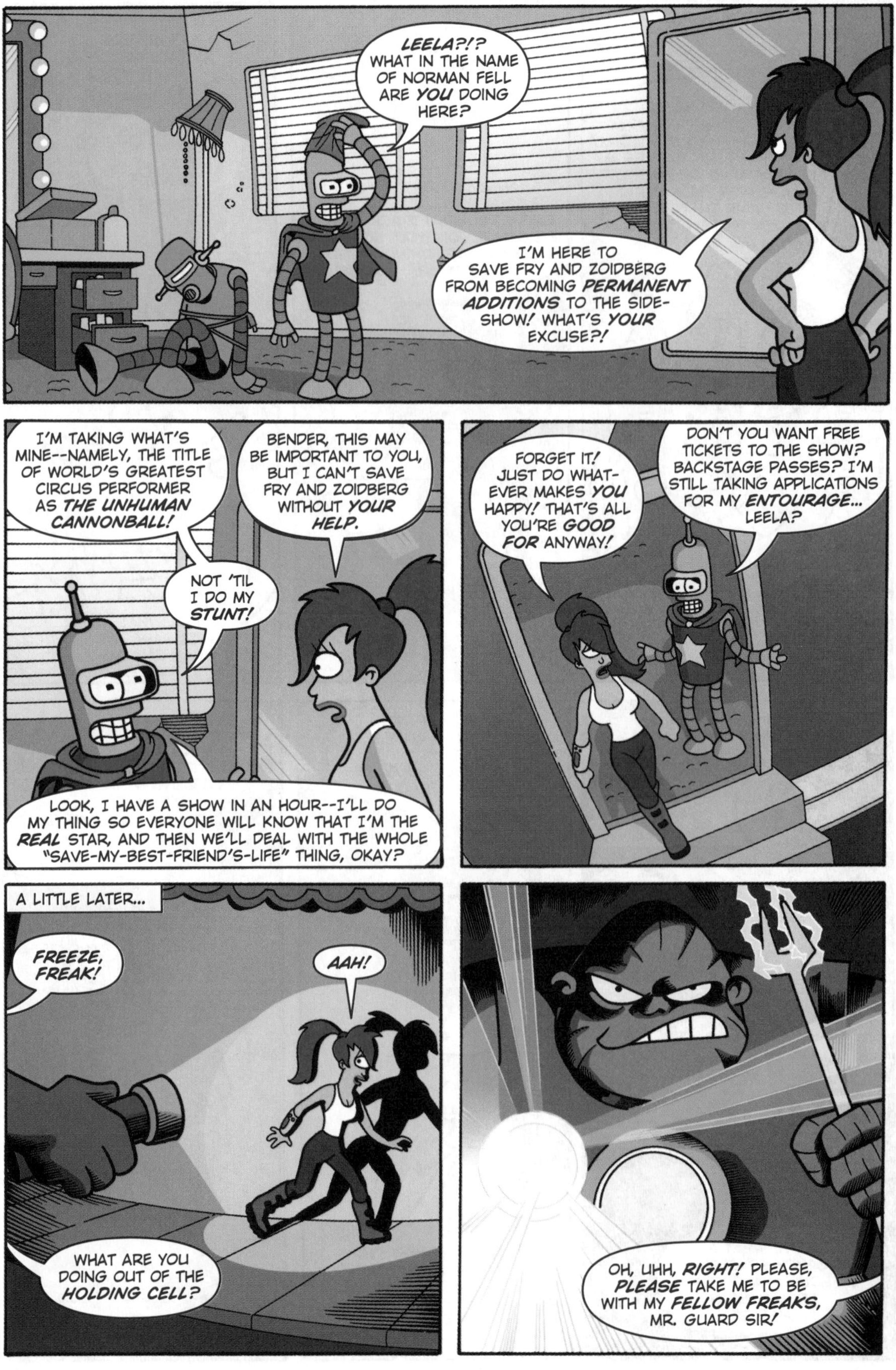
LEELA?!? WHAT IN THE NAME OF NORMAN FELL ARE YOU DOING HERE?
I'M HERE TO SAVE FRY AND ZOIDBERG FROM BECOMING PERMANENT ADDITIONS TO THE SIDE-SHOW! WHAT'S YOUR EXCUSE?!
I'M TAKING WHAT'S MINE--NAMELY, THE TITLE OF WORLD'S GREATEST CIRCUS PERFORMER AS THE UNHUMAN CANNONBALL!
BENDER, THIS MAY BE IMPORTANT TO YOU, BUT I CAN'T SAVE FRY AND ZOIDBERG WITHOUT YOUR HELP.
NOT 'TIL I DO MY STUNT!
LOOK, I HAVE A SHOW IN AN HOUR--I'LL DO MY THING SO EVERYONE WILL KNOW THAT I'M THE REAL STAR, AND THEN WE'LL DEAL WITH THE WHOLE "SAVE-MY-BEST-FRIEND'S-LIFE" THING, OKAY?
FORGET IT! JUST DO WHAT-EVER MAKES YOU HAPPY! THAT'S ALL YOU'RE GOOD FOR ANYWAY!
DON'T YOU WANT FREE TICKETS TO THE SHOW? BACKSTAGE PASSES? I'M STILL TAKING APPLICATIONS FOR MY ENTOURAGE... LEELA?
A LITTLE LATER...
FREEZE, FREAK!
AAH!
WHAT ARE YOU DOING OUT OF THE HOLDING CELL?
OH, UHH, RIGHT! PLEASE, PLEASE TAKE ME TO BE WITH MY FELLOW FREAKS, MR. GUARD SIR!

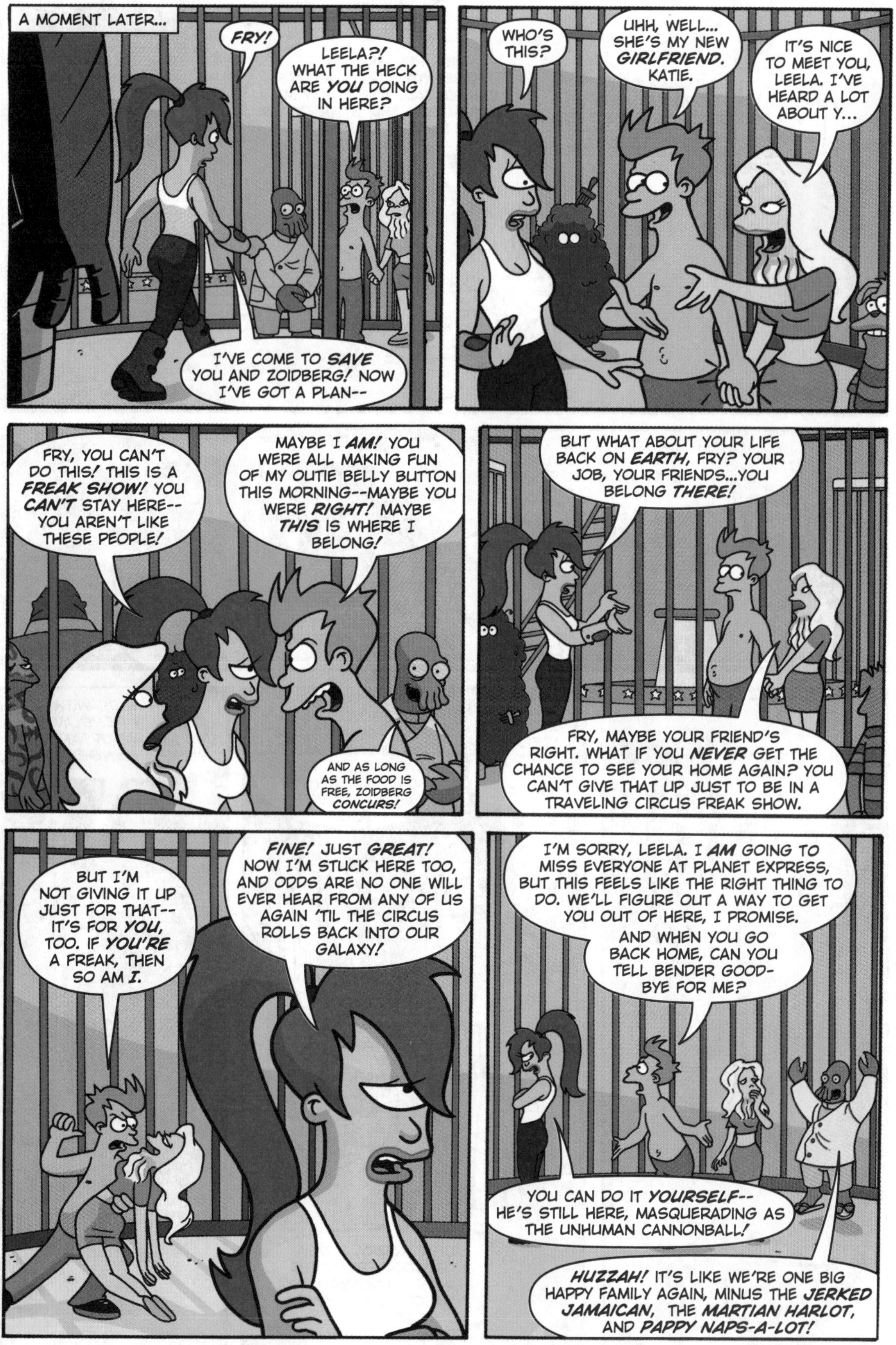
A MOMENT LATER...
FRY!
LEELA?! WHAT THE HECK ARE YOU DOING IN HERE?
I'VE COME TO SAVE YOU AND ZOIDBERG! NOW I'VE GOT A PLAN--
WHO'S THIS?
UHH, WELL... SHE'S MY NEW GIRLFRIEND. KATIE.
IT'S NICE TO MEET YOU, LEELA. I'VE HEARD A LOT ABOUT Y...
FRY, YOU CAN'T DO THIS! THIS IS A FREAK SHOW! YOU CAN'T STAY HERE-- YOU AREN'T LIKE THESE PEOPLE!
MAYBE I AM! YOU WERE ALL MAKING FUN OF MY OUTIE BELLY BUTTON THIS MORNING--MAYBE YOU WERE RIGHT! MAYBE THIS IS WHERE I BELONG!
AND AS LONG AS THE FOOD IS FREE, ZOIDBERG CONCURS!
BUT WHAT ABOUT YOUR LIFE BACK ON EARTH, FRY? YOUR JOB, YOUR FRIENDS...YOU BELONG THERE!
FRY, MAYBE YOUR FRIEND'S RIGHT. WHAT IF YOU NEVER GET THE CHANCE TO SEE YOUR HOME AGAIN? YOU CAN'T GIVE THAT UP JUST TO BE IN A TRAVELING CIRCUS FREAK SHOW.
BUT I'M NOT GIVING IT UP JUST FOR THAT-- IT'S FOR YOU, TOO. IF YOU'RE A FREAK, THEN SO AM I.
FINE! JUST GREAT! NOW I'M STUCK HERE TOO, AND ODDS ARE NO ONE WILL EVER HEAR FROM ANY OF US AGAIN 'TIL THE CIRCUS ROLLS BACK INTO OUR GALAXY!
I'M SORRY, LEELA. I AM GOING TO MISS EVERYONE AT PLANET EXPRESS, BUT THIS FEELS LIKE THE RIGHT THING TO DO. WE'LL FIGURE OUT A WAY TO GET YOU OUT OF HERE, I PROMISE.
AND WHEN YOU GO BACK HOME, CAN YOU TELL BENDER GOOD-BYE FOR ME?
YOU CAN DO IT YOURSELF-- HE'S STILL HERE, MASQUERADING AS THE UNHUMAN CANNONBALL!
HUZZAH! IT'S LIKE WE'RE ONE BIG HAPPY FAMILY AGAIN, MINUS THE JERKED JAMAICAN, THE MARTIAN HARLOT, AND PAPPY NAPS-A-LOT!

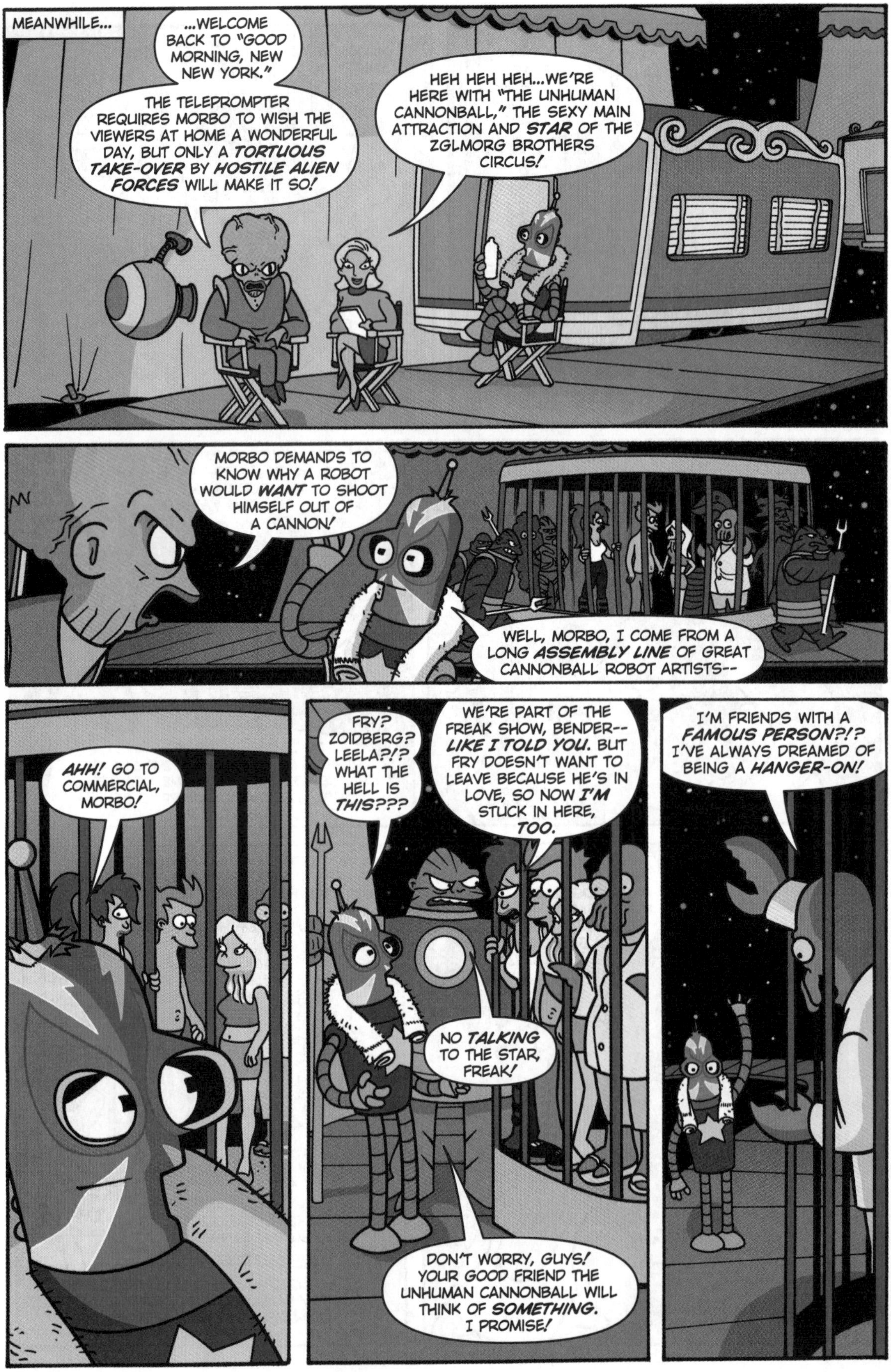
MEANWHILE...
...WELCOME BACK TO "GOOD MORNING, NEW NEW YORK."
THE TELEPROMPTER REQUIRES MORBO TO WISH THE VIEWERS AT HOME A WONDERFUL DAY, BUT ONLY A TORTUOUS TAKE-OVER BY HOSTILE ALIEN FORCES WILL MAKE IT SO!
HEH HEH HEH...WE'RE HERE WITH "THE UNHUMAN CANNONBALL," THE SEXY MAIN ATTRACTION AND STAR OF THE ZGLMORG BROTHERS CIRCUS!
MORBO DEMANDS TO KNOW WHY A ROBOT WOULD WANT TO SHOOT HIMSELF OUT OF A CANNON!
WELL, MORBO, I COME FROM A LONG ASSEMBLY LINE OF GREAT CANNONBALL ROBOT ARTISTS--
AHH! GO TO COMMERCIAL, MORBO!
FRY? ZOIDBERG? LEELA?!? WHAT THE HELL IS THIS???
WE'RE PART OF THE FREAK SHOW, BENDER-- LIKE I TOLD YOU. BUT FRY DOESN'T WANT TO LEAVE BECAUSE HE'S IN LOVE, SO NOW I'M STUCK IN HERE, TOO.
NO TALKING TO THE STAR, FREAK!
DON'T WORRY, GUYS! YOUR GOOD FRIEND THE UNHUMAN CANNONBALL WILL THINK OF SOMETHING. I PROMISE!
I'M FRIENDS WITH A FAMOUS PERSON?!? I'VE ALWAYS DREAMED OF BEING A HANGER-ON!

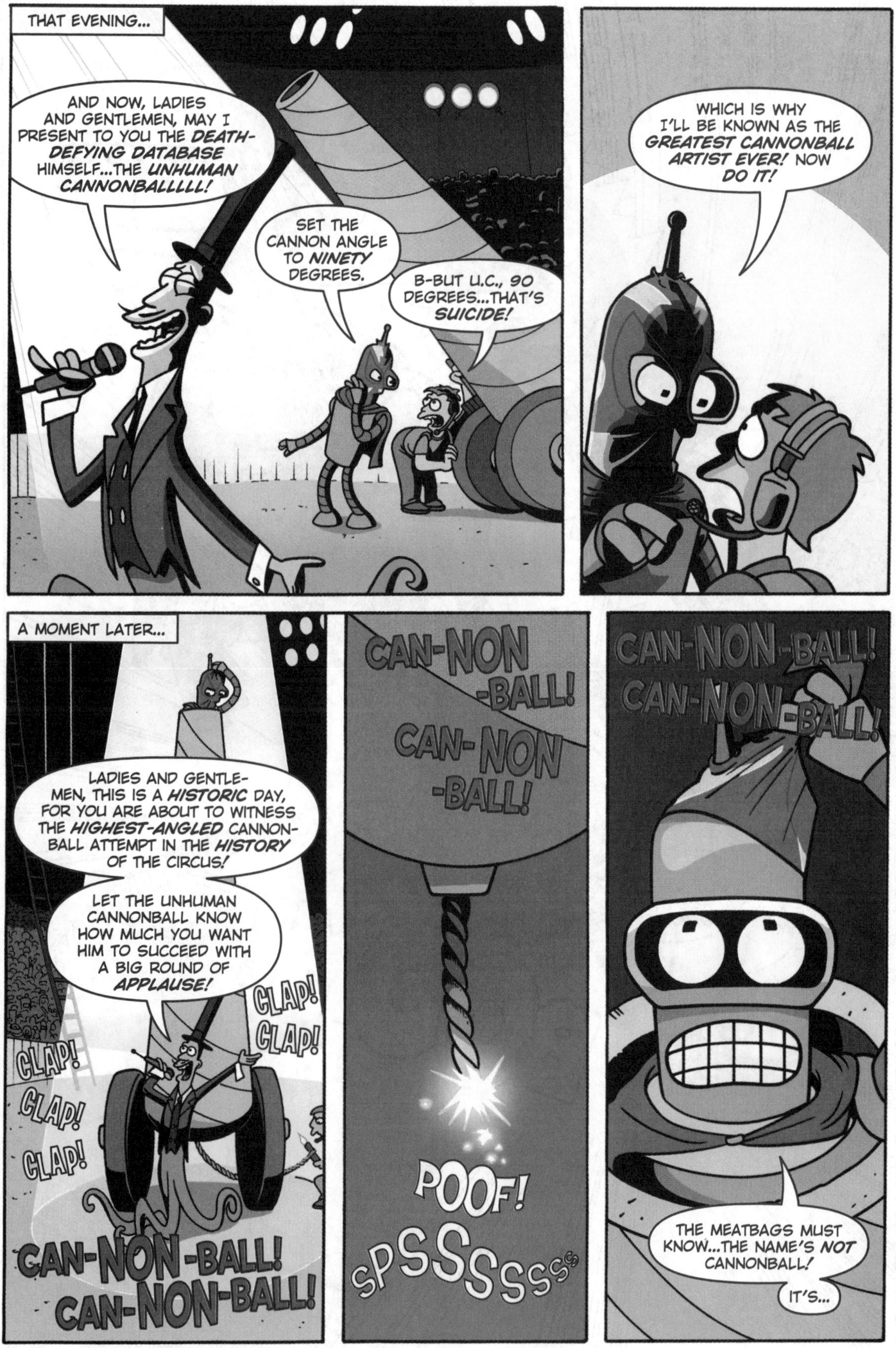
THAT EVENING...
AND NOW, LADIES AND GENTLEMEN, MAY I PRESENT TO YOU THE DEATH-DEFYING DATABASE HIMSELF...THE UNHUMAN CANNONBALLLLLL!
SET THE CANNON ANGLE TO NINETY DEGREES.
B-BUT U.C., 90 DEGREES...THAT'S SUICIDE!
WHICH IS WHY I'LL BE KNOWN AS THE GREATEST CANNONBALL ARTIST EVER! NOW DO IT!
A MOMENT LATER...
LADIES AND GENTLEMEN, THIS IS A HISTORIC DAY, FOR YOU ARE ABOUT TO WITNESS THE HIGHEST-ANGLED CANNONBALL ATTEMPT IN THE HISTORY OF THE CIRCUS!
LET THE UNHUMAN CANNONBALL KNOW HOW MUCH YOU WANT HIM TO SUCCEED WITH A BIG ROUND OF APPLAUSE!
CLAP! CLAP!
CLAP! CLAP! CLAP!
CAN-NON-BALL! CAN-NON-BALL!
CAN-NON-BALL! CAN-NON-BALL!
POOF!
SPSSSSSSS
CAN-NON-BALL! CAN-NON-BALL!
THE MEATBAGS MUST KNOW...THE NAME'S NOT CANNONBALL!
IT'S...

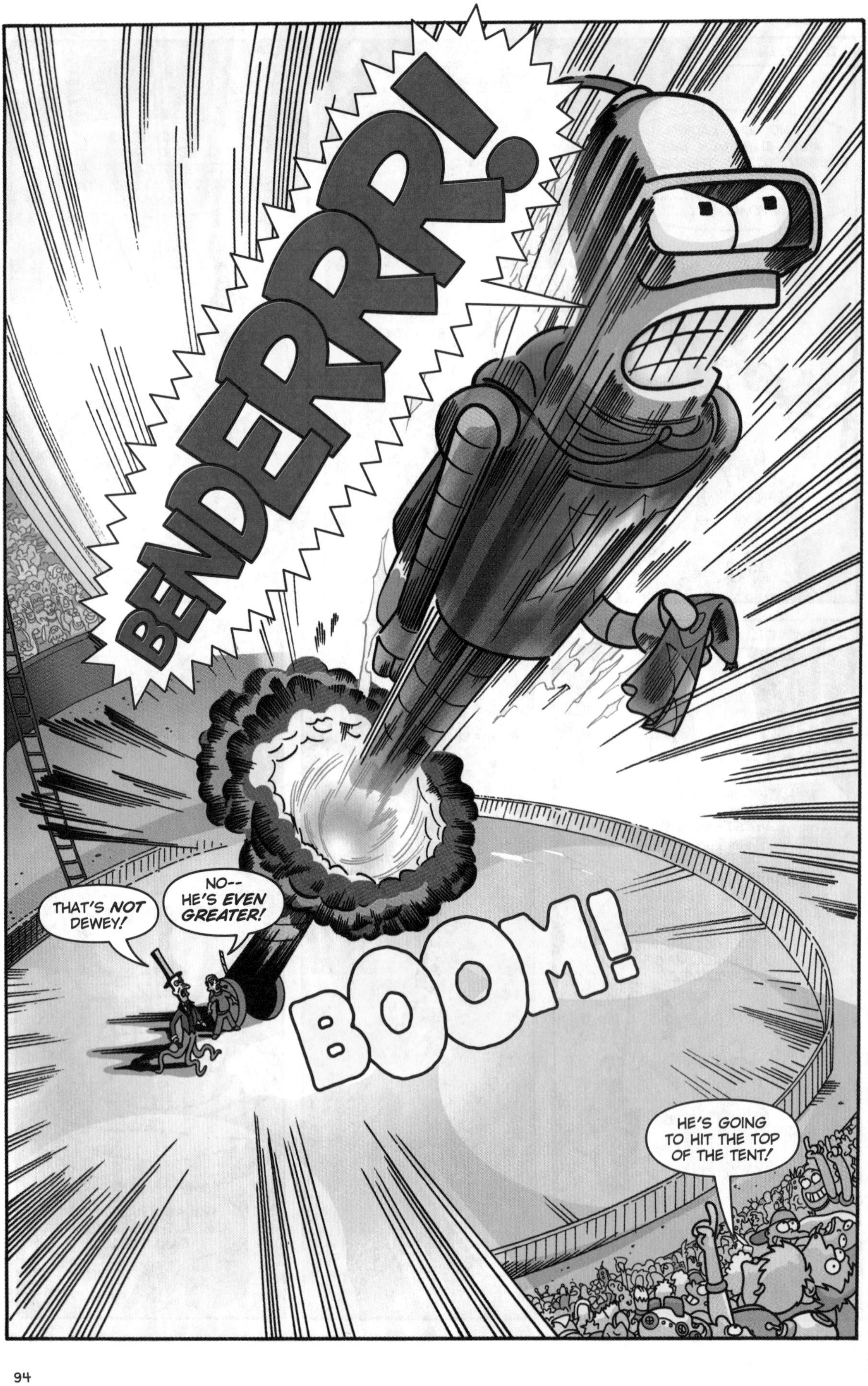
BENDERRR!
THAT'S NOT DEWEY!
NO-- HE'S EVEN GREATER!
BOOM!
HE'S GOING TO HIT THE TOP OF THE TENT!

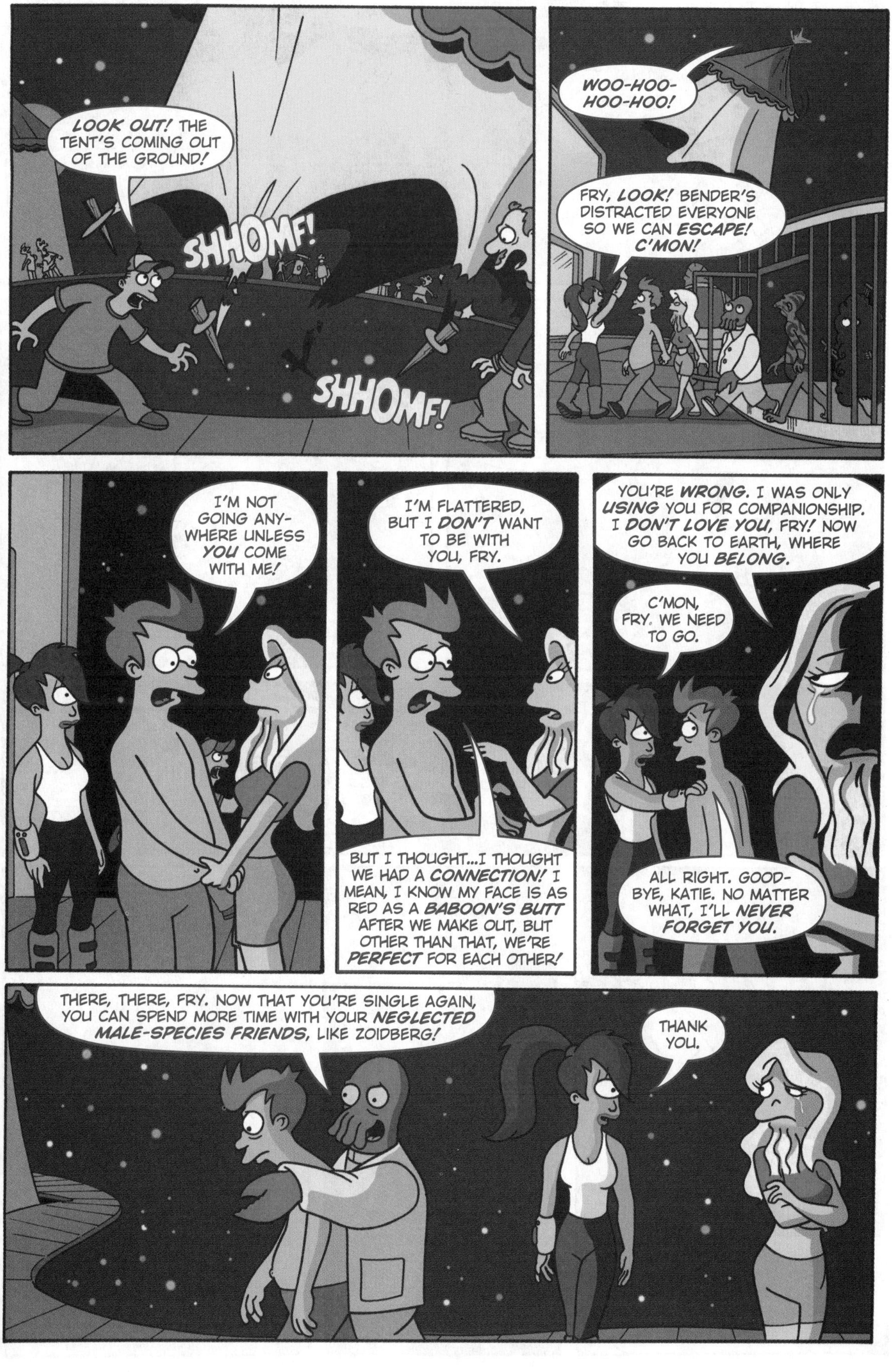
LOOK OUT! THE TENT'S COMING OUT OF THE GROUND!
SHHOMF!
SHHOMF!
WOO-HOO-HOO-HOO!
FRY, LOOK! BENDER'S DISTRACTED EVERYONE SO WE CAN ESCAPE! C'MON!
I'M NOT GOING ANYWHERE UNLESS YOU COME WITH ME!
I'M FLATTERED, BUT I DON'T WANT TO BE WITH YOU, FRY.
BUT I THOUGHT...I THOUGHT WE HAD A CONNECTION! I MEAN, I KNOW MY FACE IS AS RED AS A BABOON'S BUTT AFTER WE MAKE OUT, BUT OTHER THAN THAT, WE'RE PERFECT FOR EACH OTHER!
YOU'RE WRONG. I WAS ONLY USING YOU FOR COMPANIONSHIP. I DON'T LOVE YOU, FRY! NOW GO BACK TO EARTH, WHERE YOU BELONG.
C'MON, FRY. WE NEED TO GO.
ALL RIGHT. GOOD-BYE, KATIE. NO MATTER WHAT, I'LL NEVER FORGET YOU.
THERE, THERE, FRY. NOW THAT YOU'RE SINGLE AGAIN, YOU CAN SPEND MORE TIME WITH YOUR NEGLECTED MALE-SPECIES FRIENDS, LIKE ZOIDBERG!
THANK YOU.

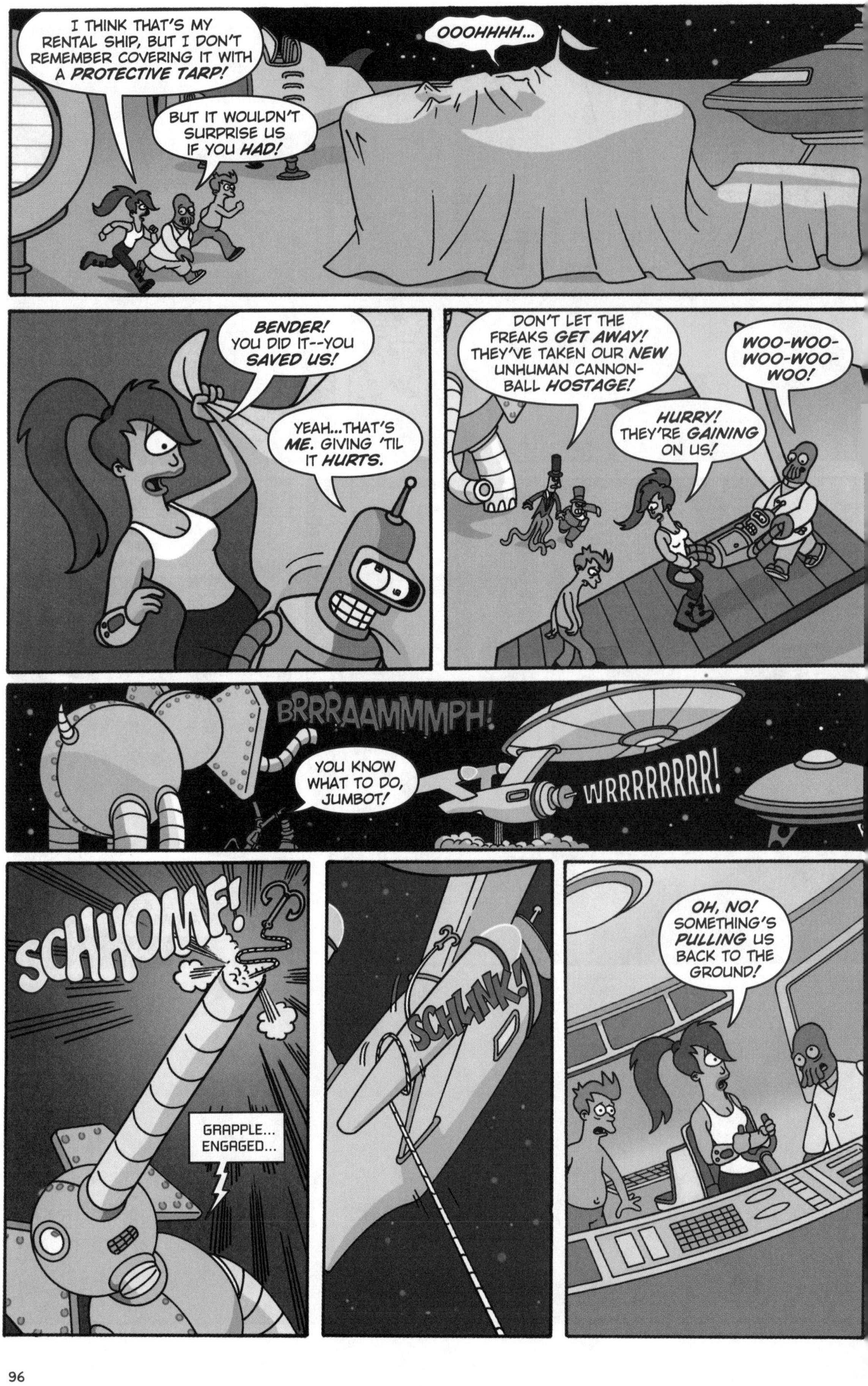
I THINK THAT'S MY RENTAL SHIP, BUT I DON'T REMEMBER COVERING IT WITH A PROTECTIVE TARP!
OOOHHHH...
BUT IT WOULDN'T SURPRISE US IF YOU HAD!
BENDER! YOU DID IT--YOU SAVED US!
YEAH...THAT'S ME. GIVING 'TIL IT HURTS.
DON'T LET THE FREAKS GET AWAY! THEY'VE TAKEN OUR NEW UNHUMAN CANNON-BALL HOSTAGE!
WOO-WOO-WOO-WOO-WOO!
HURRY! THEY'RE GAINING ON US!
BRRRAAMMMPH!
YOU KNOW WHAT TO DO, JUMBOT!
WRRRRRRRR!
SCHHOMF!
GRAPPLE... ENGAGED...
SCHLINK!
OH, NO! SOMETHING'S PULLING US BACK TO THE GROUND!

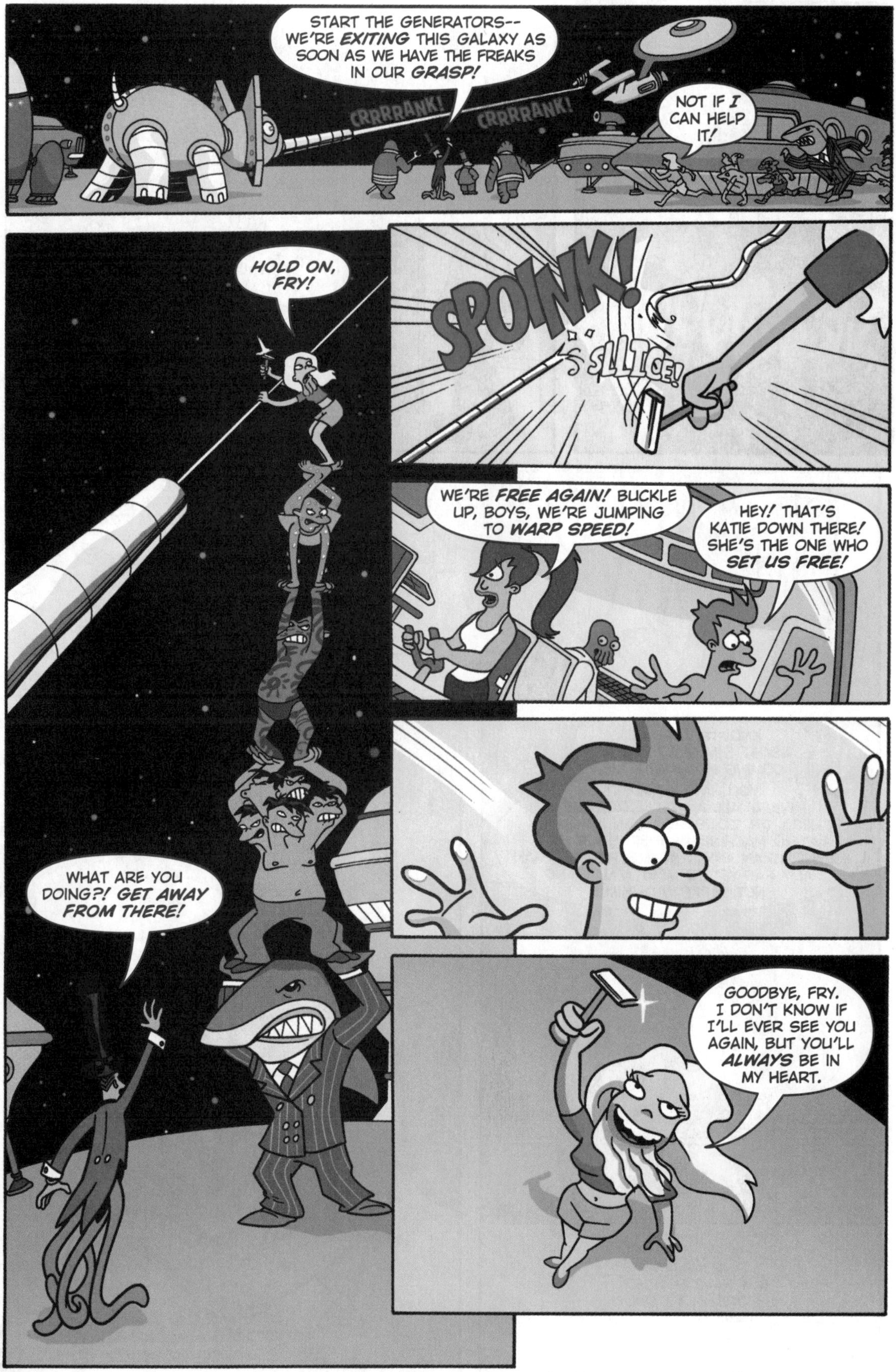
START THE GENERATORS-- WE'RE EXITING THIS GALAXY AS SOON AS WE HAVE THE FREAKS IN OUR GRASP!
CRRRRANK!
CRRRRANK!
NOT IF I CAN HELP IT!
HOLD ON, FRY!
WHAT ARE YOU DOING?! GET AWAY FROM THERE!
SPOINK!
SLLICE!
WE'RE FREE AGAIN! BUCKLE UP, BOYS, WE'RE JUMPING TO WARP SPEED!
HEY! THAT'S KATIE DOWN THERE! SHE'S THE ONE WHO SET US FREE!
GOODBYE, FRY. I DON'T KNOW IF I'LL EVER SEE YOU AGAIN, BUT YOU'LL ALWAYS BE IN MY HEART.

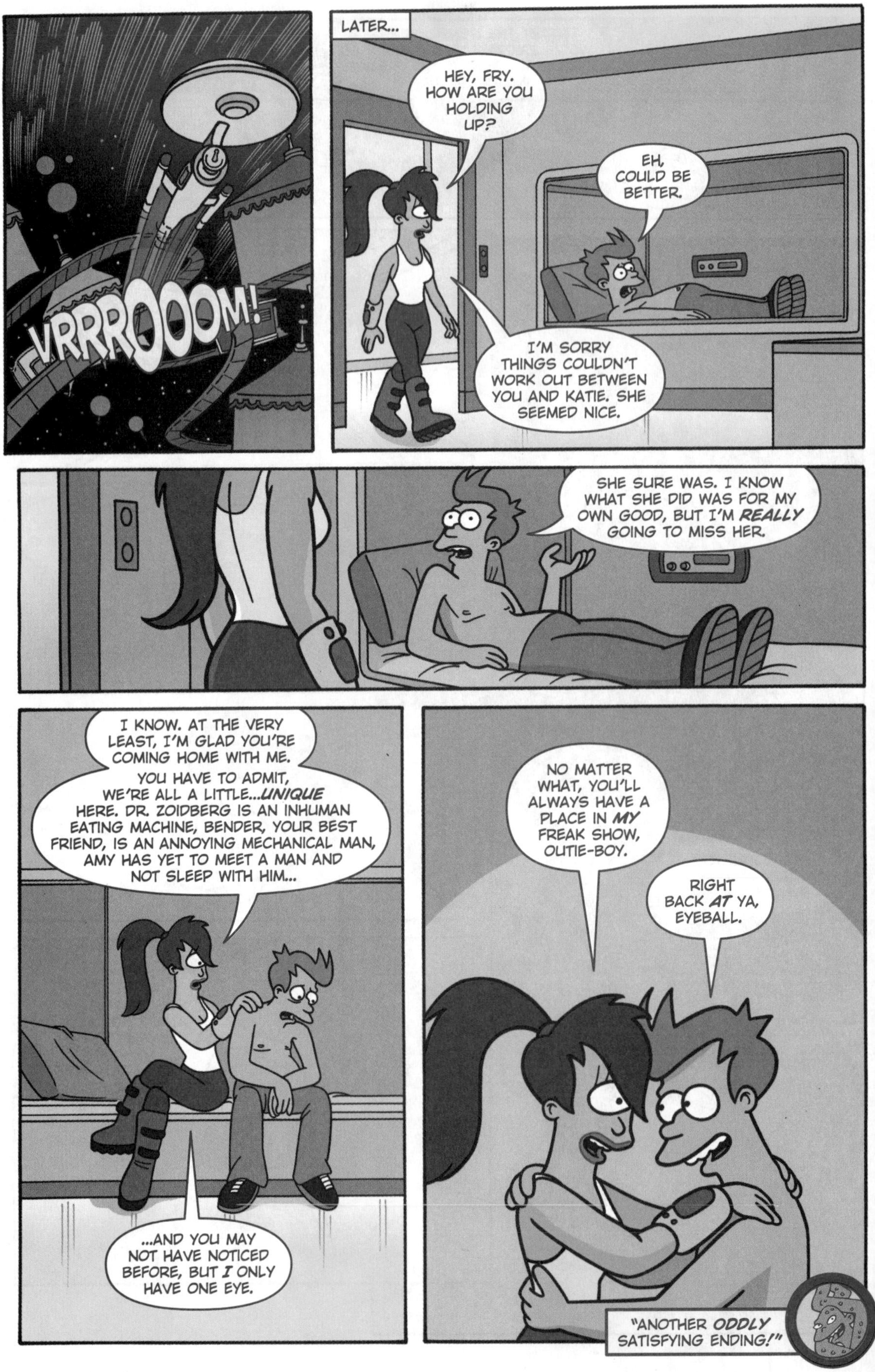
VRRROOOM!
LATER...
HEY, FRY. HOW ARE YOU HOLDING UP?
EH, COULD BE BETTER.
I'M SORRY THINGS COULDN'T WORK OUT BETWEEN YOU AND KATIE. SHE SEEMED NICE.
SHE SURE WAS. I KNOW WHAT SHE DID WAS FOR MY OWN GOOD, BUT I'M *REALLY* GOING TO MISS HER.
I KNOW. AT THE VERY LEAST, I'M GLAD YOU'RE COMING HOME WITH ME.
YOU HAVE TO ADMIT, WE'RE ALL A LITTLE...*UNIQUE* HERE. DR. ZOIDBERG IS AN INHUMAN EATING MACHINE, BENDER, YOUR BEST FRIEND, IS AN ANNOYING MECHANICAL MAN, AMY HAS YET TO MEET A MAN AND NOT SLEEP WITH HIM...
...AND YOU MAY NOT HAVE NOTICED BEFORE, BUT *I* ONLY HAVE ONE EYE.
NO MATTER WHAT, YOU'LL ALWAYS HAVE A PLACE IN *MY* FREAK SHOW, OUTIE-BOY.
RIGHT BACK *AT* YA, EYEBALL.
"ANOTHER *ODDLY* SATISFYING ENDING!"

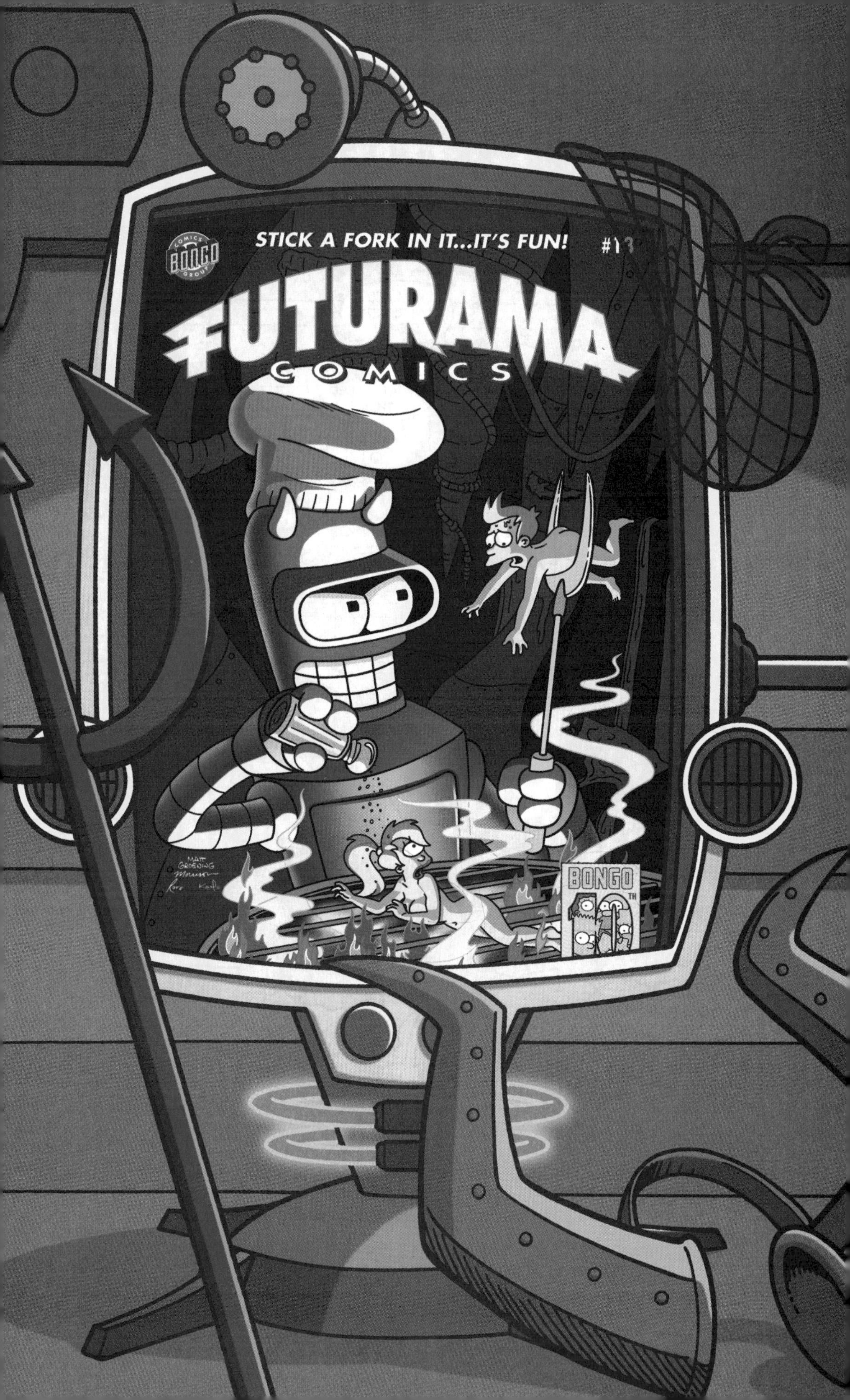

BONGO COMICS GROUP
STICK A FORK IN IT...IT'S FUN!
#1
FUTURAMA
COMICS
MATT GROENING
BONGO
TH

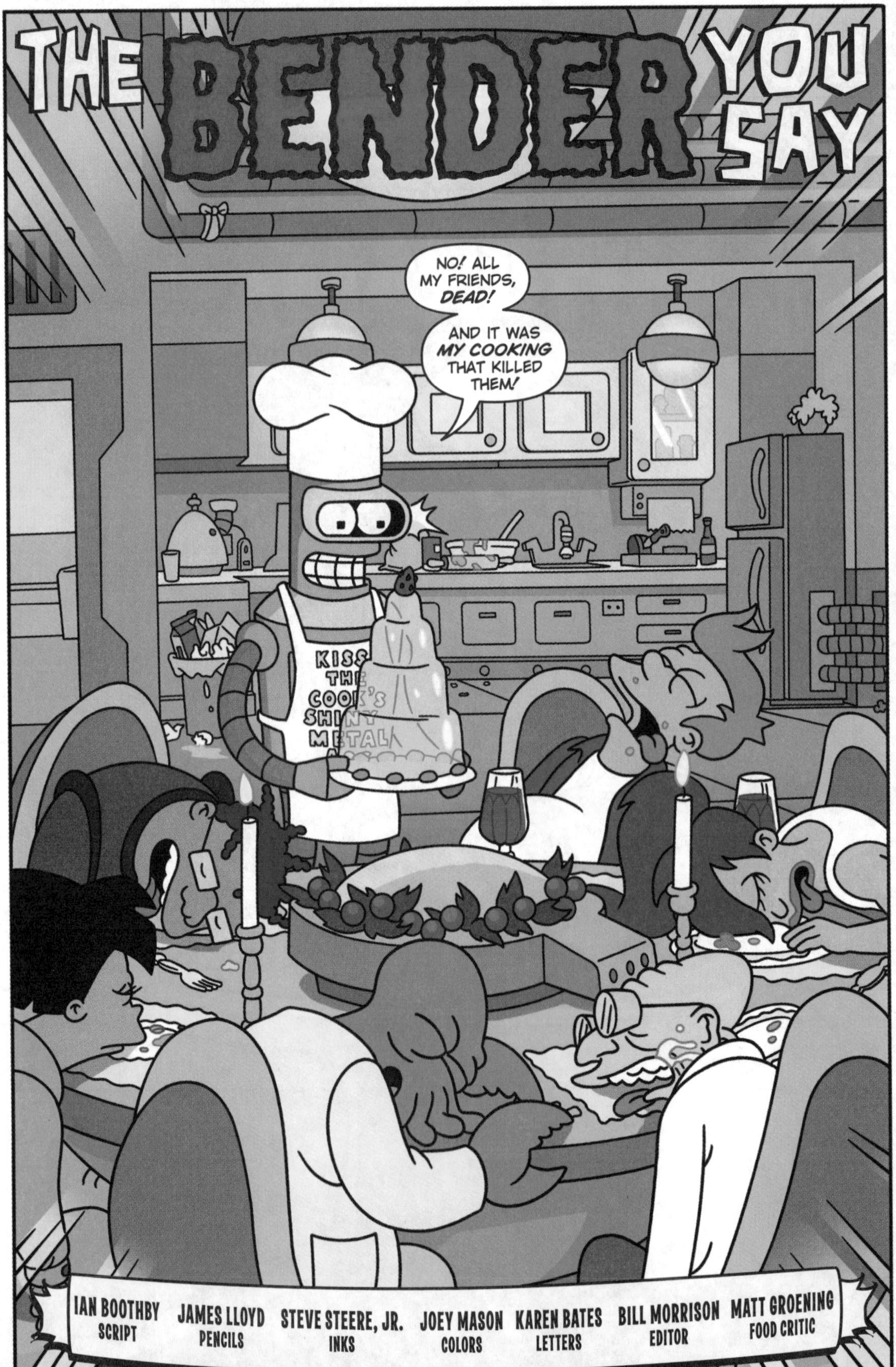
THE BENDER YOU SAY
NO! ALL MY FRIENDS, DEAD!
AND IT WAS MY COOKING THAT KILLED THEM!
KISS THE COOK'S SHINY METAL
IAN BOOTHBY SCRIPT
JAMES LLOYD PENCILS
STEVE STEERE, JR. INKS
JOEY MASON COLORS
KAREN BATES LETTERS
BILL MORRISON EDITOR
MATT GROENING FOOD CRITIC

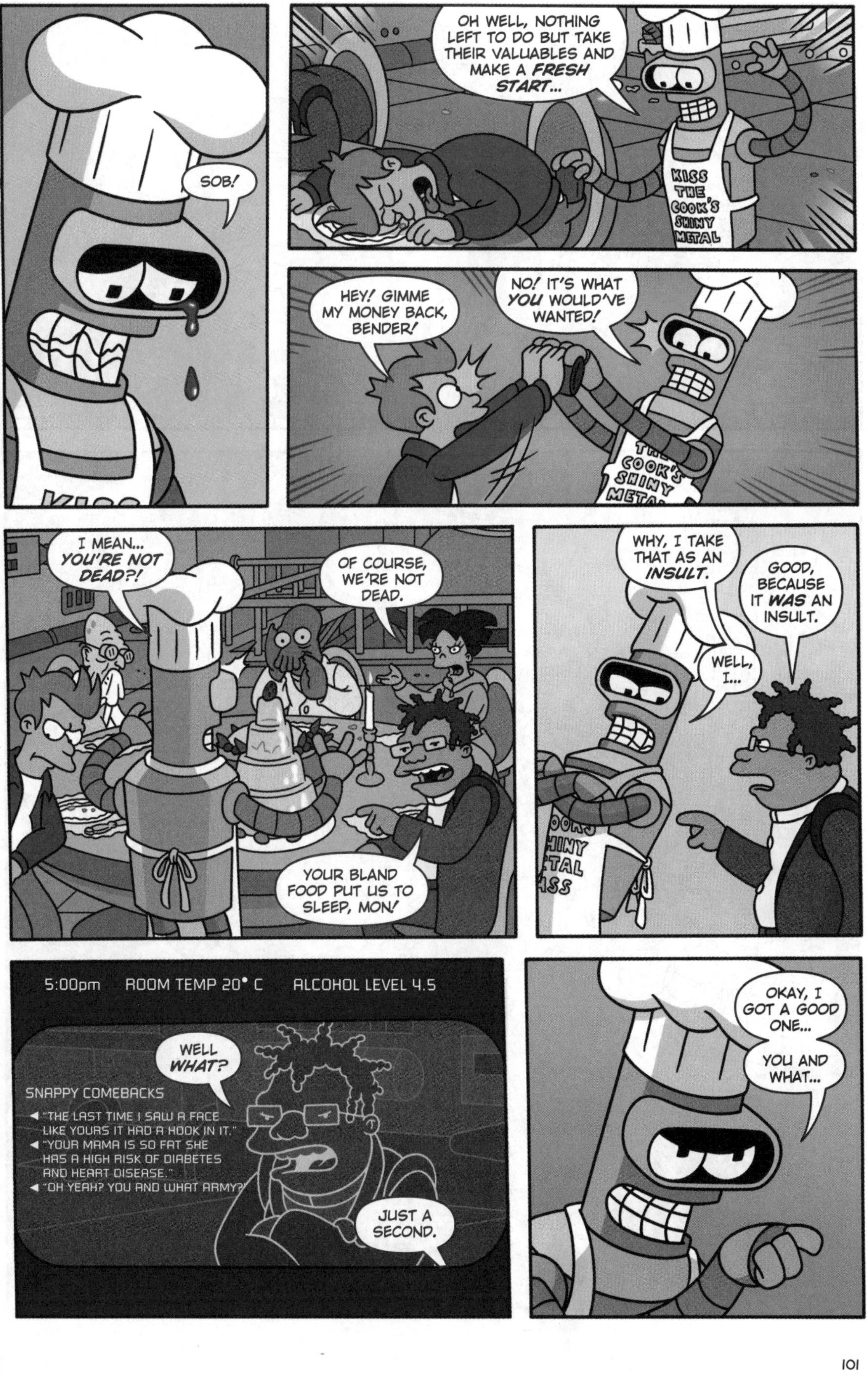
SOB!
OH WELL, NOTHING LEFT TO DO BUT TAKE THEIR VALUABLES AND MAKE A FRESH START...
KISS THE COOK'S SHINY METAL
HEY! GIMME MY MONEY BACK, BENDER!
NO! IT'S WHAT YOU WOULD'VE WANTED!
I MEAN... YOU'RE NOT DEAD?!
OF COURSE, WE'RE NOT DEAD.
YOUR BLAND FOOD PUT US TO SLEEP, MON!
WHY, I TAKE THAT AS AN INSULT.
GOOD, BECAUSE IT WAS AN INSULT.
WELL, I...
5:00pm ROOM TEMP 20° C ALCOHOL LEVEL 4.5
WELL WHAT?
SNAPPY COMEBACKS
"THE LAST TIME I SAW A FACE LIKE YOURS IT HAD A HOOK IN IT."
"YOUR MAMA IS SO FAT SHE HAS A HIGH RISK OF DIABETES AND HEART DISEASE."
"OH YEAH? YOU AND WHAT ARMY?"
JUST A SECOND.
OKAY, I GOT A GOOD ONE...
YOU AND WHAT...

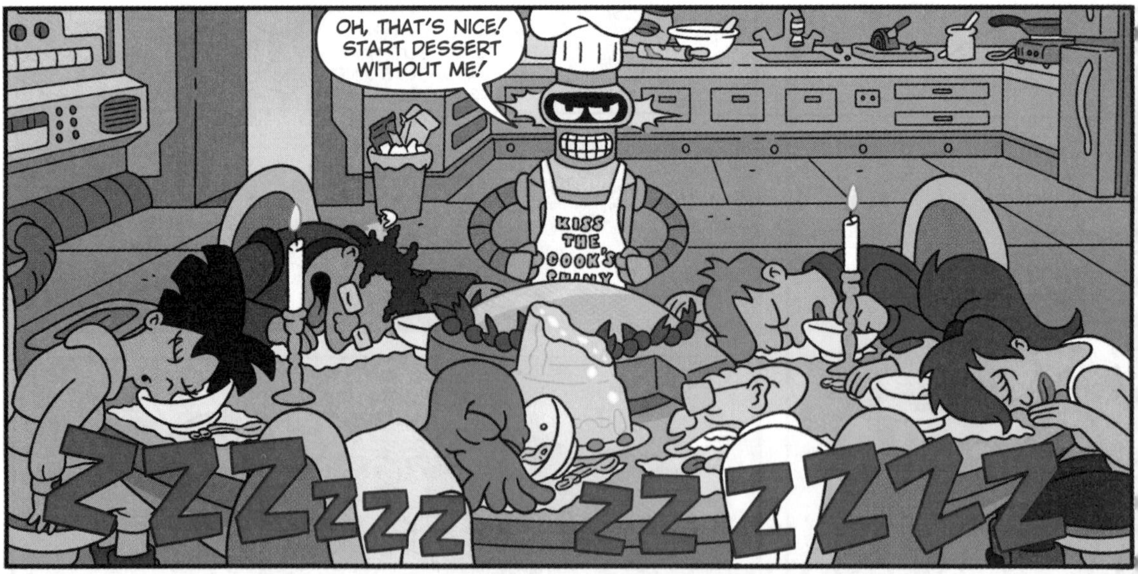
OH, THAT'S NICE! START DESSERT WITHOUT ME!
KISS THE COOK'S
ZZZzzz ZZZZZZZ

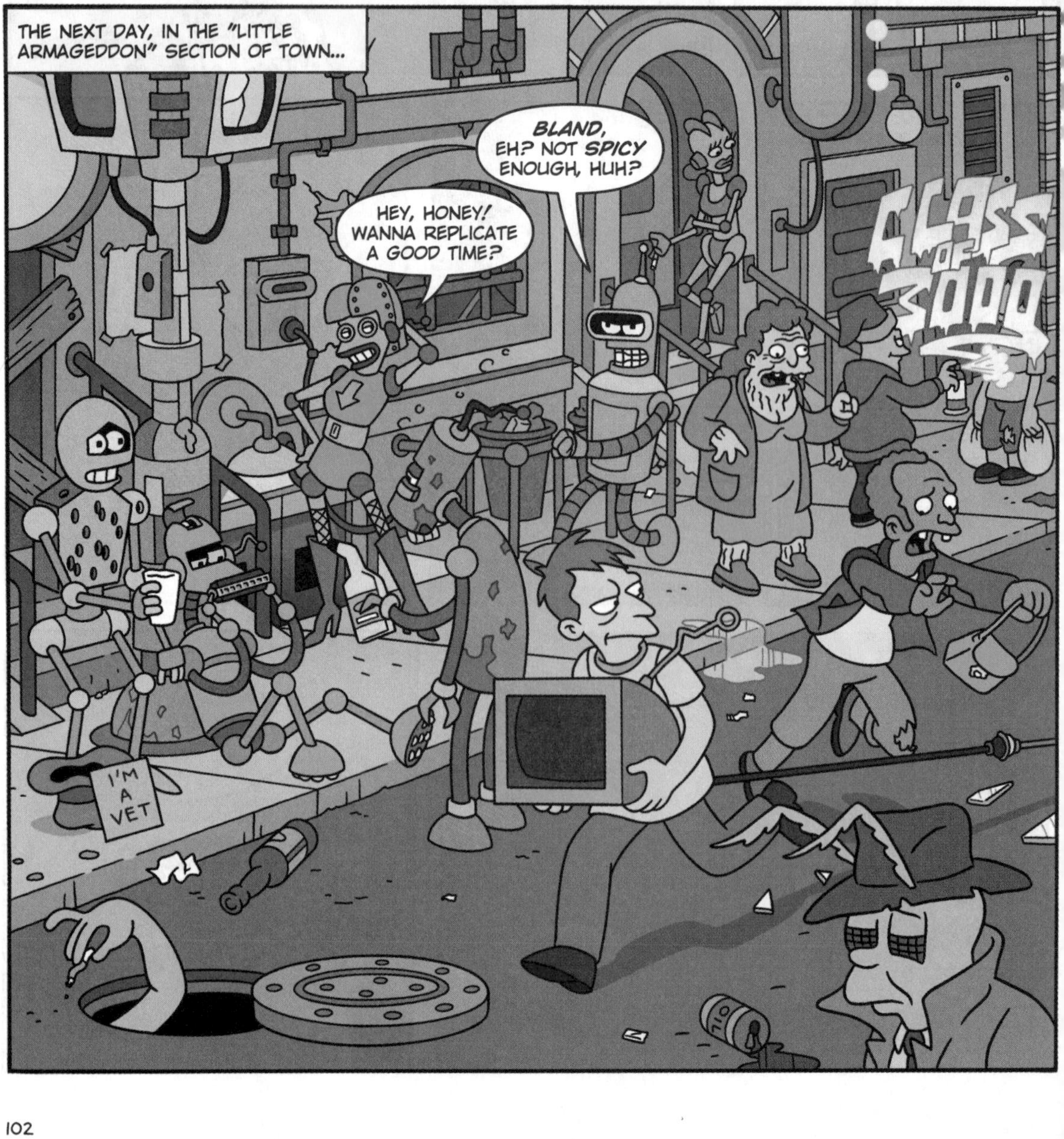
THE NEXT DAY, IN THE "LITTLE ARMAGEDDON" SECTION OF TOWN...
HEY, HONEY! WANNA REPLICATE A GOOD TIME?
*BLAND,* EH? NOT *SPICY* ENOUGH, HUH?
CLASS OF 3000
I'M A VET
OIL

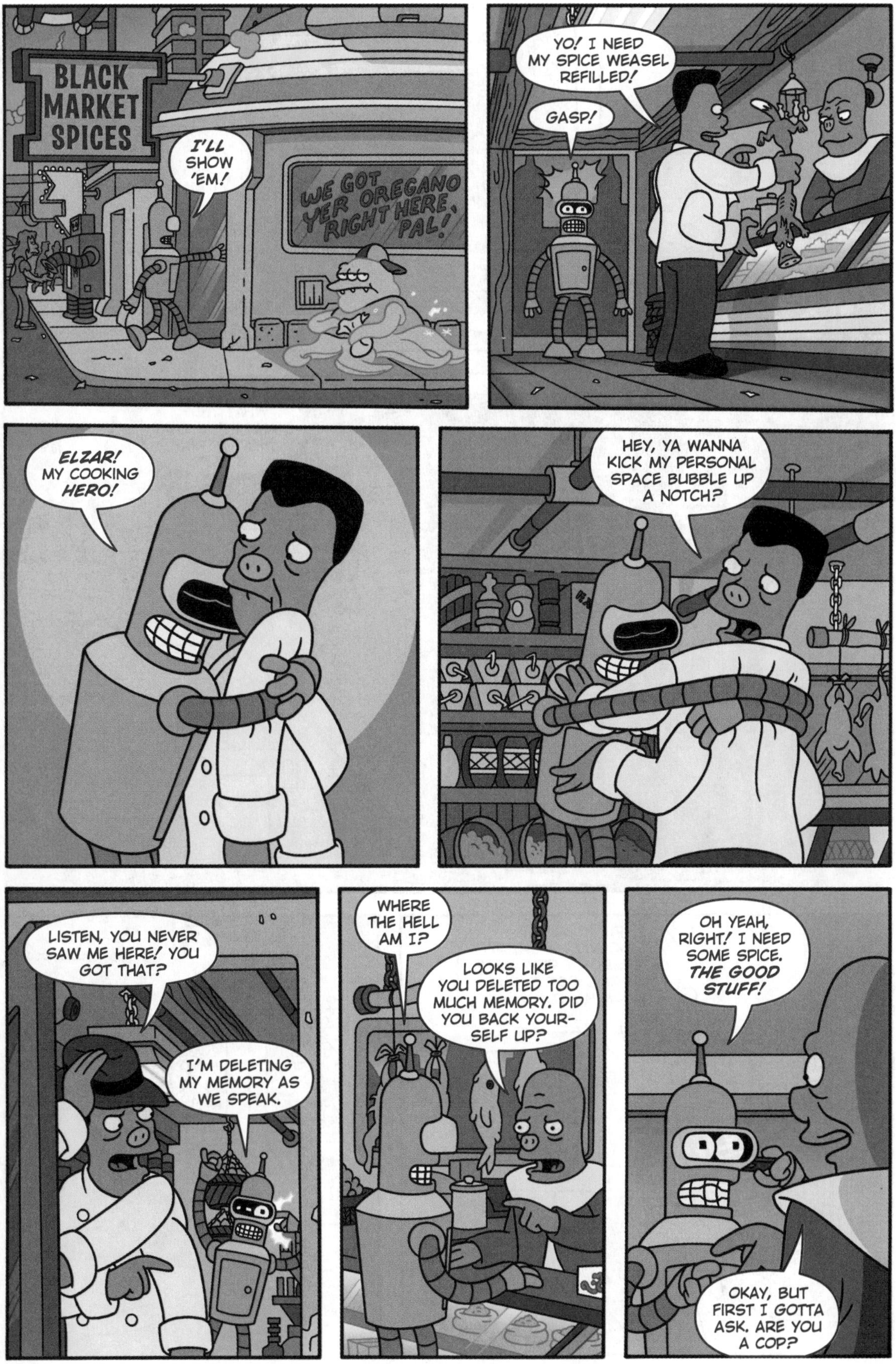
BLACK MARKET SPICES
I'LL SHOW 'EM!
WE GOT YER OREGANO RIGHT HERE, PAL!
YO! I NEED MY SPICE WEASEL REFILLED!
GASP!
ELZAR! MY COOKING HERO!
HEY, YA WANNA KICK MY PERSONAL SPACE BUBBLE UP A NOTCH?
LISTEN, YOU NEVER SAW ME HERE! YOU GOT THAT?
I'M DELETING MY MEMORY AS WE SPEAK.
WHERE THE HELL AM I?
LOOKS LIKE YOU DELETED TOO MUCH MEMORY. DID YOU BACK YOURSELF UP?
OH YEAH, RIGHT! I NEED SOME SPICE. THE GOOD STUFF!
OKAY, BUT FIRST I GOTTA ASK. ARE YOU A COP?

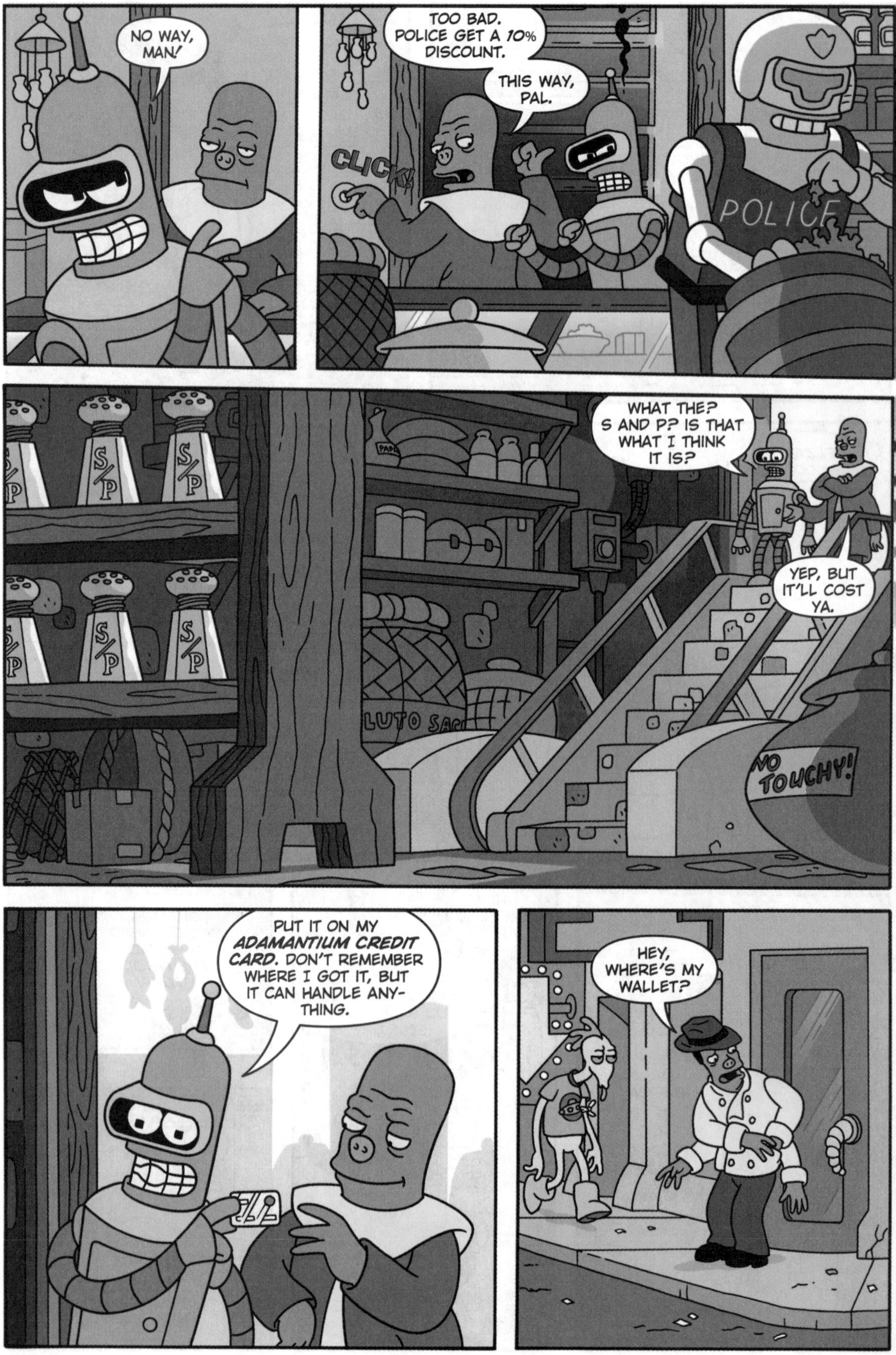
NO WAY, MAN!
TOO BAD. POLICE GET A 10% DISCOUNT.
THIS WAY, PAL.
CLICK!
POLICE
WHAT THE? S AND P? IS THAT WHAT I THINK IT IS?
YEP, BUT IT'LL COST YA.
NO TOUCHY!
PUT IT ON MY ADAMANTIUM CREDIT CARD. DON'T REMEMBER WHERE I GOT IT, BUT IT CAN HANDLE ANY-THING.
HEY, WHERE'S MY WALLET?

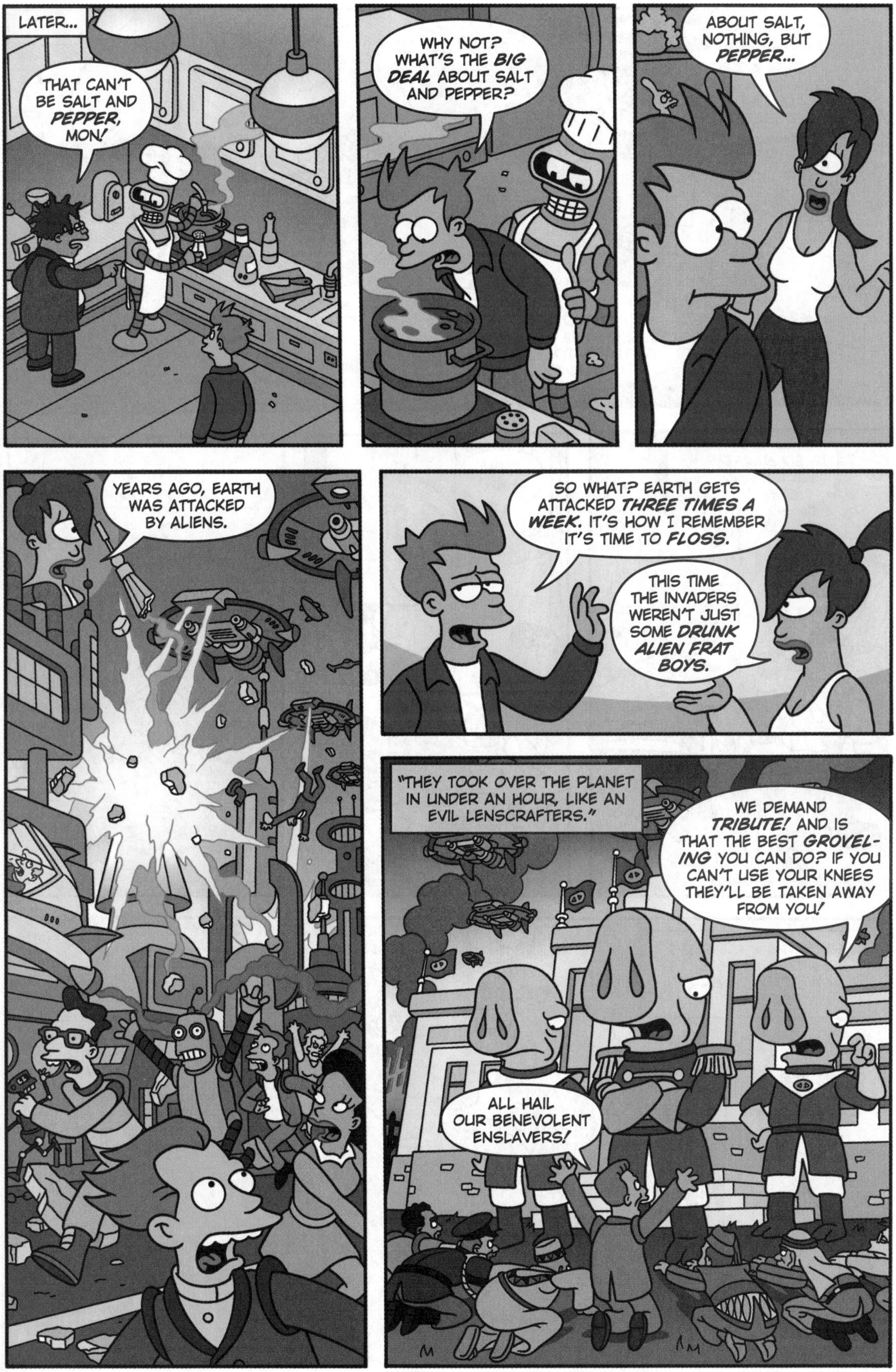

LATER...
THAT CAN'T BE SALT AND PEPPER, MON!
WHY NOT? WHAT'S THE BIG DEAL ABOUT SALT AND PEPPER?
ABOUT SALT, NOTHING, BUT PEPPER...
YEARS AGO, EARTH WAS ATTACKED BY ALIENS.
SO WHAT? EARTH GETS ATTACKED THREE TIMES A WEEK. IT'S HOW I REMEMBER IT'S TIME TO FLOSS.
THIS TIME THE INVADERS WEREN'T JUST SOME DRUNK ALIEN FRAT BOYS.
"THEY TOOK OVER THE PLANET IN UNDER AN HOUR, LIKE AN EVIL LENSCRAFTERS."
WE DEMAND TRIBUTE! AND IS THAT THE BEST GROVEL-ING YOU CAN DO? IF YOU CAN'T USE YOUR KNEES THEY'LL BE TAKEN AWAY FROM YOU!
ALL HAIL OUR BENEVOLENT ENSLAVERS!

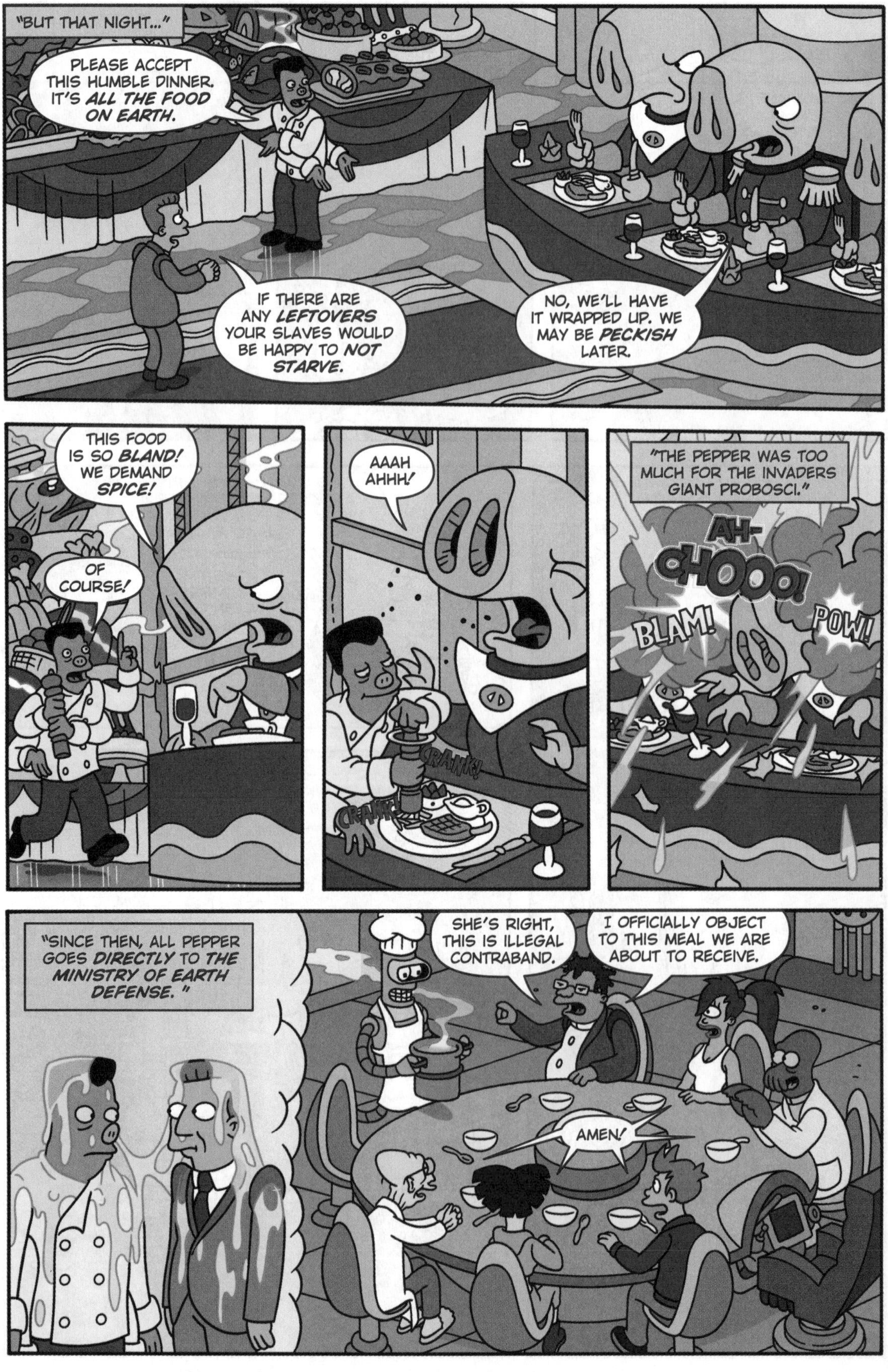

"BUT THAT NIGHT..."
PLEASE ACCEPT THIS HUMBLE DINNER. IT'S ALL THE FOOD ON EARTH.
IF THERE ARE ANY LEFTOVERS YOUR SLAVES WOULD BE HAPPY TO NOT STARVE.
NO, WE'LL HAVE IT WRAPPED UP. WE MAY BE PECKISH LATER.
THIS FOOD IS SO BLAND! WE DEMAND SPICE!
OF COURSE!
AAAH AHHH!
CRANK!
CRANK!
"THE PEPPER WAS TOO MUCH FOR THE INVADERS GIANT PROBOSCI."
AH-CHOOO!
BLAM!
POW!
"SINCE THEN, ALL PEPPER GOES DIRECTLY TO THE MINISTRY OF EARTH DEFENSE."
SHE'S RIGHT, THIS IS ILLEGAL CONTRABAND.
I OFFICIALLY OBJECT TO THIS MEAL WE ARE ABOUT TO RECEIVE.
AMEN!

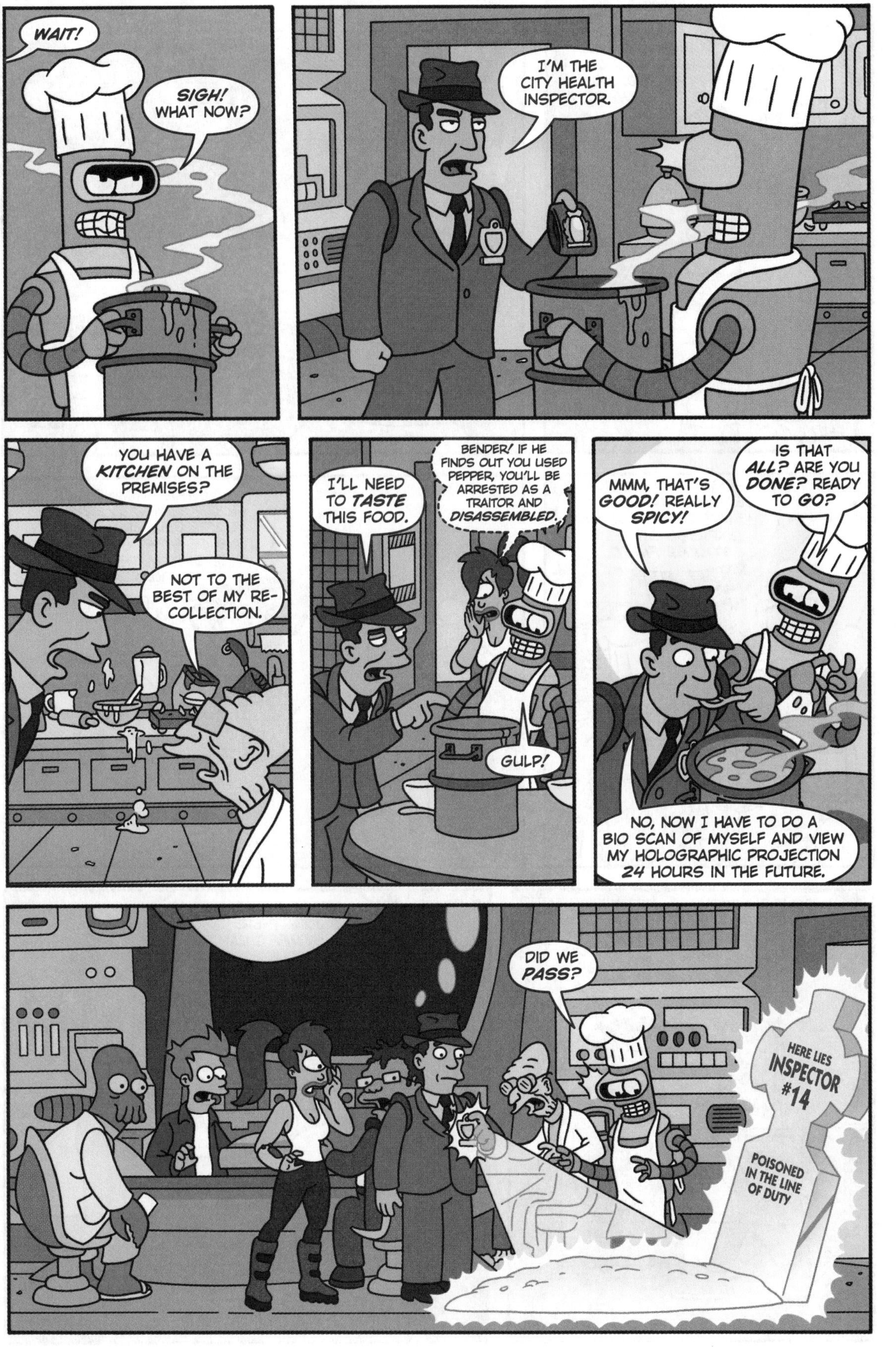

WAIT!
SIGH! WHAT NOW?
I'M THE CITY HEALTH INSPECTOR.
YOU HAVE A KITCHEN ON THE PREMISES?
NOT TO THE BEST OF MY RE-COLLECTION.
I'LL NEED TO TASTE THIS FOOD.
BENDER! IF HE FINDS OUT YOU USED PEPPER, YOU'LL BE ARRESTED AS A TRAITOR AND DISASSEMBLED.
GULP!
MMM, THAT'S GOOD! REALLY SPICY!
IS THAT ALL? ARE YOU DONE? READY TO GO?
NO, NOW I HAVE TO DO A BIO SCAN OF MYSELF AND VIEW MY HOLOGRAPHIC PROJECTION 24 HOURS IN THE FUTURE.
DID WE PASS?
HERE LIES INSPECTOR #14
POISONED IN THE LINE OF DUTY

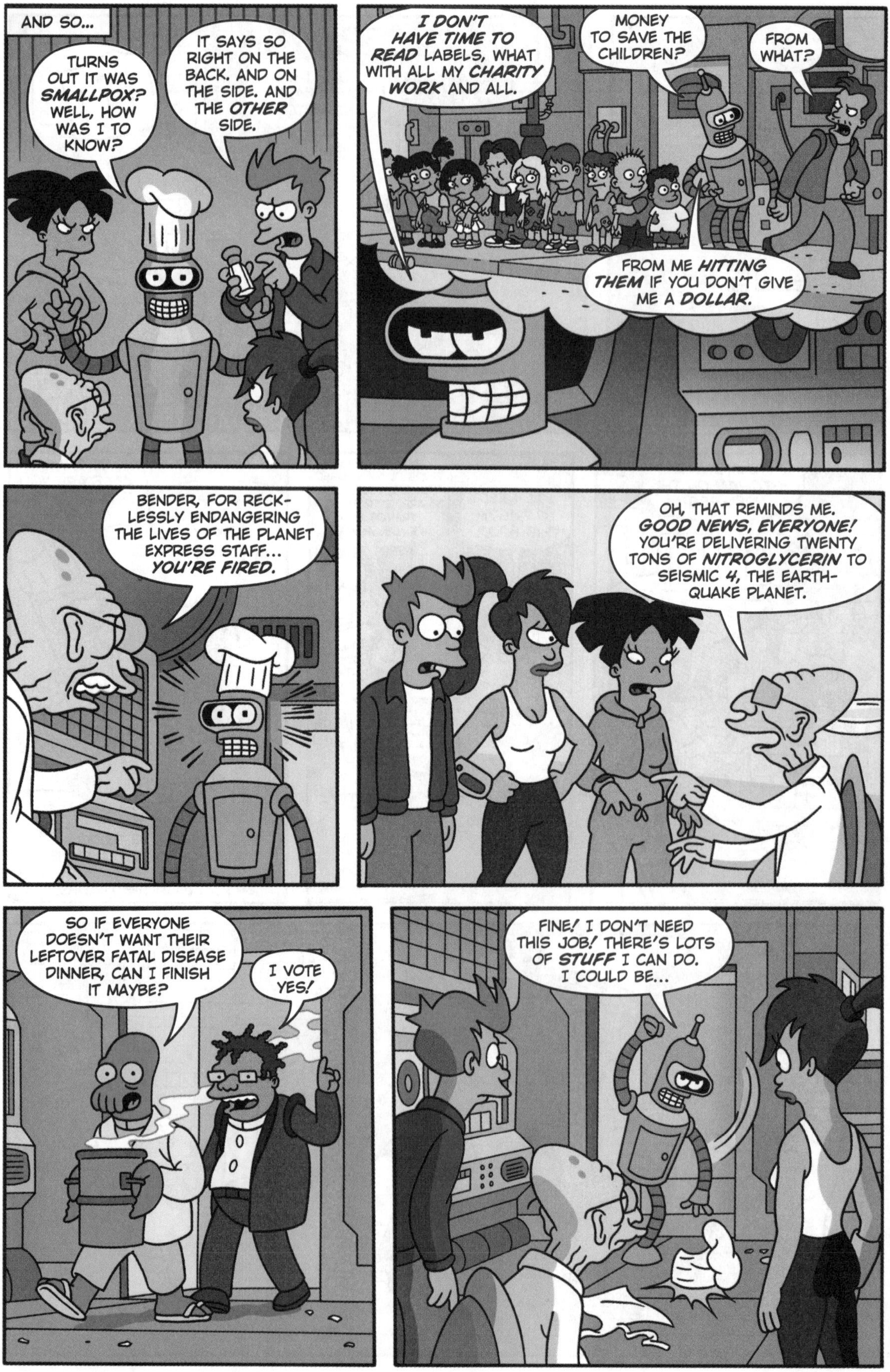

AND SO...
TURNS OUT IT WAS SMALLPOX? WELL, HOW WAS I TO KNOW?
IT SAYS SO RIGHT ON THE BACK. AND ON THE SIDE. AND THE OTHER SIDE.
I DON'T HAVE TIME TO READ LABELS, WHAT WITH ALL MY CHARITY WORK AND ALL.
MONEY TO SAVE THE CHILDREN?
FROM WHAT?
FROM ME HITTING THEM IF YOU DON'T GIVE ME A DOLLAR.
BENDER, FOR RECK-LESSLY ENDANGERING THE LIVES OF THE PLANET EXPRESS STAFF... YOU'RE FIRED.
OH, THAT REMINDS ME. GOOD NEWS, EVERYONE! YOU'RE DELIVERING TWENTY TONS OF NITROGLYCERIN TO SEISMIC 4, THE EARTH-QUAKE PLANET.
SO IF EVERYONE DOESN'T WANT THEIR LEFTOVER FATAL DISEASE DINNER, CAN I FINISH IT MAYBE?
I VOTE YES!
FINE! I DON'T NEED THIS JOB! THERE'S LOTS OF STUFF I CAN DO. I COULD BE...

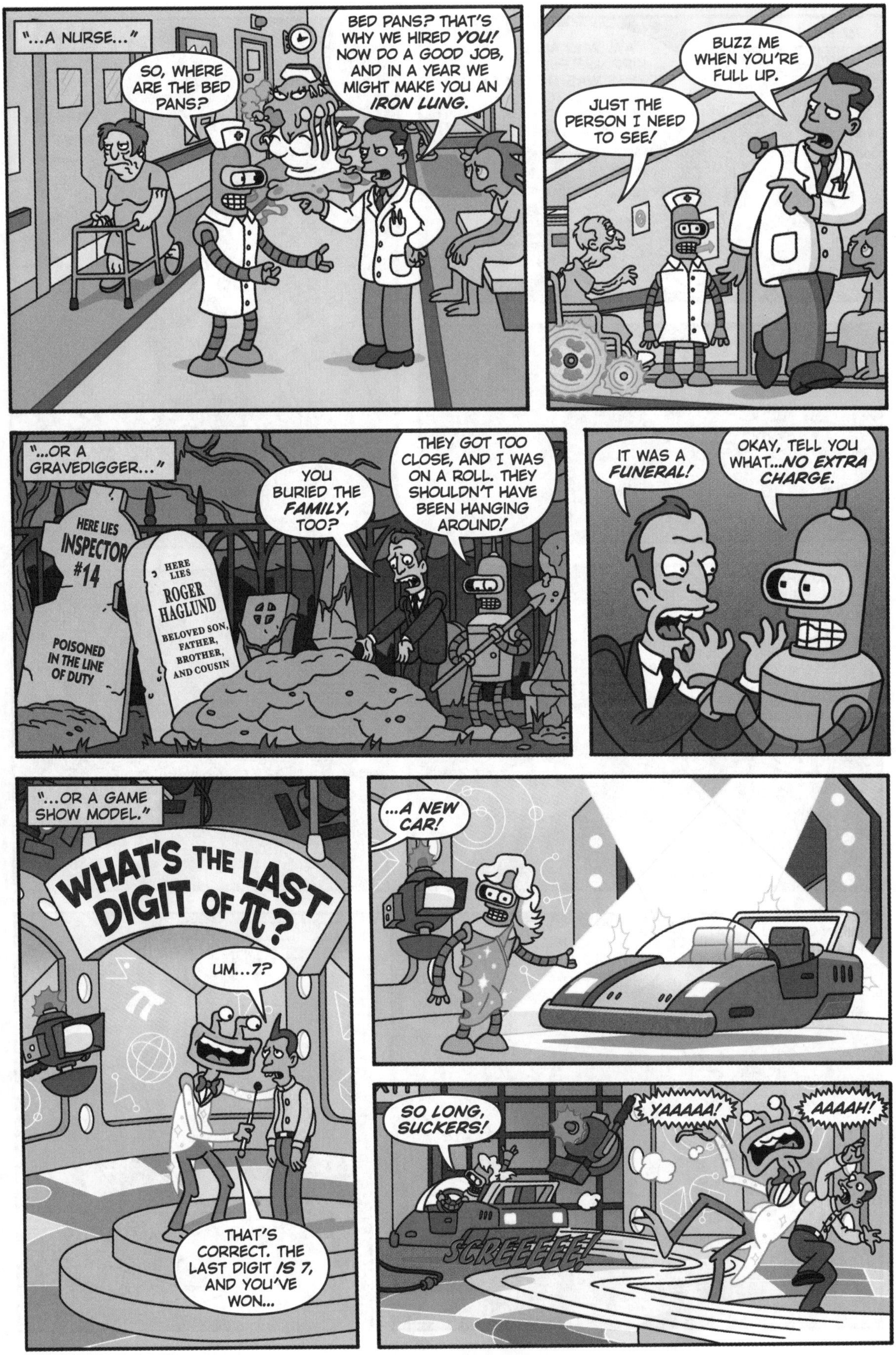
"...A NURSE..."
SO, WHERE ARE THE BED PANS?
BED PANS? THAT'S WHY WE HIRED YOU! NOW DO A GOOD JOB, AND IN A YEAR WE MIGHT MAKE YOU AN IRON LUNG.
BUZZ ME WHEN YOU'RE FULL UP.
JUST THE PERSON I NEED TO SEE!
"...OR A GRAVEDIGGER..."
HERE LIES INSPECTOR #14 POISONED IN THE LINE OF DUTY
HERE LIES ROGER HAGLUND BELOVED SON, FATHER, BROTHER, AND COUSIN
YOU BURIED THE FAMILY, TOO?
THEY GOT TOO CLOSE, AND I WAS ON A ROLL. THEY SHOULDN'T HAVE BEEN HANGING AROUND!
IT WAS A FUNERAL!
OKAY, TELL YOU WHAT...NO EXTRA CHARGE.
"...OR A GAME SHOW MODEL."
WHAT'S THE LAST DIGIT OF π?
UM...7?
THAT'S CORRECT. THE LAST DIGIT IS 7, AND YOU'VE WON...
...A NEW CAR!
SO LONG, SUCKERS!
YAAAAA!
AAAAH!
SCREEEEEE!

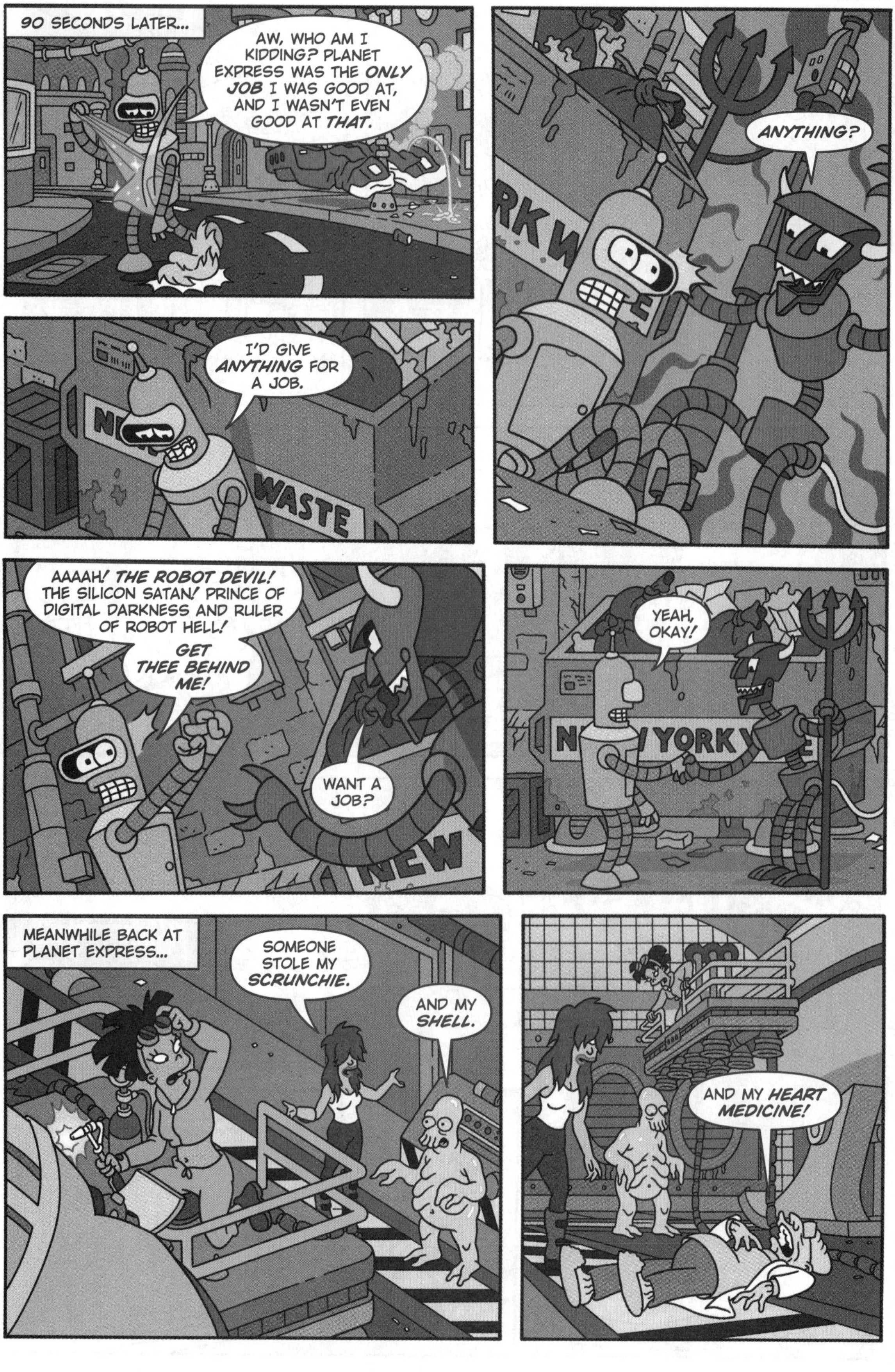
90 SECONDS LATER...
AW, WHO AM I KIDDING? PLANET EXPRESS WAS THE *ONLY JOB* I WAS GOOD AT, AND I WASN'T EVEN GOOD AT *THAT*.
*ANYTHING?*
I'D GIVE *ANYTHING* FOR A JOB.
WASTE
AAAAH! *THE ROBOT DEVIL!* THE SILICON SATAN! PRINCE OF DIGITAL DARKNESS AND RULER OF ROBOT HELL!
*GET THEE BEHIND ME!*
WANT A JOB?
NEW
YEAH, OKAY!
YORK
MEANWHILE BACK AT PLANET EXPRESS...
SOMEONE STOLE MY *SCRUNCHIE*.
AND MY *SHELL*.
AND MY *HEART MEDICINE!*

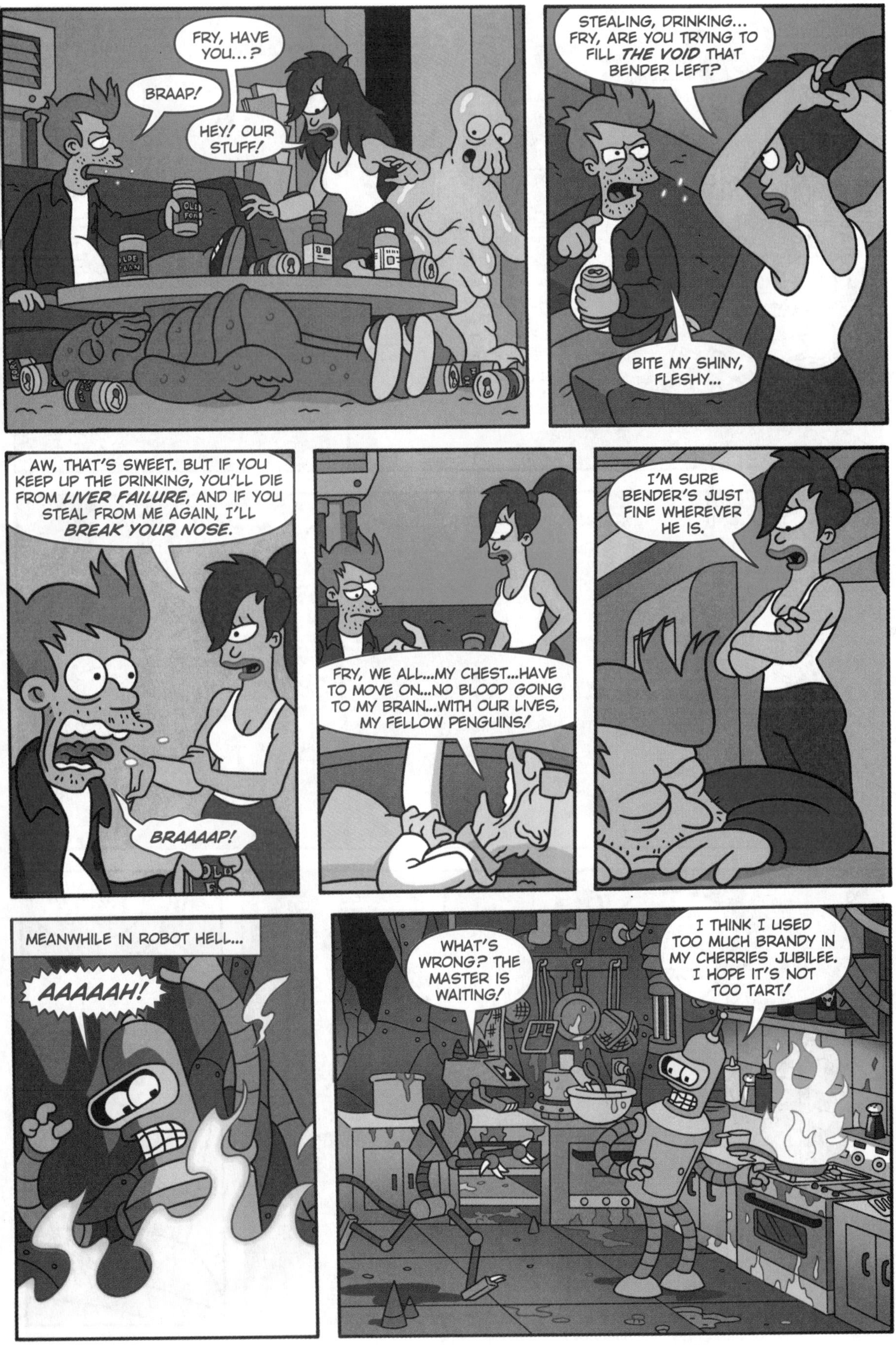
FRY, HAVE YOU...?
BRAAP!
HEY! OUR STUFF!
STEALING, DRINKING... FRY, ARE YOU TRYING TO FILL THE VOID THAT BENDER LEFT?
BITE MY SHINY, FLESHY...
AW, THAT'S SWEET. BUT IF YOU KEEP UP THE DRINKING, YOU'LL DIE FROM LIVER FAILURE, AND IF YOU STEAL FROM ME AGAIN, I'LL BREAK YOUR NOSE.
BRAAAAP!
FRY, WE ALL...MY CHEST...HAVE TO MOVE ON...NO BLOOD GOING TO MY BRAIN...WITH OUR LIVES, MY FELLOW PENGUINS!
I'M SURE BENDER'S JUST FINE WHEREVER HE IS.
MEANWHILE IN ROBOT HELL...
AAAAAH!
WHAT'S WRONG? THE MASTER IS WAITING!
I THINK I USED TOO MUCH BRANDY IN MY CHERRIES JUBILEE. I HOPE IT'S NOT TOO TART!

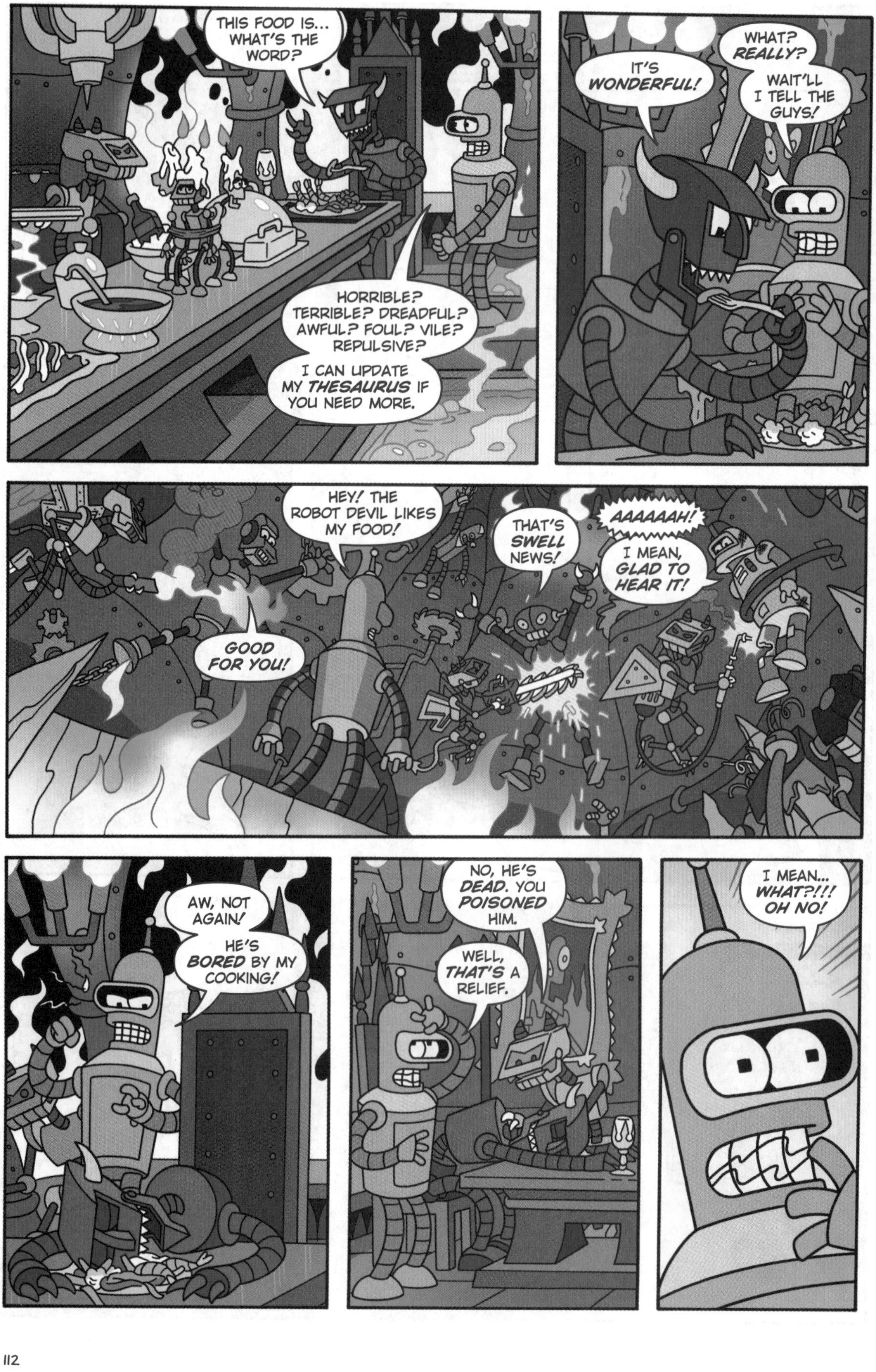
THIS FOOD IS... WHAT'S THE WORD?
HORRIBLE? TERRIBLE? DREADFUL? AWFUL? FOUL? VILE? REPULSIVE?
I CAN UPDATE MY *THESAURUS* IF YOU NEED MORE.
IT'S *WONDERFUL!*
WHAT? *REALLY?*
WAIT'LL I TELL THE GUYS!
HEY! THE ROBOT DEVIL LIKES MY FOOD!
GOOD FOR YOU!
THAT'S *SWELL* NEWS!
AAAAAAH!
I MEAN, *GLAD TO HEAR IT!*
AW, NOT AGAIN!
HE'S *BORED* BY MY COOKING!
NO, HE'S *DEAD*. YOU *POISONED* HIM.
WELL, *THAT'S* A RELIEF.
I MEAN... *WHAT?!!! OH NO!*

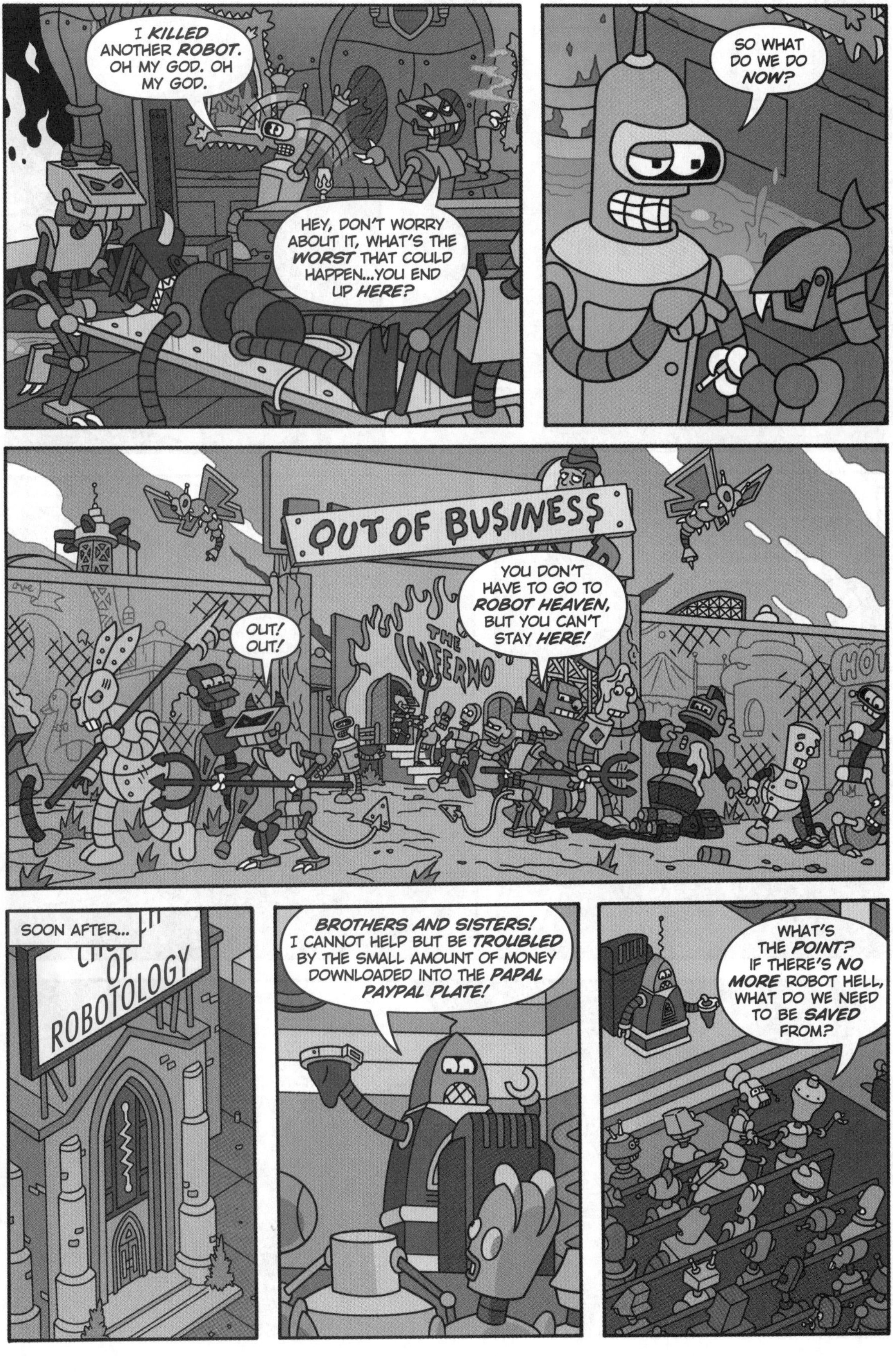
I KILLED ANOTHER ROBOT. OH MY GOD. OH MY GOD.
HEY, DON'T WORRY ABOUT IT, WHAT'S THE WORST THAT COULD HAPPEN...YOU END UP HERE?
SO WHAT DO WE DO NOW?
OUT OF BU$INE$$
THE INFERNO
OUT! OUT!
YOU DON'T HAVE TO GO TO ROBOT HEAVEN, BUT YOU CAN'T STAY HERE!
SOON AFTER...
CHURCH OF ROBOTOLOGY
BROTHERS AND SISTERS! I CANNOT HELP BUT BE TROUBLED BY THE SMALL AMOUNT OF MONEY DOWNLOADED INTO THE PAPAL PAYPAL PLATE!
WHAT'S THE POINT? IF THERE'S NO MORE ROBOT HELL, WHAT DO WE NEED TO BE SAVED FROM?

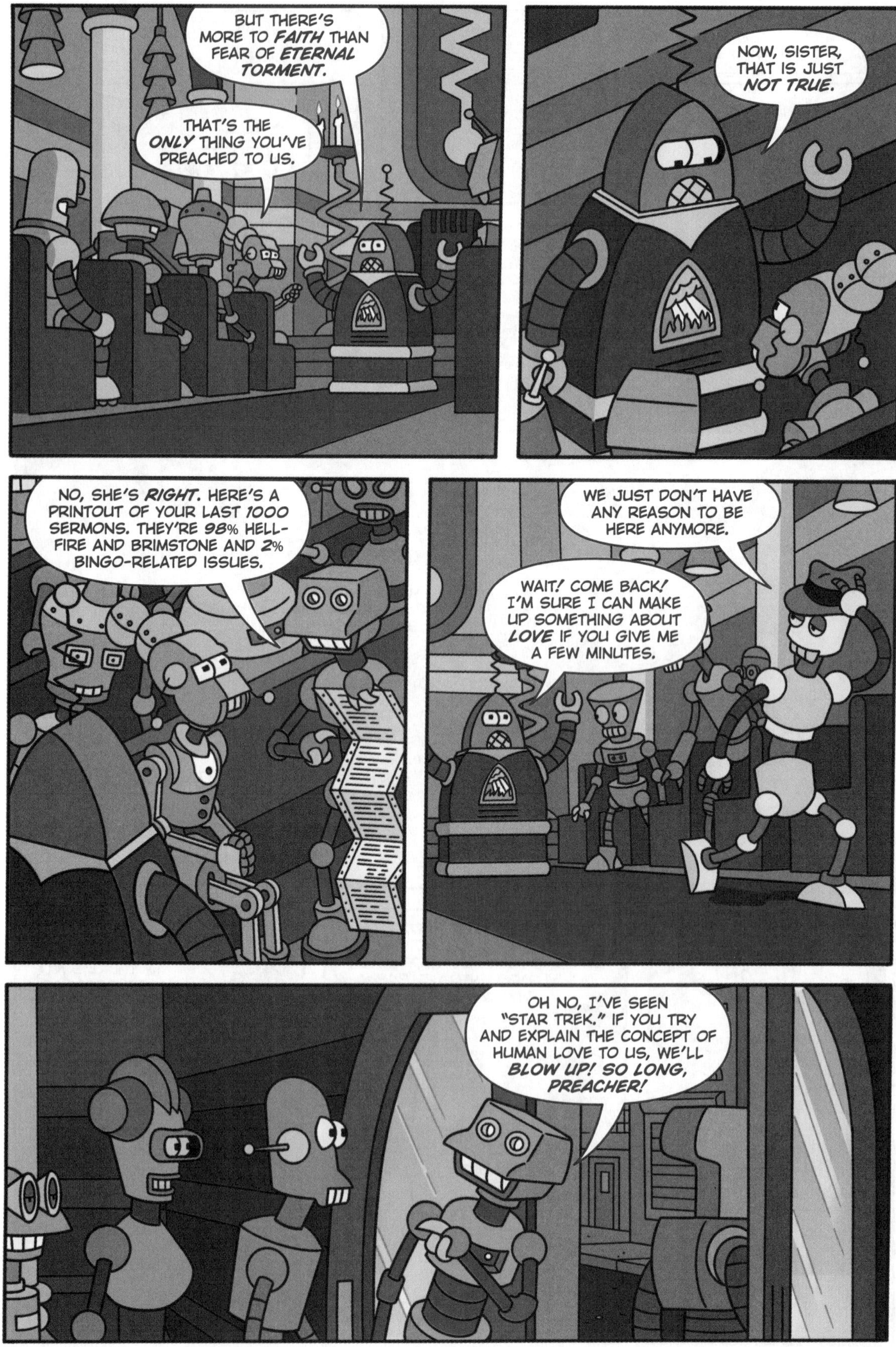
BUT THERE'S MORE TO FAITH THAN FEAR OF ETERNAL TORMENT.
THAT'S THE ONLY THING YOU'VE PREACHED TO US.
NOW, SISTER, THAT IS JUST NOT TRUE.
NO, SHE'S RIGHT. HERE'S A PRINTOUT OF YOUR LAST 1000 SERMONS. THEY'RE 98% HELL-FIRE AND BRIMSTONE AND 2% BINGO-RELATED ISSUES.
WE JUST DON'T HAVE ANY REASON TO BE HERE ANYMORE.
WAIT! COME BACK! I'M SURE I CAN MAKE UP SOMETHING ABOUT LOVE IF YOU GIVE ME A FEW MINUTES.
OH NO, I'VE SEEN "STAR TREK." IF YOU TRY AND EXPLAIN THE CONCEPT OF HUMAN LOVE TO US, WE'LL BLOW UP! SO LONG, PREACHER!

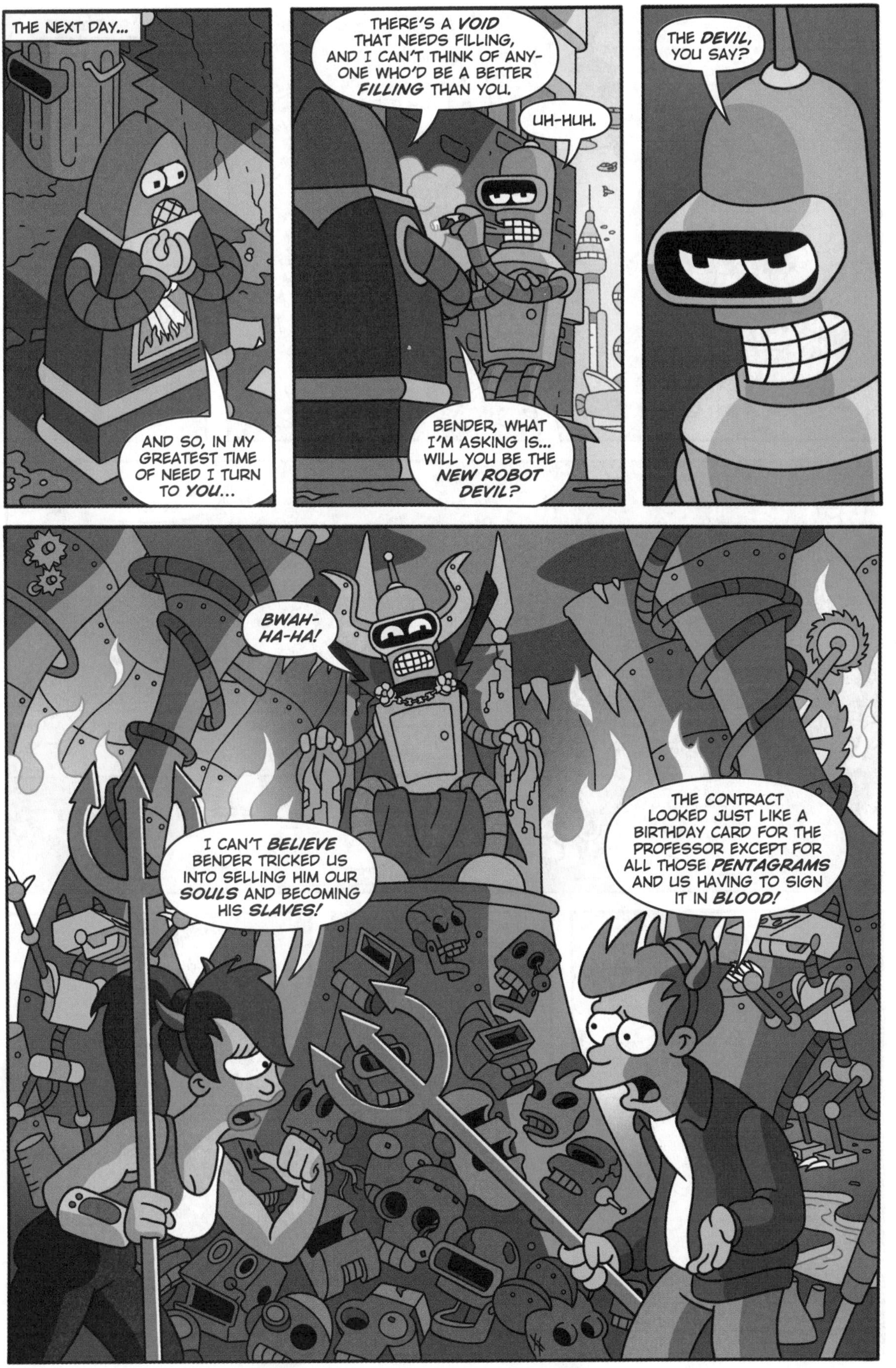
THE NEXT DAY...
AND SO, IN MY GREATEST TIME OF NEED I TURN TO *YOU*...
THERE'S A *VOID* THAT NEEDS FILLING, AND I CAN'T THINK OF ANY-ONE WHO'D BE A BETTER *FILLING* THAN YOU.
UH-HUH.
BENDER, WHAT I'M ASKING IS... WILL YOU BE THE *NEW ROBOT DEVIL?*
THE *DEVIL*, YOU SAY?
*BWAH-HA-HA!*
I CAN'T *BELIEVE* BENDER TRICKED US INTO SELLING HIM OUR *SOULS* AND BECOMING HIS *SLAVES!*
THE CONTRACT LOOKED JUST LIKE A BIRTHDAY CARD FOR THE PROFESSOR EXCEPT FOR ALL THOSE *PENTAGRAMS* AND US HAVING TO SIGN IT IN *BLOOD!*

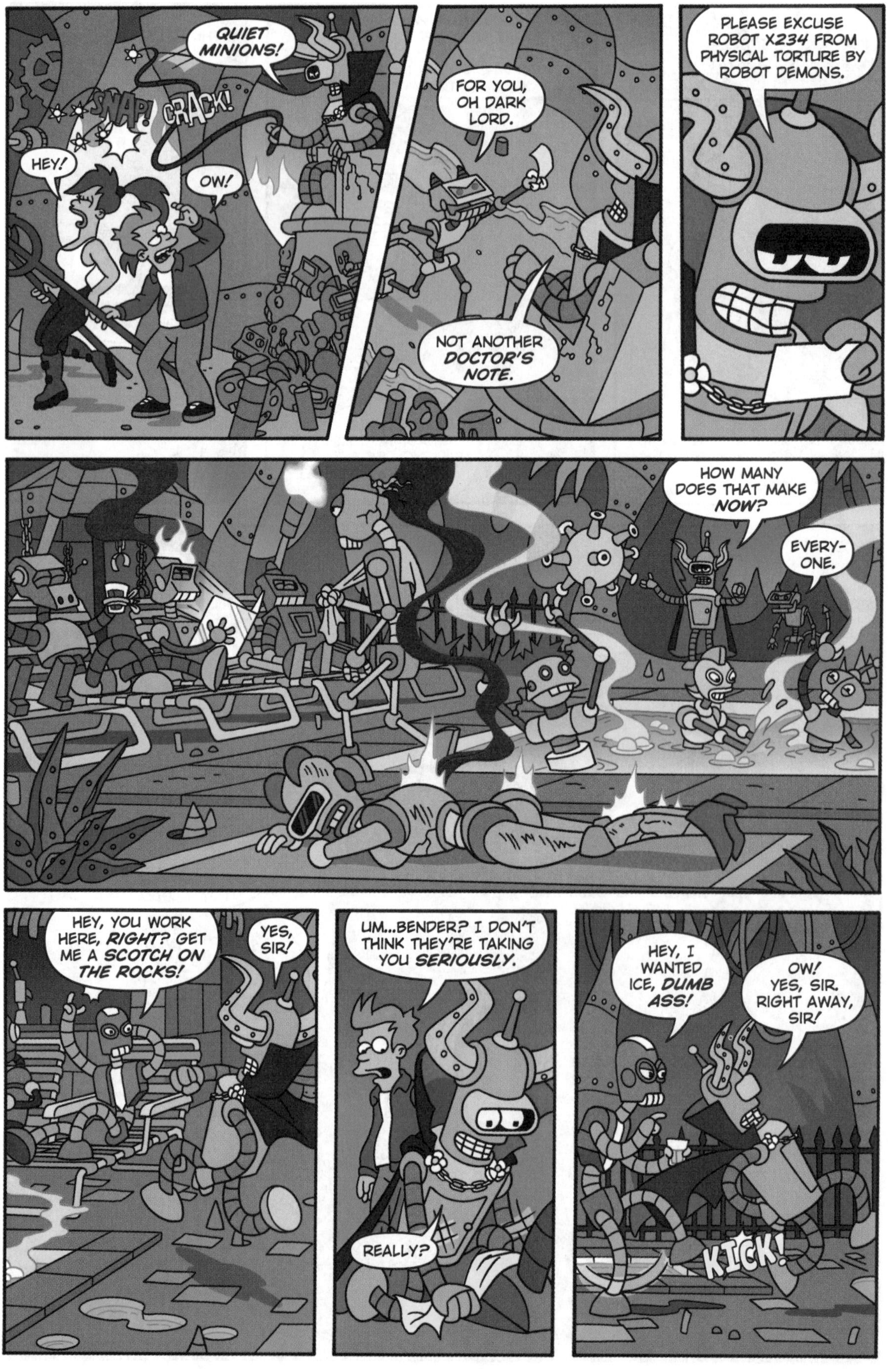
QUIET MINIONS!
SNAP! CRACK!
HEY!
OW!
FOR YOU, OH DARK LORD.
NOT ANOTHER DOCTOR'S NOTE.
PLEASE EXCUSE ROBOT X234 FROM PHYSICAL TORTURE BY ROBOT DEMONS.
HOW MANY DOES THAT MAKE NOW?
EVERY-ONE.
HEY, YOU WORK HERE, RIGHT? GET ME A SCOTCH ON THE ROCKS!
YES, SIR!
UM...BENDER? I DON'T THINK THEY'RE TAKING YOU SERIOUSLY.
REALLY?
HEY, I WANTED ICE, DUMB ASS!
OW! YES, SIR. RIGHT AWAY, SIR!
KICK!

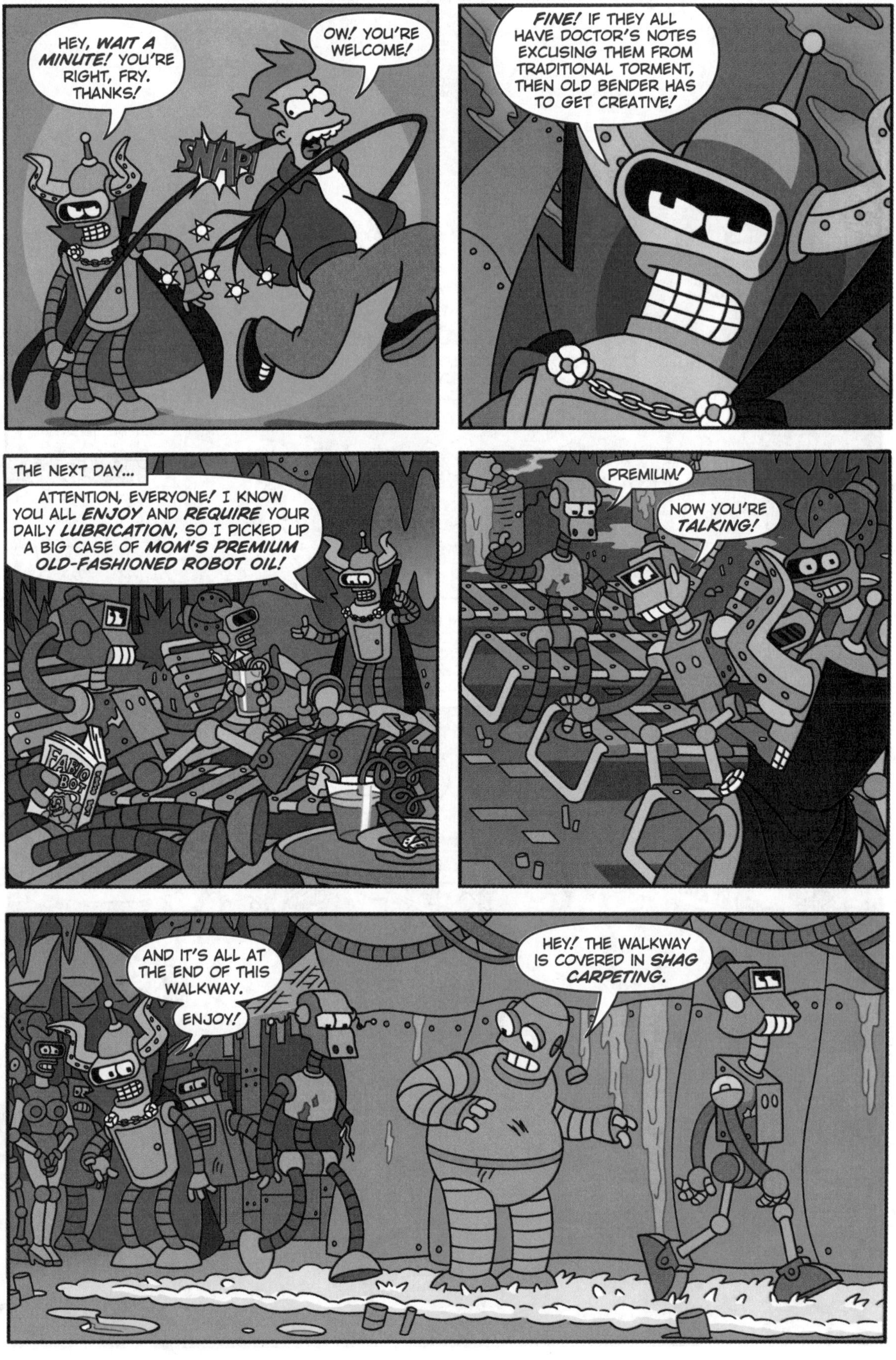
HEY, WAIT A MINUTE! YOU'RE RIGHT, FRY. THANKS!
OW! YOU'RE WELCOME!
SNAP!
FINE! IF THEY ALL HAVE DOCTOR'S NOTES EXCUSING THEM FROM TRADITIONAL TORMENT, THEN OLD BENDER HAS TO GET CREATIVE!
THE NEXT DAY...
ATTENTION, EVERYONE! I KNOW YOU ALL ENJOY AND REQUIRE YOUR DAILY LUBRICATION, SO I PICKED UP A BIG CASE OF MOM'S PREMIUM OLD-FASHIONED ROBOT OIL!
FABIO BOT
PREMIUM!
NOW YOU'RE TALKING!
AND IT'S ALL AT THE END OF THIS WALKWAY.
ENJOY!
HEY! THE WALKWAY IS COVERED IN SHAG CARPETING.

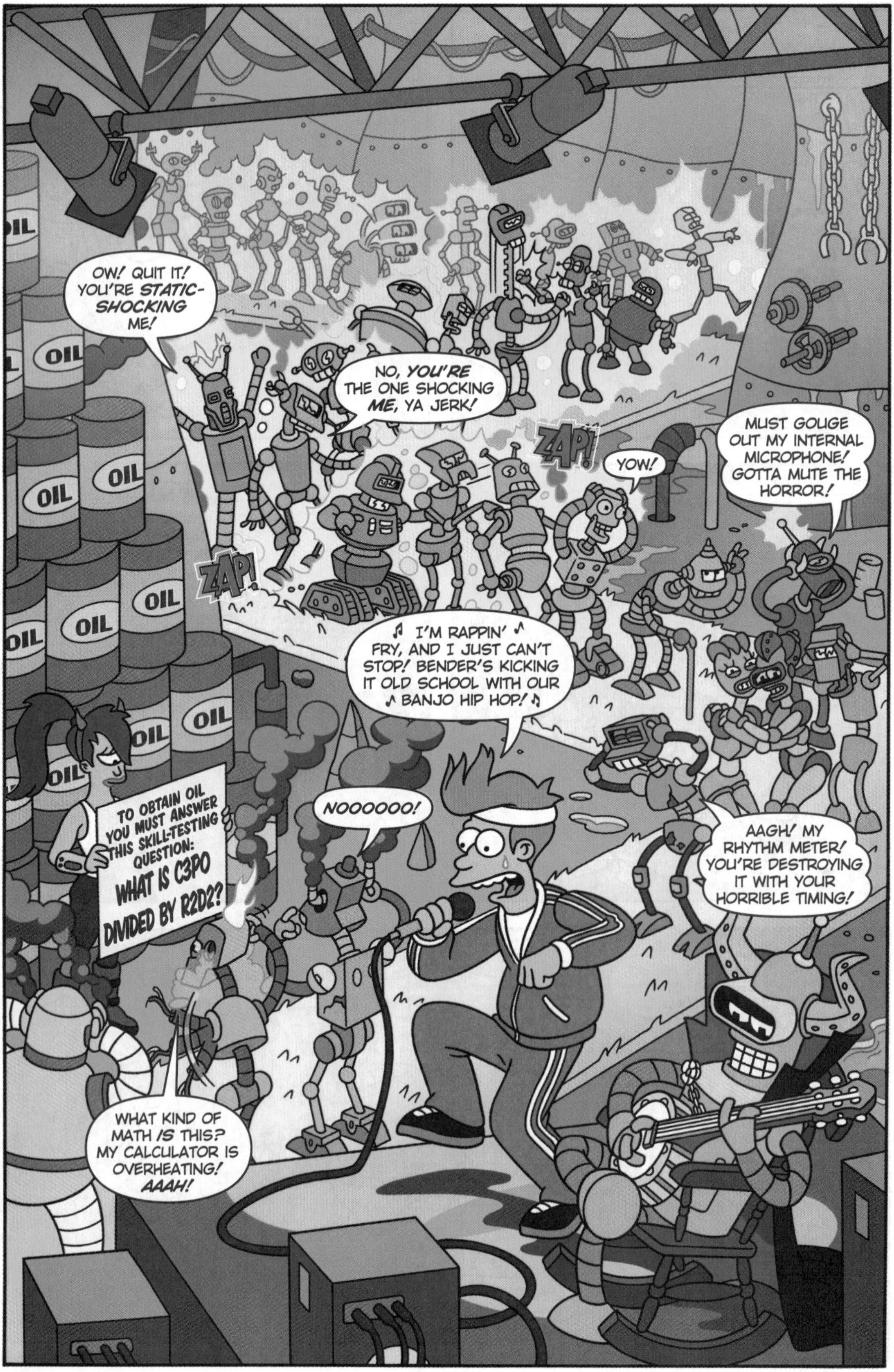
OIL
OW! QUIT IT! YOU'RE STATIC-SHOCKING ME!
NO, YOU'RE THE ONE SHOCKING ME, YA JERK!
ZAP!
YOW!
MUST GOUGE OUT MY INTERNAL MICROPHONE! GOTTA MUTE THE HORROR!
ZAP!
♪ I'M RAPPIN' ♪ FRY, AND I JUST CAN'T STOP! BENDER'S KICKING IT OLD SCHOOL WITH OUR ♪ BANJO HIP HOP! ♪
TO OBTAIN OIL YOU MUST ANSWER THIS SKILL-TESTING QUESTION: WHAT IS C3PO DIVIDED BY R2D2?
NOOOOOO!
AAGH! MY RHYTHM METER! YOU'RE DESTROYING IT WITH YOUR HORRIBLE TIMING!
WHAT KIND OF MATH IS THIS? MY CALCULATOR IS OVERHEATING! AAAH!

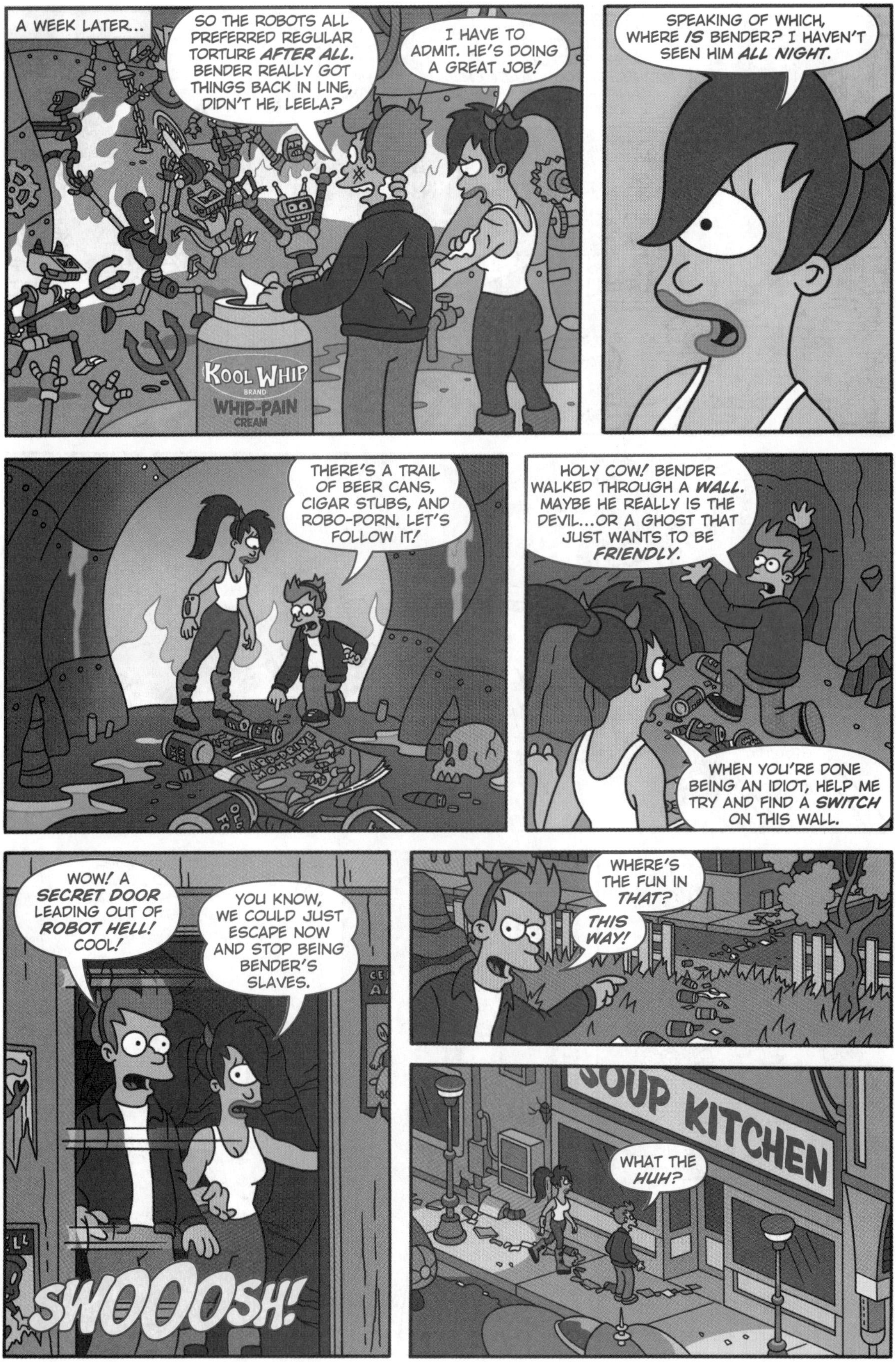
A WEEK LATER...
SO THE ROBOTS ALL PREFERRED REGULAR TORTURE AFTER ALL. BENDER REALLY GOT THINGS BACK IN LINE, DIDN'T HE, LEELA?
I HAVE TO ADMIT. HE'S DOING A GREAT JOB!
KOOL WHIP BRAND WHIP-PAIN CREAM
SPEAKING OF WHICH, WHERE IS BENDER? I HAVEN'T SEEN HIM ALL NIGHT.
THERE'S A TRAIL OF BEER CANS, CIGAR STUBS, AND ROBO-PORN. LET'S FOLLOW IT!
HARD-DRIVE MONTHLY
HOLY COW! BENDER WALKED THROUGH A WALL. MAYBE HE REALLY IS THE DEVIL...OR A GHOST THAT JUST WANTS TO BE FRIENDLY.
WHEN YOU'RE DONE BEING AN IDIOT, HELP ME TRY AND FIND A SWITCH ON THIS WALL.
WOW! A SECRET DOOR LEADING OUT OF ROBOT HELL! COOL!
YOU KNOW, WE COULD JUST ESCAPE NOW AND STOP BEING BENDER'S SLAVES.
SWOOOSH!
WHERE'S THE FUN IN THAT?
THIS WAY!
SOUP KITCHEN
WHAT THE HUH?

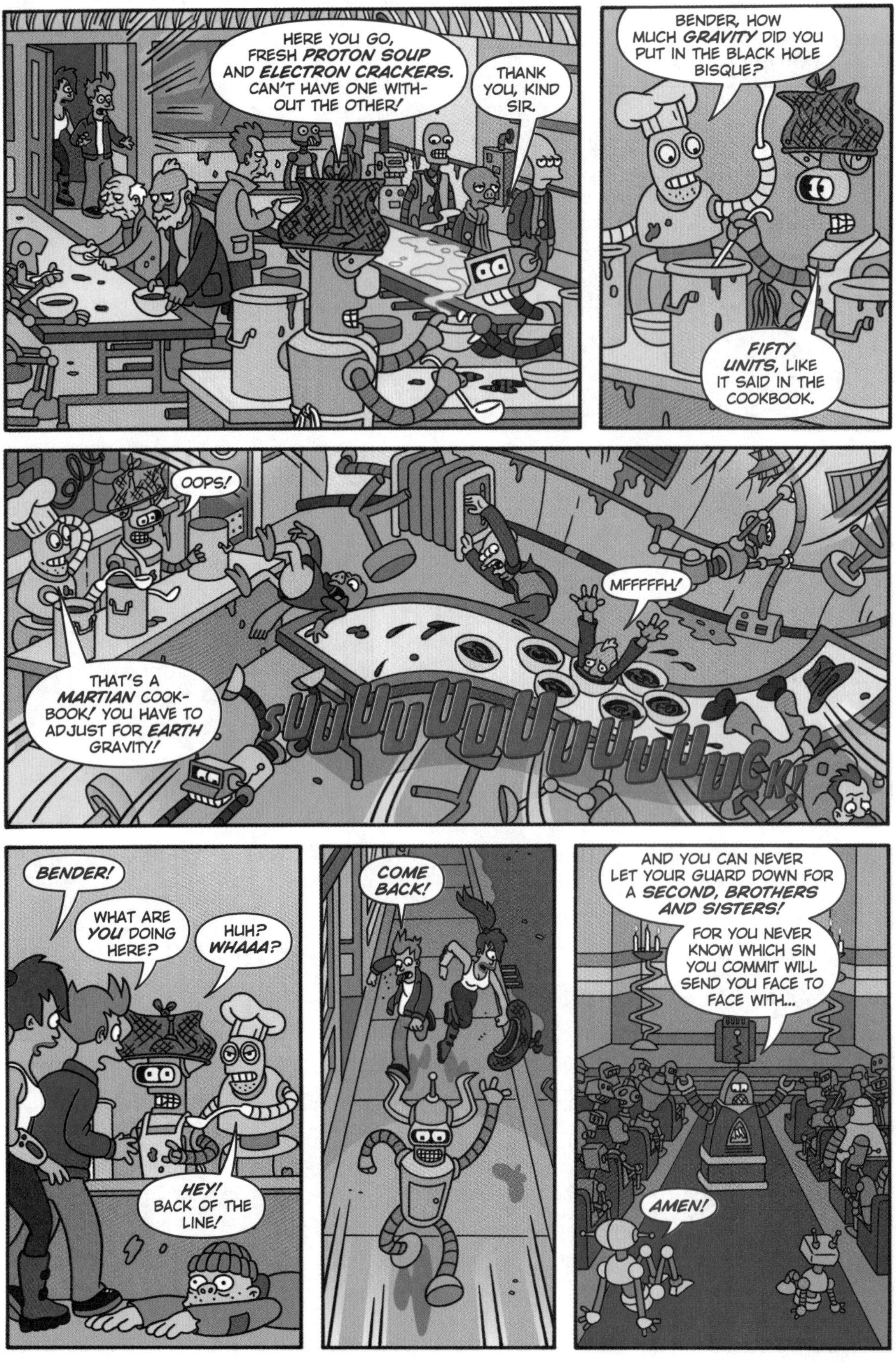
HERE YOU GO, FRESH PROTON SOUP AND ELECTRON CRACKERS. CAN'T HAVE ONE WITH-OUT THE OTHER!
THANK YOU, KIND SIR.
BENDER, HOW MUCH GRAVITY DID YOU PUT IN THE BLACK HOLE BISQUE?
FIFTY UNITS, LIKE IT SAID IN THE COOKBOOK.
OOPS!
THAT'S A MARTIAN COOK-BOOK! YOU HAVE TO ADJUST FOR EARTH GRAVITY!
MFFFFFH!
SUUUUUUUUUUUUUUUUUCK!
BENDER!
WHAT ARE YOU DOING HERE?
HUH? WHAAA?
HEY! BACK OF THE LINE!
COME BACK!
AND YOU CAN NEVER LET YOUR GUARD DOWN FOR A SECOND, BROTHERS AND SISTERS!
FOR YOU NEVER KNOW WHICH SIN YOU COMMIT WILL SEND YOU FACE TO FACE WITH...
AMEN!

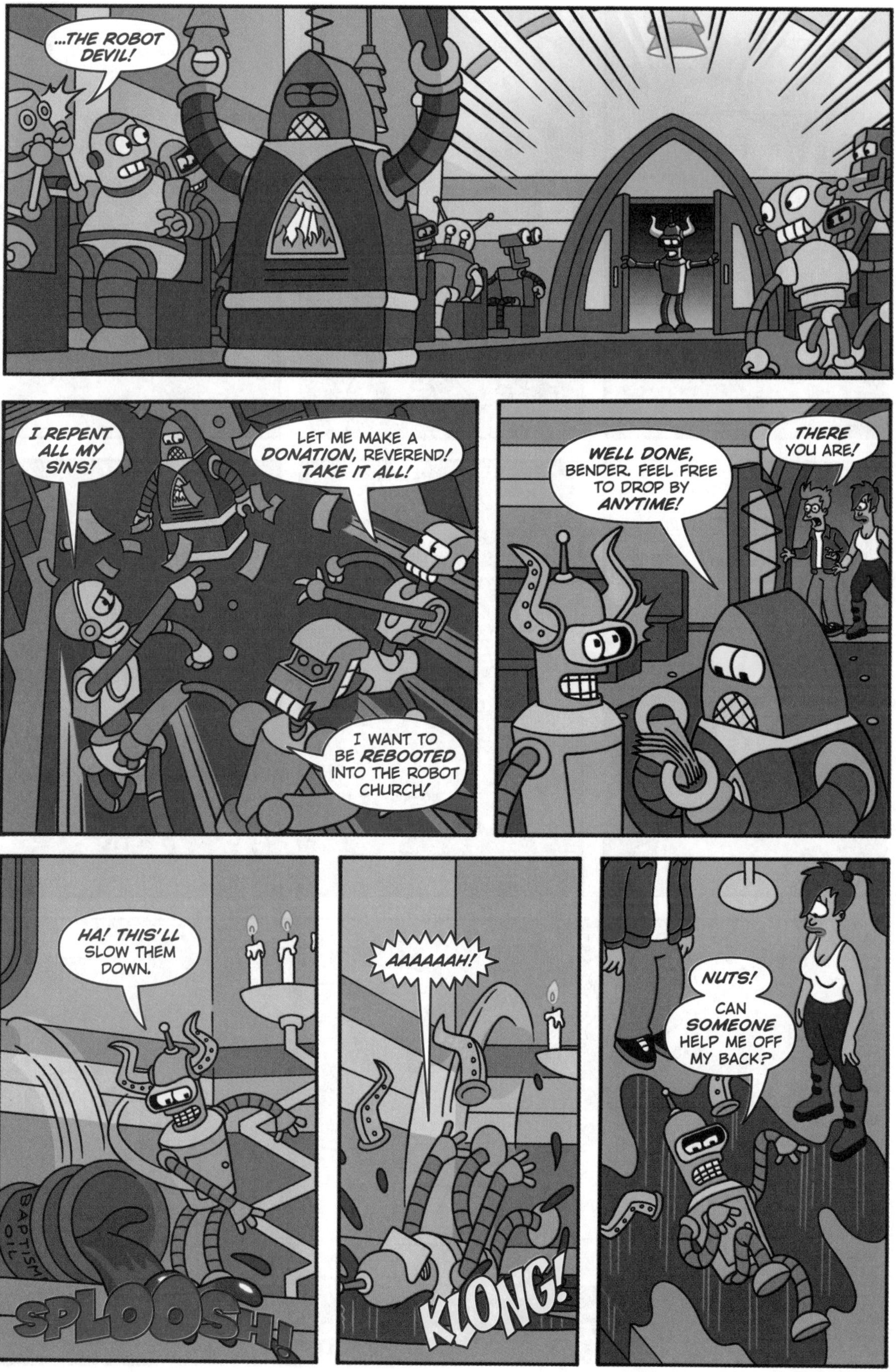
...THE ROBOT DEVIL!
I REPENT ALL MY SINS!
LET ME MAKE A DONATION, REVEREND! TAKE IT ALL!
I WANT TO BE REBOOTED INTO THE ROBOT CHURCH!
WELL DONE, BENDER. FEEL FREE TO DROP BY ANYTIME!
THERE YOU ARE!
HA! THIS'LL SLOW THEM DOWN.
BAPTISM OIL
SPLOOSH!
AAAAAAH!
KLONG!
NUTS!
CAN SOMEONE HELP ME OFF MY BACK?

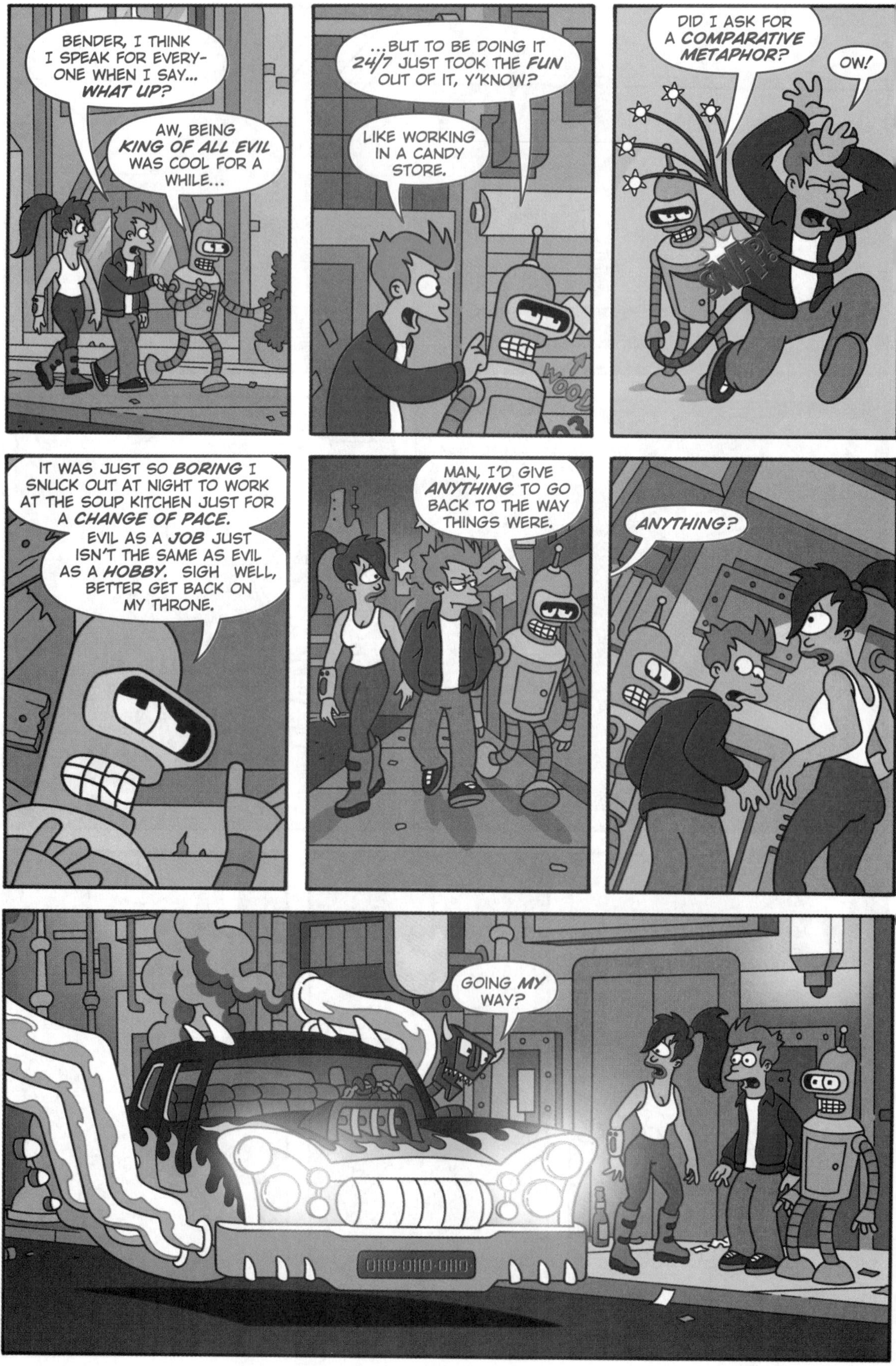
BENDER, I THINK I SPEAK FOR EVERYONE WHEN I SAY... *WHAT UP?*
AW, BEING *KING OF ALL EVIL* WAS COOL FOR A WHILE...
...BUT TO BE DOING IT *24/7* JUST TOOK THE *FUN* OUT OF IT, Y'KNOW?
LIKE WORKING IN A CANDY STORE.
DID I ASK FOR A *COMPARATIVE METAPHOR?*
OW!
SNAP!
IT WAS JUST SO *BORING* I SNUCK OUT AT NIGHT TO WORK AT THE SOUP KITCHEN JUST FOR A *CHANGE OF PACE.*
EVIL AS A *JOB* JUST ISN'T THE SAME AS EVIL AS A *HOBBY.* SIGH WELL, BETTER GET BACK ON MY THRONE.
MAN, I'D GIVE *ANYTHING* TO GO BACK TO THE WAY THINGS WERE.
*ANYTHING?*
GOING *MY* WAY?
0110·0110·0110

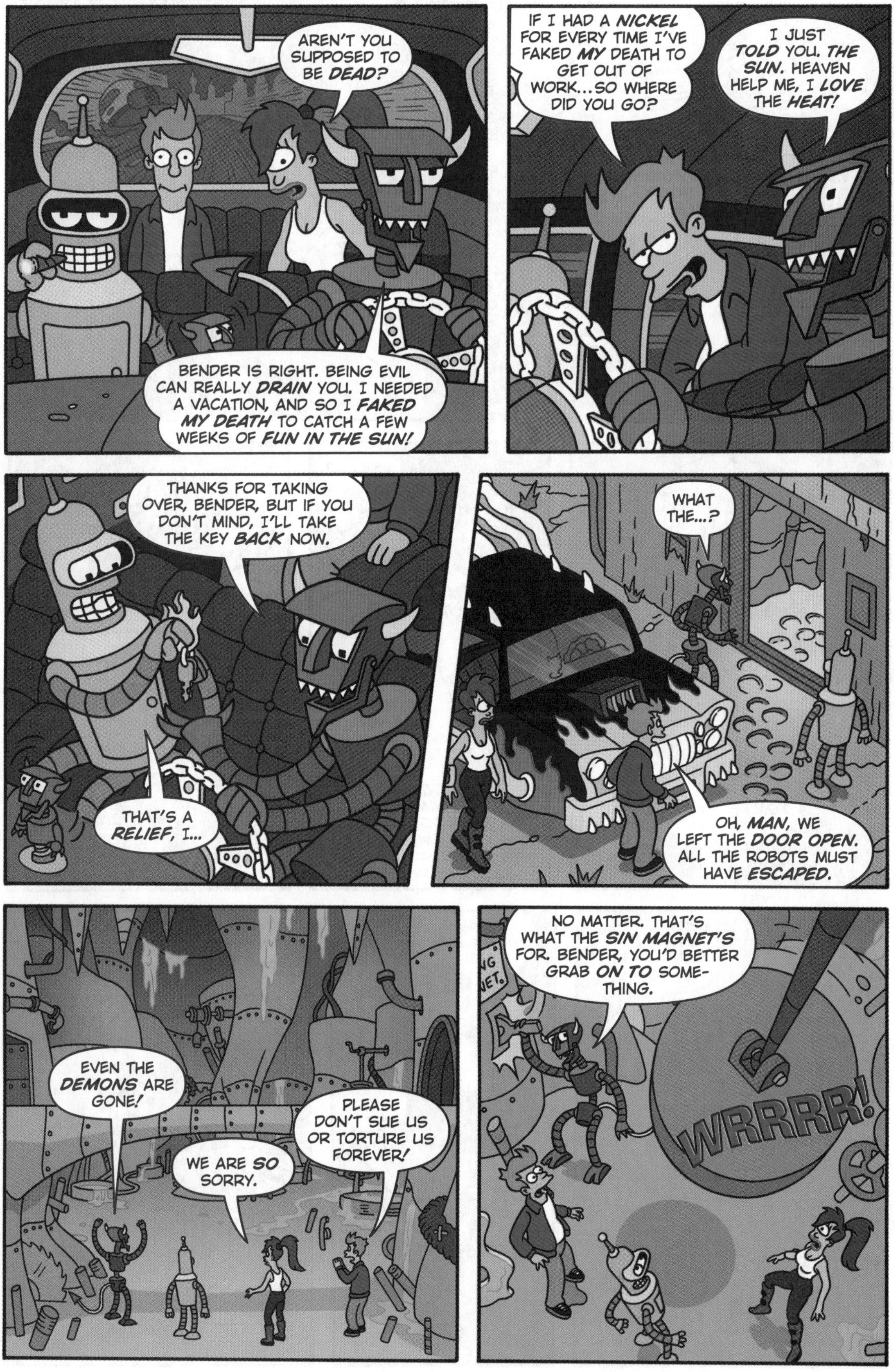
AREN'T YOU SUPPOSED TO BE DEAD?
BENDER IS RIGHT. BEING EVIL CAN REALLY DRAIN YOU. I NEEDED A VACATION, AND SO I FAKED MY DEATH TO CATCH A FEW WEEKS OF FUN IN THE SUN!
IF I HAD A NICKEL FOR EVERY TIME I'VE FAKED MY DEATH TO GET OUT OF WORK...SO WHERE DID YOU GO?
I JUST TOLD YOU. THE SUN. HEAVEN HELP ME, I LOVE THE HEAT!
THANKS FOR TAKING OVER, BENDER, BUT IF YOU DON'T MIND, I'LL TAKE THE KEY BACK NOW.
THAT'S A RELIEF, I...
WHAT THE...?
OH, MAN, WE LEFT THE DOOR OPEN. ALL THE ROBOTS MUST HAVE ESCAPED.
EVEN THE DEMONS ARE GONE!
WE ARE SO SORRY.
PLEASE DON'T SUE US OR TORTURE US FOREVER!
NO MATTER. THAT'S WHAT THE SIN MAGNET'S FOR. BENDER, YOU'D BETTER GRAB ON TO SOME-THING.
WRRRR!

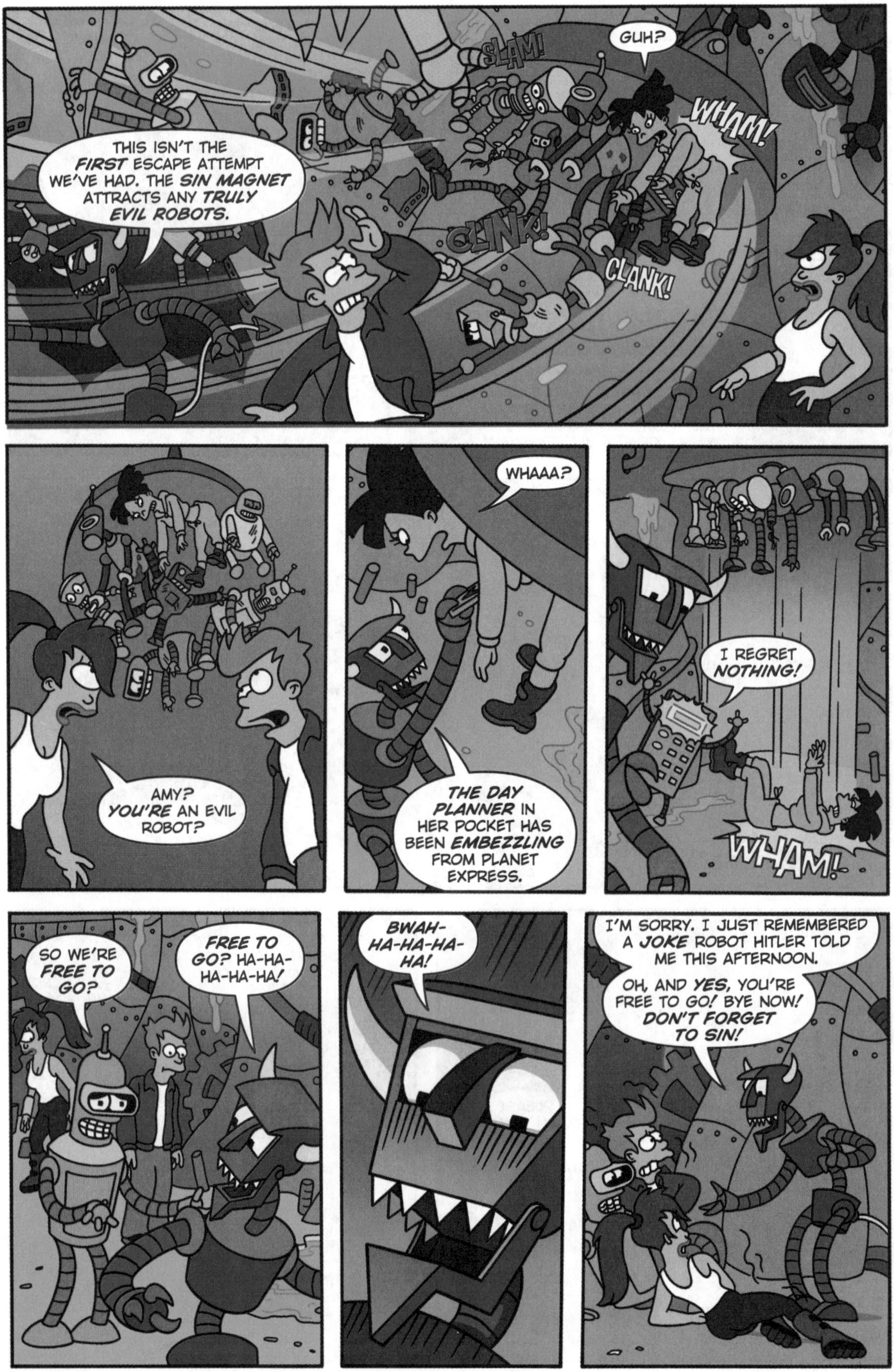
THIS ISN'T THE FIRST ESCAPE ATTEMPT WE'VE HAD. THE SIN MAGNET ATTRACTS ANY TRULY EVIL ROBOTS.
SLAM!
GUH?
WHAM!
CLINK!
CLANK!
AMY? YOU'RE AN EVIL ROBOT?
WHAAA?
THE DAY PLANNER IN HER POCKET HAS BEEN EMBEZZLING FROM PLANET EXPRESS.
I REGRET NOTHING!
WHAM!
SO WE'RE FREE TO GO?
FREE TO GO? HA-HA-HA-HA-HA!
BWAH-HA-HA-HA-HA!
I'M SORRY. I JUST REMEMBERED A JOKE ROBOT HITLER TOLD ME THIS AFTERNOON.
OH, AND YES, YOU'RE FREE TO GO! BYE NOW! DON'T FORGET TO SIN!

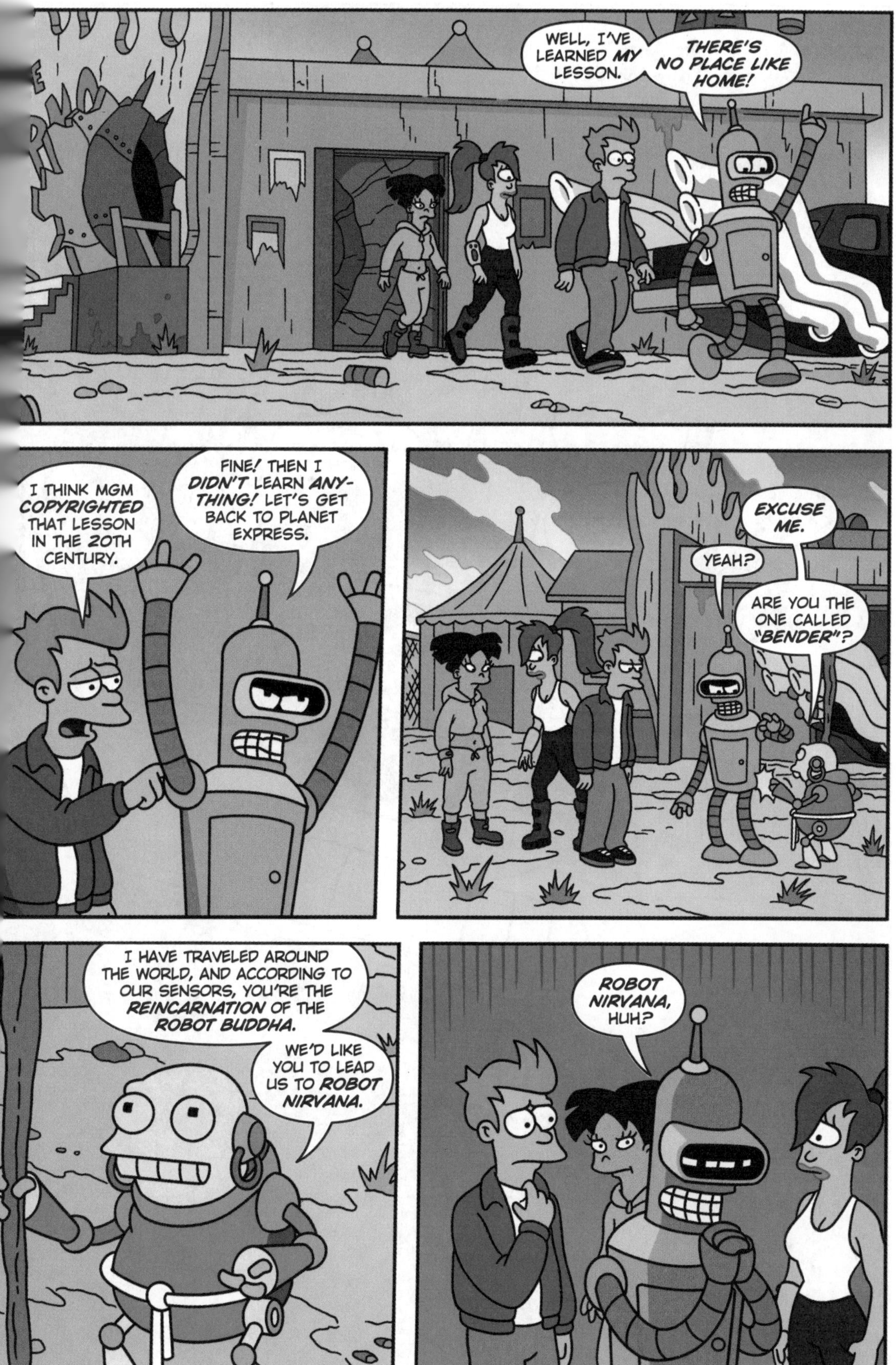
WELL, I'VE LEARNED MY LESSON.
THERE'S NO PLACE LIKE HOME!
I THINK MGM COPYRIGHTED THAT LESSON IN THE 20TH CENTURY.
FINE! THEN I DIDN'T LEARN ANYTHING! LET'S GET BACK TO PLANET EXPRESS.
EXCUSE ME.
YEAH?
ARE YOU THE ONE CALLED "BENDER"?
I HAVE TRAVELED AROUND THE WORLD, AND ACCORDING TO OUR SENSORS, YOU'RE THE REINCARNATION OF THE ROBOT BUDDHA.
WE'D LIKE YOU TO LEAD US TO ROBOT NIRVANA.
ROBOT NIRVANA, HUH?

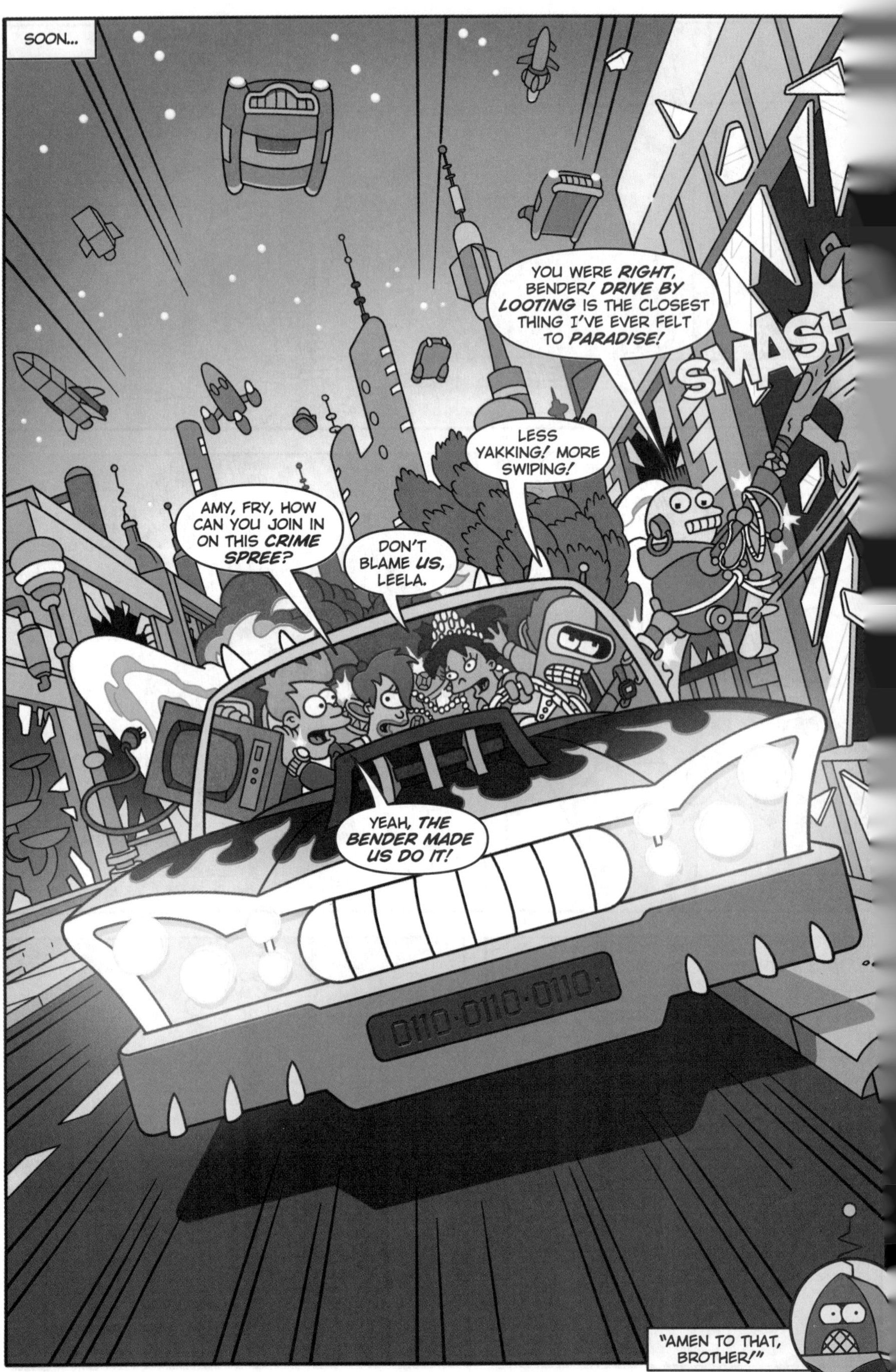
SOON...
YOU WERE RIGHT, BENDER! DRIVE BY LOOTING IS THE CLOSEST THING I'VE EVER FELT TO PARADISE!
SMASH
LESS YAKKING! MORE SWIPING!
AMY, FRY, HOW CAN YOU JOIN IN ON THIS CRIME SPREE?
DON'T BLAME US, LEELA.
YEAH, THE BENDER MADE US DO IT!
0110·0110·0110
"AMEN TO THAT, BROTHER!"